Making Publics, Making Places

This book is available as a free fully-searchable ebook from
www.adelaide.edu.au/press

Making Publics, Making Places

Edited by

Mary Griffiths and Kim Barbour

THE UNIVERSITY
of ADELAIDE

UNIVERSITY OF
ADELAIDE PRESS

Published in Adelaide by

University of Adelaide Press
Barr Smith Library
The University of Adelaide
South Australia 5005
press@adelaide.edu.au
www.adelaide.edu.au/press

The University of Adelaide Press publishes peer reviewed scholarly books. It aims to maximise access to the best research by publishing works through the internet as free downloads and for sale as high quality printed volumes.

For the full Cataloguing-in-Publication data please contact the National Library of Australia: cip@nla.gov.au

ISBN (paperback) 978-1-925261-42-4
ISBN (ebook: pdf) 978-1-925261-43-1
ISBN (ebook: epub) 978-1-925261-44-8
ISBN (ebook: kindle) 978-1-925261-45-5
DOI: http://dx.doi.org/10.20851/publics

Editor: Rebecca Burton
Editorial support: Julia Keller
Book design: Zoë Stokes
Cover design: Emma Spoehr
Cover image: © Casey Reas, www.reas.com

Contents

Preface

The impetus for *Making Publics, Making Places* was a desire to map the connections and disjunctions between scholarly approaches to understanding the making of publics and places. Primarily, the approaches in this collection represent the broad field of media scholarship complemented by perspectives from adjacent disciplines. The collection is exploratory, a boldly heterogeneous reaffirmation that places and publics continue to be the focus of investigations into cultural practices in a hypermediated era.

In accounts of mediation and societal change, digital technologies are often framed as taking on an agency of their own. Nigel Thrift's (2014) editorial commentary for an issue of *Environment and Planning A* on data, space and place notes an important limitation in taking up either side of the Manichean divide on technological and human determinism. He argues that not only is technology 'more mundane than it is generally portrayed, it is part of people's practices and adapts to them'. Its impact is therefore more likely to result in a 'slow upheaval' of change made by mostly invisible technology infrastructure, rather than 'some kind of ecstatic change' (p. 1264). Taking on Thrift's argument about the symbiotic nature of advances in technology and people's practices of use, our aim in the call for chapters was to invite contributors to help shape a collection illustrating the breadth and variety of approaches to understanding new media's generative power in everyday life.

The volume thus attends to two specific areas of disruption and generative change which are often taken up separately, despite their intrinsically linked nature: understandings of publics, and understandings of place. Following Couldry's advice on the opening up of cultural theory, we aimed to include perspectives beyond those in our disciplinary location as new media researchers — perspectives with the potential to 'open up possible empirical work on culture' (2000, p. 14). Couldry notes the benefits of stepping out of theoretical straightjackets, and refers to Stuart Hall's advice that 'the only theory worth having is the theory you have to fight off, not the one you speak with profound fluency' (1992 in Couldry 2000, p. 280). This advice was also persuasive in shaping the call. We invited contributions from any discipline that accounted for the contexts, moments and practices that shape places and publics in the digital age. Contributors responded creatively, by assessing the impact of specific practices, and by identifying the diverse ways in which users and makers respond to their empowerment through technologies.

This final editorial selection, through the thematic connections described in Chapter One, addresses the challenges and potential changes to power relations and cultural practices inherent in the production of publics and places, interrogating how these terms come into play, how they are resisted, and how they are remade. Contributors approach these areas of change from research areas as diverse as heritage studies, television audiences, film, comics and news, to high speed broadband, online diplomacy, online activism, ethnic media and democratic governance.

The book develops into an overall narrative about the pervasiveness and diversity of human innovation and the generative nature of technology, which is formative in connecting people to others and to place. The freshness and depth of individual perspectives are underpinned by the collection's shared concerns and emphases, which help shape a collective understanding of how people's most significant connections are made.

References

Couldry, N 2000, *Inside culture: Reimagining the method of cultural studies*, Sage Publications, London.

Hall, S 1992, 'Cultural studies and its theoretical legacies', in L Grossberg, C Nelson & P Treichler (eds.), *Cultural studies*, Routledge, New York, pp. 277-285.

Thrift, N 2014, 'The promise of urban informatics: Some speculations', *Environment and Planning A*, vol. 46, pp. 1263-1266, viewed 6 June 2016, <http://epn.sagepub.com/content/46/6/1263.full.pdf+html>.

Abstracts

2 — The elasticity of the public sphere: Expansion, contraction and 'other' media

John Budarick

This chapter traces the shifting conceptual contours and parameters of the public sphere as they relate to ethnic minority, transnational and diasporic media. The chapter focuses on two developments in understandings of the public sphere, and the communicative landscapes so central to rational debate. The first concerns the fragmentation of the public sphere into smaller sphericules or spheres, coalescing with ideas of subnational publics and identity politics (Fraser 1990; Gitlin 1998; Cunningham 2001). The second concerns what Fraser calls the transnationalisation of the public sphere — that is, the way that, through increasingly prominent movements of people, goods and media across borders, the ideas of society, nation and community have been wrenched clear of their nation-state home (Cammaerts & van Audenhove 2005; Fraser 2014). The aim of this chapter is to examine these reconceptualisations and to think about the place of ethnic, transnational and diasporic media in each.

3 — 'Imagine if our cities talked to us': Questions about the making of 'responsive' places and urban publics.

Mary Griffiths

A key feature of the urban Internet of Things and 'smartification' is the immediacy of the information collected from, and deliverable to, city inhabitants in ambient environments. These flows create, according to proponents, a smart city that 'talks back' efficiently to the public by eliminating human error, simplifying and automating decision making, and thus solving the problems that municipalities face in times of exponential urban population growth and diminishing resources. The chapter explores what follows from considering big data as a 'collective achievement' (Ruppert 2015), arguing that liveable, sustainable and participatory cities are created when based on a partnership between governments and urban publics, appropriate public engagement strategies and citizen-user advocacy. Beginning with a brief overview of the UN's Urban Renewal initiative as it pertains to guiding principles for the protection of rights to the city and the encouragement of transparent, multilevel governance, the chapter moves through a series of illustrations and propositions about traditions of placemaking, ambient environments and smart cities.

4 — Picturing placelessness: Online graphic narratives and Australia's refugee detention centres

Aaron Humphrey

Theorists such as Edward Relph and Melvin Webber have argued that an industrial emphasis on accessibility and efficiency has eroded our sense of place. Online communication is frequently 'placeless' in this respect, but also provides ways of thinking about identities as detached from places, nations and nationalities. This chapter will explore these themes by examining an online comic, 'At Work inside our Detention Centres — A Guard's Story', which focuses on the existential placelessness faced by asylum seekers in Australia's detention centres. To depict the dilemma of detention, this comic mimics some of the design elements of online communication which facilitate placelessness. At the same time, the drawings in this comic by Sam Wallman depart from the standardised and industrialised norms of online communication. Centred on the place where pen meets paper, comics can act as a powerful tool for both picturing and resisting the placelessness of industrialised online communication.

5 — Reclaiming heritage for UNESCO: Discursive practices and community building in northern Italy

Maria Cristina Paganoni

This chapter discusses the impact of web-mediated communication in enhancing cultural actions for heritage promotion, focusing on UNESCO's World Heritage List. The analytic field embraces three sites in the Lombardy region of Italy. A World Heritage Site since 1995, the model workers' village of Crespi d'Adda needs massive regeneration and an inclusive project for its future civic destination. Heading a transnational nomination file of Venetian fortifications from the fifteenth to the seventeenth century, the municipality of Bergamo now seeks citizen engagement. On the outskirts of Milan, Sesto San Giovanni, a former heavy industrial district of the twentieth century, is applying to be recognised by UNESCO as an organically evolved landscape. The investigation of visual/verbal materials retrieved online is carried out by means of discourse analysis and heritage studies in order to better understand the contribution of digital media to the synergic making of places and publics.

6 — Find your Adelaide: Digital placemaking with *Adelaide City Explorer*

Darren Peacock and Jill MacKenzie

Mobile locative technologies have radically altered the ways in which we access and share place-based information. The mobile digital revolution opens many new opportunities for creating richly informated spaces. *Adelaide City Explorer* is a working experiment in digital cultural informatics designed to enhance the ways people discover and engage with the built, cultural and natural environment of a city. The *Adelaide City Explorer* website and mobile apps support the discovery and sharing of place-based narratives and information and the construction of pathways through the city and its architectural, environmental, historical and cultural evolution. They enable a new approach to the curation and exploration of urban environments which is less linear and didactic and more exploratory, collaborative and open-ended. By recontextualising heritage information within the physical places and spaces they describe, we aim to create digital artefacts and place-based experiences that maximise the encyclopaedic, spatial, procedural and participatory properties identified by Murray (1997, 2012) as the key 'affordances' of digital media. This 'here and now heritage' enables new ways to engage with and to read both past and present through heritage places.

7 — Chinese films and the sense of place: Beijing as 'Thirdspace' from *In the Heat of the Sun* to *Mr Six*

Hongyan Zou and Peter C Pugsley

This chapter explores two films set in Beijing, to examine how the city's protagonists are contextualised within the landscape of China's state capital, and how the city has been spatially depicted and imagined amidst a time of immense technological, economic and social change. Our investigation of *Mr Six* (*Lao Paoer*, dir. Guan Hu, 2015) illustrates how city-based films shape perceptions of a city by drawing from Edward W Soja's discussions on the trialectical relation between space, social relations and history — particularly the 'Thirdspace' (based on Lefebvre's *Production of Space*), which combines material, physical and cognitive spaces into a conceptual site. *Mr Six* serves as a postscript to an earlier Beijing-based film about disaffected youth, *In the Heat of the Sun* (*Yangguang can lan de rizi*, dir. Jiang Wen, 1994). In these films the symbolic spaces of Beijing are depicted through their streetscapes and dwelling spaces where transforming economies and technologies increasingly impact on day-to-day contemporary Chinese public and private life. These cinematic places mirror the complexities of urbanisation and globalisation, and a comparison of the two films shows how the production of space in the cinematic world reflects a changing public.

8 — Social media and news media: Building new publics or fragmenting audiences?

Kathryn Bowd

Social media have provided news outlets with unprecedented opportunities to expand their networks of communication and build audience and participation. The capacity for immediacy and interaction inherent in social media platforms is shifting understandings of news communities and of ways in which news media can engage with 'the people formerly known as the audience', to use the term coined by US academic Jay Rosen (2006). However, the extent to which news outlets are capitalising on these opportunities varies widely. This is particularly evident among Australia's regional newspapers. Their engagement with social media ranged from multiple daily posts on both Facebook and Twitter, incorporating photos, videos and requests for comment, to sporadic posts updating audiences on news events. However, even where comment was sought, it was often through a broad-ranging request for information rather than an invitation to engage more deeply in debate. This suggests that regional newspapers continue preferencing traditional one-to-many forms of communication rather than fully utilising the communicative capacities of social media. This in turn raises questions about whether news media are using social media to expand their reach and develop new publics or merely fragmenting existing audiences across a growing range of communication platforms.

9 — The use of Chinese social media by foreign embassies: How 'generative technologies' are offering opportunities for modern diplomacy

Ying Jiang

Social media provide the opportunity to reach youth populations of other countries. In foreign embassies in China, for example, there are more than forty embassies that use the most popular Chinese social media platform — Weibo — to engage with 'online publics' in China. This chapter examines how 'generative technologies' are offering opportunities for modern diplomacy. Engagement and interactivity have been emphasised in using social media in public relation works. However, this chapter argues that interactivity is not necessarily linked to the success of engagement with online publics via social media accounts. This chapter examines the interactivity of those embassies' Weibo accounts by looking at two aspects: the number of comments or retweets that each post receives, and the number of negative and positive comments that each post receives.

10 — An opinion leader and the making of a city on China's Sina Weibo

Wilfred Yang Wang

This chapter examines the role of an opinion leader on Sina Weibo (a microblog) in mobilising the countercampaign against nationwide anti-Japan demonstrations in 2012. Specifically, the chapter focuses on those online practices by the opinion leader and his followers which facilitated the process of remaking Guangzhou, the southern Chinese city near Hong Kong and Macau. Using data collected from Sina Weibo during the anti-Japan demonstrations, the chapter argues that the countercampaign in Guangzhou was successful due to the opinion leader's ability to manipulate the technological affordances of Weibo and the socialites of the city, to construct himself as a spatial subject of Guangzhou, and to construct a geopublic that contested and questioned the legitimacy of a state-imposed notion of nationalism. The online practices of posting, reposting, commenting, and uploading visual audio materials mapped Guangzhou city during the nationalistic movements. The mapping constructs an alternative sense of Chinese nationalism which encapsulates both local values and the national agenda of border sovereignty.

11 — Public audiencing: Using Twitter to study audience engagement with characters and actors

Kim Barbour

The current fascination with social media sites has undoubtedly made many parts of our lives more public. We are increasingly publicising not only our activities, relationships and cultural preferences, but also the way we think and understand the world. These new data streams provide avenues for researchers to gather insight into both personal and public opinion and behaviour. One particular space that has attracted scholarly attention is the live tweeting of television. As audiences discuss television shows through second-screen applications, researchers have an opportunity to gain insight into the way viewers engage with elements of a media text without soliciting or directing the discussion. With second-screen use becoming increasingly common through a range of audience types, a wider approach is necessary, in order to encompass a fuller range of audience behaviour, than the current tendency to examine the audience as members of a fandom. This chapter reports on a focused study of tweets relating to the first broadcast of the second season of *Love Child* (Nine Network, 2015). This analysis focuses specifically on how the collected tweets reference actors and characters, demonstrating that Twitter studies can make visible audience identification practices. In particular, the analysis identifies three key behavioural elements: direct address to the actors, either inside or outside the diegetic space; tagging actors while referencing character behaviour; and character bleed.

12 — Overcoming the tyranny of distance? High speed broadband and the significance of place

Jenny Kennedy, Rowan Wilken, Bjorn Nansen, Michael Arnold and Mitchell Harrop

This chapter draws on relational understandings of place as a productive theoretical context for framing an examination of the increasingly crucial role that high speed broadband plays in mediating and shaping place-based interactions and experiences. A relational approach emphasises the processual qualities of place: how place can be understood as a bounded but open and contested site, a complex product of competing discourses, ever-shifting social relations, and internal (and external) events and influences. According to this understanding, any given 'place' is a product of, and dependent on, 'the interconnectedness of the elements within it', as well as being dependent on 'its interconnection with other places'. Nowhere is the tension between connectedness and distinction more apparent than in the socially, technically, economically and geographically varied Australian landscape. Drawing on these conceptions of place, this paper examines how high speed broadband intersects with the other elements that make place meaningful.

List of contributors

Michael Arnold is an associate professor in the History and Philosophy of Science Programme in the School of Historical and Philosophical Studies at the University of Melbourne. His ongoing teaching and research activities lie at the intersection of contemporary technologies and our society and culture. In recent years his research projects have included a comparative study of social networking in six locations across the Asia-Pacific; several studies of high speed broadband in the domestic context; a study to develop methods to assess social returns on investments in technologies; a study of ethical and governance issues associated with the electronic health record; a study of digital storytelling by young Indigenous Australians; and a study of online memorials. This research has formed the basis of a monograph published by Routledge, and more than fifty peer-reviewed papers.

Kim Barbour is a qualitative new media scholar and lecturer in the Department of Media at the University of Adelaide. Kim's research looks at online persona, the strategic production of identity through digital media, and the use of social media, while her teaching covers media history, media theory and digital storytelling, including media production practices. Kim is a founding editor of the online, Open Access journal *Persona Studies*. She has published a chapter in the edited book *Media, Margins and Popular Culture* (Palgrave), articles in *Celebrity Studies*, *M/C Journal* (guest editor), *First Monday*, and elsewhere, and her paper 'Performing Professionalism|Validating Artistness' won the Grant Noble Award for best postgraduate paper at ANZCA 2014. She is co-author of a book on persona studies to be published in 2017 by Wiley.

Kathryn Bowd is a senior lecturer in journalism and media at the University of Adelaide. Her research focus is on non-metropolitan media, with an emphasis on journalism practice and the relationships between smaller media outlets and their communities. Before making the move to academia, she spent seventeen years as a newspaper journalist in Australia and the UK, working for both regional and metropolitan publications. She is associate editor of the leading Australian academic journal focused on journalism and journalism studies, *Australian Journalism Review*, and is on the Executive of the Journalism Education and Research Association of Australia.

John Budarick is a lecturer in the Department of Media at the University of Adelaide. His research interests include transnational and diasporic media, ethnic and migrant media, and social theory and communication. With a background in sociology, he completed his PhD at Monash University in 2011. His research has been published in leading Australian and international academic journals, including *Journal of Sociology*, *Media International Australian*, *Global Media and Communication*, *International Journal of Communication*, and *Media, Culture and Society*. He is the co-editor of a forthcoming book with Palgrave Macmillan, entitled *Minorities and Media: Producers, Industries, Audiences*.

Mary Griffiths is an associate professor in media at the University of Adelaide. Research interests include the civic and political uptake of digital and smart technologies in democracies; and smart cities and urban informatics. Recent projects include: 'Cultural Heritage and Smart Technologies' and 'The Google Cultural Institute and Public Participation'. She is Associate Editor of *EJEG: The Electronic Journal of E-Government* and is guest editor for its special issue on 'Smart Cities' (Winter 2017). She has served on *Communication, Politics & Culture* in various editorial roles since 1991. Her work has been published by both journals, and in *MIA*, *New Media & Society*, *International Journal of Media and Cultural Politics*, and the *Journal of Community Informatics*. Her research affiliations include the JM Coetzee Centre for Creative Practice, the Australian Centre for Smart Cities, and the China-Australia Centre for Transcultural Studies, Beijing Foreign Studies University, Beijing.

Mitchell Harrop is a researcher and lecturer in the Interaction Design Lab in the Department of Computing and Information Systems at The University of Melbourne.

Aaron Humphrey recently completed his PhD at the University of Adelaide, where his dissertation on comics and education was awarded the Dean's Commendation for Thesis Excellence. Combining critical analysis with creative practice, his work investigates the relationship between words, images and multimodal communication. His research has been published in *Media International Australia*, *Composition Studies*, *Digital Humanities Quarterly*, *The Comics Grid* and *The Conversation*. As a cartoonist, his comics are currently used in digital rhetoric courses and for postgraduate medical education. As a filmmaker, his short films have screened in festivals in Australasia and North America. He is member of the JM Coetzee Centre for Creative Practice and is a co-founder and co-organiser of 'Inkers and Thinkers,' Australasia's annual academic conference devoted to comics and graphic narratives.

Jenny Kennedy is a research fellow in the Department of Computing and Information Systems at the University of Melbourne. Jenny's research interests are media theories of everyday life, social discourses around technology use, and material culture. She has published in *Information, Culture & Society*; *Convergence: The International Journal of*

Research into New Media Technologies; *Continuum: Journal of Media & Cultural Studies*; and *Communication, Politics & Culture*.

Ying Jiang is a senior lecturer in media at the University of Adelaide. In 2008, Ying was selected as one of the 100 outstanding young Chinese leaders in the world by the Hong Kong Dragon Foundation. Ying's research interests and publications mainly include cyber-nationalism, cross-cultural communication, social media and public relations. Ying's first book in 2012, *Cyber-nationalism in China: Challenging Western Media Portrayals of Chinese Censorship*, has achieved more than 15 000 downloads so far. Ying's article '"Reversed Agenda-Setting Effects" in China: Case Studies of Weibo Trending Topics and the Effects on State-Owned Media in China', published by *Journal of International Communications*, has become one of the most read articles on *Taylor & Francis Online*.

Jill MacKenzie has held curatorial, public programming, education and online services roles in social history museums in Western Canada and Australia. Since 2011, she has worked as a researcher and consultant for community and volunteer-run museums and organisations in South Australia. She recently submitted a PhD in history at the University of Adelaide.

Bjorn Nansen is a lecturer in the Department of Media and Communication at the University of Melbourne. He is a researcher of digital media and culture, with interests in technology adoption, tangible computing and natural user interfaces, children's media use, material culture studies and critical theory of technology. He holds a Discovery Early Career Researcher Award [DECRA] funded by the Australian Research Council. His most recent publications have featured in *New Media & Society*; *Journal of Children and Media*; *Environment and Planning D*; *Media International Australia*; and *M/C*.

Maria Cristina Paganoni is an associate professor of English language and translation at Università degli Studi di Milano, her alma mater. Her current research focuses on web-mediated communication and urban branding, heritage discourse in the new media, and the smart city, drawing on linguistics, discourse and multimodal analysis, and social semiotics. She has authored several contributions on these topics in books and peer-reviewed journals. Her latest publications include the monograph *City Branding and New Media: Linguistic Perspectives, Discursive Strategies and Multimodality* (Palgrave Macmillan 2015).

Darren Peacock is chief executive officer at the National Trust of South Australia.

Peter C Pugsley is an associate professor and head of media and teaches Asian screen media at the University of Adelaide. He is the author of *Morality and Sexuality in Asian Cinema: Cinematic Boundaries* (Routledge 2015) and *Tradition, Culture and Aesthetics in Contemporary Asian Cinema* (Ashgate 2013).

Wilfred Yang Wang teaches digital media studies at universities across Melbourne and he is affiliated with the Digital Media Research Centre at the Queensland University of Technology, Australia. His current research projects include migrant media in Australia, Chinese social media and digital media in Asia. He has a specific interest in the field of internet geography.

Rowan Wilken is an associate professor in media and communication, at the Swinburne Institute for Social Research, Swinburne University of Technology. He is author of *Cultural Economies of Locative Media* (forthcoming) and *Teletechnologies, Place, and Community* (2011), and is co-editor of *Location Technologies in International Context* (forthcoming), *The Afterlives of Georges Perec* (forthcoming), *Locative Media* (2015), and *Mobile Technology and Place* (2012).

Hongyan Zou is a PhD candidate in the Department of Media at the University of Adelaide. Her thesis looks at the dynamic relationship between cinema and city, specifically mainland Chinese films set in or about different regions across China since the 1980s.

Making publics, making places

1

Mary Griffiths and Kim Barbour

Key concepts

The media landscape is in a profound moment of transition. Perhaps this statement has been true since the development of moveable type, but the impact of the transformation in media environments as a result of digital technologies, particularly those which are utilised through internet services, is significant in all realms of everyday life, and in the organisation of forms of modernity.

What constitutes 'publics' is contextual and contested, as Warner's work on the concept convincingly illustrates (2002). His analysis begins by examining the many confusing overlapping uses of the terms 'the public', 'publics' and 'a public'. He notes that individuals may belong simultaneously to many publics, and that this fact contributes to the ambiguity and circularity of many publics constituting 'the public', making research 'difficult'. In dealing with defining elements of a public, he states, 'space and physical presence do not make much difference; a public is understood to be different from a crowd, an audience, or any other group that requires co-presence' (p. 53). His argument is that a public is best understood as formed around textual practices and self-organised relationships with strangers.

In the last decade of burgeoning many-to-many communications, as the chapters in this collection show, publics are forming and fragmenting around access to particular technology — platform, website, application, game, profile, group, hashtag — although accessibility to information, space and discourse has always been a determinant to one's membership within a public. Such publics have an increasingly nebulous quality, forming and dispersing, being created and fractured through adoption, insertion or rejection. The fragmentation of mass audiences since the turn of the century has accelerated in the last decade. What replaces the mass audience includes the ubiquitous mobilisations of social media; the segmentation of readerships during the adaptation of print and broadcast media to internet delivery; and the increasing power of media technology companies like Google and Facebook as content providers and corporate stewards of the 'walled gardens', where publics form around news, entertainment and politics. The process of making and unmaking publics continues to be dynamic, initiating this book's explorations of the ways they can be conceptualised, how makers of publics function, and the practices of inclusion and exclusion, which shape disparate, sometimes ephemeral, and geographically distant publics.

The making of places is equally fluid, and the individuals who frequent them may be conceptualised as publics if their point of assembly is a shared interest, or if they are visible — however fleetingly — to each other. Placemaking can be personal, corporate and civic. It occurs in online space, through embodied experiences and in the design of built environment. The relationship between space and place is one that has attracted considerable scholarly attention. Several chapters in the collection speak primarily to the issues of reimagining places, emerging as an important consideration for governing bodies and populations. Digital technologies are the basis for 'place' planning, for multiple reasons including connecting the nation, offering the means to preserve public goods including heritage, and enhancing the enjoyment of culture. The collective stewardship of shared assets is made possible through digital technologies, and in the smart city, the re-establishment of collective and civic values is being envisioned. Issues of inclusion and participation are critical for the design of place.

In the chapters that follow, we take up these broad areas of investigation through four key concepts, which connect these studies with different disciplinary histories:

1. The use of, and access to, media and digital technologies continue to allow contestation of dominant ideological structures.
2. Spaces become places through lived engagement.
3. Media technologies can transform people into publics.
4. Digital connectivity facilitates understanding of physical space.

Exemplifying in Chapter Two the interconnectedness of the twin focuses of this book — publics and places — John Budarick introduces the themes of crossing global boundaries and connecting formerly dispersed publics. Budarick reconsiders critiques of the Habermassian concept of the public sphere, and assesses transcultural media's potential for constructing new, effective publics. Arguing that transnational, ethnic and diasporic media provide important new ways for people to communicate, educate and debate, Budarick demonstrates the importance of a diversity of media forms to assist in the extension and necessary complexity of the creation of new public spheres. While the inherent limitations of this type of media, particularly in connecting to those outside of their immediate target publics, must be acknowledged, the necessity of these diverse media forms in supporting marginalised voices necessitates their continued significance in the global media environment.

While Budarick deals with media publics and intangible places through the elasticity of the public sphere, Mary Griffiths in Chapter Three focuses instead on public spaces of the physical kind. Griffiths interrogates the 'non-ideological' values embedded into the design and development of responsive spaces in the 'smart city', arguing that the quality of civic experiences in such places rests on their collective makers, the inclusiveness of their designs, and the democratic commitment of their urban designers and technology enablers. A top-down partnership between technology corporations and municipalities is developing the cities of the future, where the fundamental rights to full participation and a sense of belonging depend on the invisible design of ecosystems, data flows and an infrastructure which creates different access to a sense of place for specific publics in the population. In the smart cities, the chapter asks, how will those currently marginalised be represented in the data gathered, so that a city can 'talk' to all its inhabitants? The drivers of smartification indicate that market discourses could prevail over inclusivity of participation. The chapter concludes that governance of place, the nature of publics and 'rights to the city' may need to be reconceptualised, if the ambient spaces of responsive environments are to remain democratic and sustainable.

An online practice can become an expressive 'place' for the displaced, causing a reconsideration of place and placelessness. In Chapter Four, Aaron Humphrey explores the harsh political dynamics of Australia's asylum and border protection policies. There is, as Humphrey shows, an inherent contradiction in enacting legislation which places the Australian mainland out of the 'Migration Zone'. Australia is a country populated by waves of migration, and by people who have left places where they felt at home to experience the dislocation that precedes finding a sense of belonging. There is, despite the vote-winning policy on boats, a publicly expressed empathy with those in the camps. The repression of official information about the conditions in detention centres in Nauru and Manus Island, and the dearth of reliable reportage because of restricted access, have only energised the circulation of unofficial accounts and increased numbers of supporters. The rich illustrations of the anonymous newspaper comic that this chapter contextualises and analyses, 'A Guard's Story', elucidate the desperation and resilience needed when people displaced from their homeland await confirmation of refugee status, and place. These images find different publics because, as Humphrey notes, digital publishing forms have expanded, allowing wider appreciation not only of visual illustrations of placelessness, but also of 'what it means to be citizens of the places where we live'.

The design and discursive power of online space, access to it, and what people make when they occupy it are canvassed further in the following chapter. The act of collecting memories and animating the past with stories increases popular participation and enjoyment of heritage. Citizens and visitors alike are drawn to walking around Italy's UNESCO heritage sites. For Maria Cristina Paganoni, the restoration of built heritage of global importance both suggests new media's potential to connect new publics to the richness of place, by creating social spaces to young contemporary audiences, and highlights the danger of continuing old inequalities in discursive framings of the past. Paganoni's research into promotional citizen portals and social media highlights the potential for the anchoring of class divisions. She points to a disjuncture in stakeholder power illustrated by the high levels of expertise and knowledge needed to engage fully with institutional bodies like UNESCO. Even the languages of groups involved in the renewal of sites like Crespi d'Adda, Bergamo and Sesto San Giovanni act as markers of privilege and agency, or the lack of thereof:

> Local administrators are required to use English to communicate with supranational bodies like UNESCO, and to connect with global networks and brand cities for international tourists, investors, talent, sports and cultural events. However, civic interaction with, and within, local communities takes place in Italian and pursues intents that need to be connected or reconnected with the official urban management discourse. (Paganoni, this volume, p. 80)

Darren Peacock and Jill MacKenzie continue the discussion of urban heritage in Chapter Six, by considering technology's enhancement of the sense of the distinctness and value of place. In their discussion of the role of digital media in facilitating engagement with Adelaide's past, the authors demonstrate how new technologies can take narrative approaches that shift the user past the information structures of guidebooks and heritage plaques, and instead contextualise the changes that have occurred through the city's development. Locative media and app software allows users to connect with personal stories of place as they travel on foot through the city, creating a sense of intimacy and emplacement in both physical and temporal terms:

> Digital media suggest and support much more flexible, less didactic, more dialogic approaches to interpretation, without a predetermined cognitive destination for users. There is much greater freedom to explore, to construct and configure different pathways through spaces, both mentally and physically. (Peacock and MacKenzie, this volume, p. 98)

The process of understanding a city through the soles of the feet, which is recognisable in the work of Peacock and MacKenzie, can also be visualised in film.

Discussing place as a lived experience of a physical space in Chapter Seven, Hongyan Zou and Peter C Pugsley examine how films can represent the experience of living in a city. In their analysis of two connected filmic narratives of Beijing, the authors demonstrate how the filmmakers use the cityscape, and the characters' interactions with their urban landscape, as commentary on the social and political issues of the time. In a film set during the Cultural Revolution (*In the Heat of the Sun*), the military enclosures and surrounding alleys speak to the alienation and learned violence of the youth at the centre of the story. In the film set in post-2010 Beijing (*Mr Six*), the role of consumption and commerce is challenged through the ubiquitous incursion of shops and markets. As cameras follow the characters moving through their cities, the audience sees the space of Beijing as a familiar, changing neighbourhood, a place where people live and belong. De Certeau's (1984) 'Walking in the City' connects these two chapters in this collection, speaking as it does to the capacity of walking as a generative activity, a way of making a city a place for oneself.

Film is only one media form that works to produce a sense of place. News media, particularly those that service otherwise isolated groups, connect people to the place in which they live. In Chapter Eight, again examining the overlapping nature of place and public, Kathryn Bowd tracks the readership dynamics of regional newspapers, as they use social media to retain their place as the social glue of far-flung communities in rural Australia. Publics for regional news were once conceptualised as being within range of the town that produced the paper, or certainly close enough for the paper to be collected, or alternatively delivered by a paperboy or the mail van. They were viewed as being close enough to a newspaper's office building for complaints to be made in person. Newspapers defined a region's identity through the comprehensive stories of the everyday which they told, and through the recurring themes of interest to readers. The story of the death of print news is still unfolding, but the disappearance of the 'rivers of gold' of advertising revenue in metropolitan papers has triggered online news developments and social media engagement which threaten to displace the regional paper as a primary source of local news. Bowd's research on the threats and opportunities to local newspapers posed by the necessity of adopting social media shows that most do not appear to be capitalising on the opportunities to do things differently and attract new publics. Indeed, many are replicating practices of distribution from their print legacy.

In Chapter Nine, Ying Jiang examines larger civic uses of social media. Her research explores public diplomacy on Weibo, China's most dominant social media space, and suggests that the author has similar reservations about their outreach or about whether the levels of interactivity online lead to any discernibly positive action offline. Foreign embassies in China have moved online to attract the interest of younger populations in issues important to the countries they represent, yet Jiang's findings suggest that there is no correlation between high numbers of 'followers' on Weibo and any increase in influence. There is potential for publics to form around, for example, the Canadian embassy sites, but as yet it is difficult to track these emerging groups.

Also focusing on the use of Weibo, Wilfred Yang Wang in Chapter Ten looks at how the social media site facilitates the making of place through online activism: a material city is digitally reclaimed from outsiders. As Weibo users posted, shared and commented, they built support and visibility for the work of an opinion leader who challenged not the truth of the protests on the ground, but rather their expression through violence directed at the city to which the protesters had travelled. Claiming Guangzhou city as 'ours', the opinion leader in this case refocused the public attention to recognise that this piece of physical space is important, valuable, to those who live in and through it in a way that might not be as apparent to visitors.

The connectivity inherent in the majority of online digital technologies provides users with a chance to communicate across geographical and temporal boundaries. More than that, as decades of research into online communities and fandoms has comprehensively demonstrated, new media technologies allow people to connect with those of like mind, to share interests, and to develop expertise. These online communities offer researchers a tremendous opportunity to study the way that those involved in these communities engage with each other through dedicated online forums, pages, profiles and websites. In Chapter Eleven, Kim Barbour, through a small study of Twitter users who tweeted about Australian television show *Love Child*, demonstrates how as researchers we also make the publics we study. Through analysis of this Twitter data set, Barbour was able to study how these users held characters and actors in their minds simultaneously, and how character bleed informed viewer conceptualisations of the show's plot. The researcher transformed a group of users into this nebulous public for the purposes of this single study, and as a result was able to gain insight into the way that everyday viewers of a television show — those who would not meet the criteria to be considered 'fans' — experience and engage with a particular show.

As stated at the outset of this chapter, digital technologies, specifically those that are accessed through the internet, are increasingly facilitating and defining our understanding of place and public. Therefore, it is fitting that we close this volume with a discussion of how those technologies are accessed. Chapter Twelve reports on research funded by the Australian Research Council which explores the ways that a sample of twenty-two urban and rural households actually experience high speed broadband. Jenny Kennedy, Rowan Wilken, Bjorn Nansen, Michael Arnold and Mitchell Harrop, members of a multidisciplinary Melbourne-based research team, scope the significance of place in the controversial implementation of Australia's National Broadband Network [NBN]. The NBN is the biggest infrastructure outlay in Australia's history. Inequities of access for those most remote from regional hubs are illustrated in this observation of remote Australian townships where the terrain itself interferes with residents' satellite access: 'Although there are wireless towers at a workable distance, the typography of the local area means that these houses cannot connect directly' (Kennedy et al., this volume). The researchers investigated through interviews with householders 'how place is constituted differently in each setting, especially as a result of the high speed broadband infrastructures provided in each place, and of the participants' experiences of these technologies' (Kennedy et al., this volume).

After considering variability in connectivity to high speed broadband [HSB], they conclude on a positive note:

> Even so, despite variable quality of access to HSB services across sites, the findings to date do suggest that increased bandwidth is accompanied by increased participation in the digital economy, in online activities, and in the use of entertainment and communication services and technologies; and the responses of our informants indicate that increased digital literacy emerges through experience and use of HSB. (Kennedy et al., this volume, p. 214)

Eschewing a totally technologically deterministic view of the place and future of new media, we instead show that it is people, whether conceptualised as users, audiences, publics, citizens, researchers or individuals, who determine how media is understood, utilised and abandoned. Equally, it is people's collective and individual relationships to place and to each other, whether physical, digital or imagined, that make place real and important in their lives. In bringing together these chapters, we hope to elucidate some of the connections, overlap and points of contention in the role of media technology in the making of places and publics.

References

de Certeau, M 1984, 'Walking in the city', in *The practice of everyday life*, trans. S Rendall, University of California Press, Berkeley, pp. 91-110.

Guan, H 2015, *Mr Six* [*Lao Paoer*], film, Huayi Brothers and Taihe Film Investments, China.

Jiang, W 1994, *In the Heat of the Sun* [*Yangguang can lan de rizi*], film, China Film Co-Production Corporation and Dragon Film, China.

Warner, M 2002, 'Publics and counterpublics', *Public Culture*, vol. 14, no. 1, pp. 49-90.

The elasticity of the public sphere: Expansion, contraction and 'other' media

2

John Budarick

Introduction

This chapter traces the shifting conceptual contours and parameters of the public sphere as they relate to ethnic minority, transnational and diasporic media. Each of these forms of media challenges the equation of public with nation, and nation with state, and problematises the housing of effective public policy within a bordered nation-state. Drawing on historical, political and theoretical critiques of the bourgeois public sphere ideal, several authors have taken minority media as being central to an understanding of multiple publics competing for political legitimacy and influence in increasingly diverse societies (Fraser 1990; Eley 1990; Calhoun 1992). Transnational media have been implicated in a similar process, wherein the location of the public sphere has been stretched to incorporate transnational public spheres, and even a global public sphere. Here, transnational and diasporic media are thought to be the engines upon which the expression of transnational publicness can occur. In many ways, then, this chapter engages with the question: 'What media provide what kind of public spheres?' (Butsch 2007, p. 3).

The public sphere as a critical theoretical model has undergone many changes since Habermas's original conception. Debates have raged over the idea's historical validity, its ability to incorporate differing sectors of complex modern societies into its discursive space, and its ability to capture globalising tendencies through which national borders are seemingly becoming more porous. What tends to remain central to discussions of the public sphere, however, is the centrality of questions over the communicative landscapes and structures within which deliberative debate can be said to take place. This chapter focuses on two developments in understandings of the public sphere, and the communicative landscapes so central to rational debate. The first concerns the fragmentation of the public sphere into smaller sphericules or spheres, coalescing with ideas of subnational publics and identity politics (Fraser 1990; Gitlin 1998; Cunningham 2001). The second concerns what Fraser calls the transnationalisation of the public sphere — that is, the way that, through increasingly prominent movements of people, goods and media across borders, the ideas of society, nation and community have been wrenched clear of their nation-state home (Cammaerts & van Audenhove 2005; Fraser 2014).

The aim of this chapter is to examine these reconceptualisations and to think about the place of ethnic, transnational and diasporic media in each. I seek to bring the public sphere into critical dialogue with different forms of non-'national' media. How well does the fracturing and contracting of the public sphere account for ethnic media, and are the communicative practices of minority ethnic groups best thought about through a model of multiple publics? What is the role of transnational and diasporic media in debates over the transnational public sphere, and can such a public space even be said to exist? It is hoped that by addressing such questions the chapter can contribute to an understanding of the role of a dynamic and changing media environment in the formation of publics and the facilitation of deliberative debate (Habermas 1989).

In the discussion to follow, I will argue two main points. First, in relation to the fracturing of the public sphere into counterpublics, subaltern publics and public sphericules, I will argue that debate has focused primarily on ethnic minority media for their role in self-representation and the provision of alternative discourses. This leaves unanswered the question of the relation between different publics and the ability of ethnic media to affect the practices and language of the dominant public sphere. Second, in regards to the transnationalisation of the public sphere, I will suggest that diasporic and transnational media, from satellite television to the internet, are taken as providing much of the framework upon which transnational publics can form and maintain themselves. However, the unifying potential of transnational media is often prioritised to the neglect of divisions and exclusions that reflect earlier critiques of the original bourgeois public sphere.

The contraction of the public sphere: Spheres, sphericules and subaltern publics

Rethinking the public sphere

It was not long after the English translation of *The Structural Transformation of the Public Sphere* that critiques of the public sphere model began to emerge in English academic writing (Habermas 1989). Many of these critiques were concerned with the nature of the 'public' itself; the realities of power over, and access to, the spaces of public deliberation; the specific forms of communication and debate prioritised by Habermas; and the very possibility of broad social consensus in societies experiencing increasing claims to cultural autonomy and political self-determination by different groups (Butsch 2007). One of the most notable critiques came from Nancy Fraser (1990, pp. 62-3), who took issue with Habermas's liberal bourgeois conception of *the* public sphere as a singular metaphorical space. Such an understanding, she argued, rests upon four assumptions:

1. that it is possible to ignore inequalities in a public sphere, and thus that inequality is 'not a necessary condition for political democracy'

2. that a single public sphere holds more democratic potential than a multiplicity of public spheres

3. that the public sphere debate should exclude private interests and issues

4. that the public sphere requires a distinction between civil society and the state.

Drawing on historical critiques, such as that of Geoff Eley (1990), Fraser (1990) argued that the male-dominated public sphere was constituted upon a particular mode of cultural behaviour and communication which privileged masculine norms of interaction and marginalised others based on gender, class and ethnicity. As such, *the* bourgeois public sphere came dangerously close to being a tool of gender- and class-based hegemony — a function of control that gives the illusion of consensus and inclusion but instead is based on the naturalisation of specific and contingent forms of social organisation and interaction. Eley (1990) argued that the liberal bourgeois model of the public sphere not only idealised a specific, gendered mode of social organisation and expression, but also ignored other forms of potential emancipation, rendering particular political and social movements as marginal to the bourgeois project.

The idea of a single public sphere also prioritised, in Habermas's original work, consensus and rationality over contestation and conflict. Fraser (1990) suggested that ignoring power inequalities fails to account for the diverse and sometimes conflicting social movements and groups in complex modern societies. A more useful approach would feature conflict and power as constitutional ingredients, and would thus legitimise social action that could be said to be antithetical to the rational, collective debate of the original public sphere — contest, disagreement and emotion (Butsch 2007). Such a reimagining also extends to the public/private dichotomy. In the original bourgeois public sphere, the very definition of what count as 'private' interests simply reaffirms the already established, white-male-dominated hierarchy of issues of social importance. The publication of issues which are deemed to be private, but which have important public consequences, would challenge such hierarchies and diversify and expand public discussion (Fraser 1990).

According to Eley (1990), it is misleading to talk of the fracturing of the public sphere as occurring in the late nineteenth century, as it was in fact never a unified and all-encompassing space for social debate. The public sphere was

> the structured setting where cultural and ideological contest or negotiation among a variety of publics takes place, rather than ... the spontaneous and class-specific achievement of the bourgeoisie in some sufficient sense. (p. 11)

Habermas himself has acknowledged these critiques, and has re-evaluated the historical role of non-bourgeoisie cultures and movements, and the contemporary role of political mobilisation and its potential interjection of mass media cultures (Habermas 1992 in Downey & Fenton 2003). Recognition of multiple publics has thus been widespread since 1989, and these competing publics have been given various names: public sphericules, counterpublics, Indigenous public spheres. Fraser (1990) labelled them *subaltern counterpublics* to better articulate the contestation at the heart of public debate in unequal and diverse societies. The idea of subaltern counterpublics holds that marginalised groups in society have for a long time constructed their own, relatively independent publics within which they are able to speak their own language and, through deliberation, construct their own terms and articulate their own desires and needs. Fraser (1990, p. 71) gave the example of feminist publics which, through their own networks of education, public speeches and organisations, successfully argued for the inclusion of issues such as domestic violence as an important *public*, rather than *private*, issue to be debated in the wider public arena. Such an example demonstrates the potential of counterpublics to contribute to inclusive democratic decision making and to fundamentally affect public opinion.

Neither Eley nor Fraser discounts the existence of a wider, overarching public sphere in relation to which counterpublics operate and organise themselves. Fraser's (1990) example of a feminist public sphere, for example, would make little sense unless contextualised by a dominant, masculine public space and discourse organised through the exclusion of a variety of alternative modes of interaction and publicity.

Importantly, it is this overarching public that a subaltern feminist public sphere 'spoke' to, influenced and changed (Fraser 1990). In order to appreciate such processes, however, one must abandon the idea of a single public sphere, instead acknowledging the historical existence of publics outside of the dominant mainstream.

Ethnic media and multiple public spheres

The public expression and organisation so central to the public sphere has naturally resulted in the conceptualisation of competing publics being tied to an increasingly fragmented media environment. Notions of counterpublics and public sphericules have found a home in areas of media studies which focus on minority, ethnic, Indigenous and alternative media (Butsch 2007; Cunningham 2001; Hartley & McKee 2000; Husband 1998, 2005; Sreberny 2005; Couldry & Dreher 2007). Behind such reconceptualisations lies an acknowledgement of the growth of grassroots, community and ethnic media; the exclusory nature of the early public service media charged with articulating the nation; and the rise of social movements around the world that challenge equations of 'society' with nation-state (Deuze 2006; Murdock 1992; Hallin 2008).

At a discursive and expressive level, then, minority media are seen to articulate identities and movements that cannot appropriately be cast as part of a single, all-encompassing public (Cammaerts & van Audenhove 2005). These media provide a platform through which counterpublics can form and develop and disseminate alternative discourses (Browne 2005; Cunningham 2001; Hartley & McKee 2000). Those traditionally marginalised from the dominant public sphere, and indeed its representative media system, can use these media to control the particular cultural tone of their discussions and interactions, rather than trying to be heard in a dominant public sphere that, by its very nature, requires them to adopt the language and values of the dominant public. Thus, as Cunningham (2001, p. 133) suggests in arguing for diasporic popular media as facilitating public sphericules, '[t]here are now several claims for such public sphericules. One can speak of a feminist public sphere and international public sphericules constituted around environmental or human rights issues'.

Attitudes to such fracturing vary. Authors such as Todd Gitlin (1998) seem more pessimistic, suggesting that the effectiveness of a fractured public sphere rests on assumptions of equality and the subsumption of deep social fractures that preclude collective deliberation. For others, public sphericules and subaltern publics hold the potential for a more balanced society — one based not on unattainable consensus, but rather on the recognition of contestation and inequality in a political and social environment defined by a diversity of interests and voices (Fraser 1990).

Satellite publics or public interaction

At the broader political level of the public sphere, in terms of its idealisation as a model for liberal democratic politics, there is still a need for consideration of how competing publics form part of a political consensus that allows for the effective functioning of day-to-day life in complex societies. How do these discursively distinct publics encounter each other, and the dominant modes of political action in Western societies? In other words, beyond the realities of multiple representative spaces, the question 'of the relation among them' remains (Butsch 2007, p. 5). Once again, this is a question that Habermas himself has considered, and it has been the focus of significant work in media studies (Downey & Fenton 2003; Husband 1998, 2005; Dahlgren 2000). However, to a large degree a focus on discourse and representation has meant that the role of media in discussions of public spheres is yet to expand sufficiently to a consideration of how and where these processes turn into political action, and in what ways public spheres become more than a series of 'independent and parallel' publics (Husband 1998, p. 143). While Habermas was concerned with the potential of mass media as facilitators of the opening-up of the public sphere to marginalised publics, particularly during times of crisis when the dominant public sphere was vulnerable to counterdiscourses, others have looked to alternative media.

In thinking about this through ethnic media, one can take some of Fraser's (1990) contributions as a useful starting point. She suggested that it is indeed the public nature of counterpublics that guards against separatism, or the political ineffectualness at issue here: 'After all, to interact discursively as a member of a public — subaltern or otherwise — is to disseminate one's discourse into ever widening arenas' (p. 67). Fraser holds out hope for cross-cultural communication amongst publics structured within an egalitarian, multicultural society. The existence of multiple publics in multicultural societies need not 'preclude the possibility of an additional, more comprehensive arena in which members of different, more limited publics talk across lines of cultural diversity' (p. 69). Her example of the feminist public sphere makes clear the potential for counterdiscourses to seep through to the wider society, reflecting the reality of complex social systems in which different publics and the individuals within them overlap and intermingle. Issues of concern to minorities previously neglected in mainstream media have been thrust into public and even political debates in Australia, Europe and North America through the actions of minority publics and the media at their disposal (Hartley & McKee 2000).

However, beyond the discursive range of possibilities, others have looked at the structural conditions necessary to ensure sustained cross-public dialogue and the political efficacy of minority public spheres (Husband 1998, 2005). If ethnic media are able to publicise formerly neglected issues, questions still remain as to the degree to which minority publics can turn from 'weak publics' to 'strong publics' (Fraser 1990, p. 75).

Are ethnic media able to provide the conduit through which minority publics can directly influence wider public opinion formation and the resultant policy decisions on a consistent basis? What are the structural conditions necessary for such a process to take place in a sustained way, and for changes in public discussions to be met with changes in public policy?

These questions have been addressed by Charles Husband (1998, 2005), through an attempt to recognise the realities of the power of dominant ethnic majorities whilst sufficiently acknowledging inequality and diversity amongst publics. Husband's notion of the multi-ethnic public sphere seeks to recapture a commonly shared public space in order to avoid the political ineffectualness that multiple public spheres can bring. A series of separate public spheres, it is argued, will do little to promote inclusive democracy (Husband 1998, 2005; Couldry & Dreher 2007). The publication of alternative and subaltern ideas is one thing, but there must be mechanisms in place to ensure that those ideas are heard, understood and acknowledged. The basis of publicness, in and of itself, is no guarantee that counterdiscourses will have a sustained affect on majority public opinion and policy.

Husband thus bases the multi-ethnic public sphere on two premises that go to the heart of citizenship and communication: *differentiated citizenship* and *the right to be understood*. The principle of differentiated citizenship acts as a safeguard against more 'formulaic' interpretations of multiculturalism and universal citizenship, wherein the limits of diversity are set by dominant groups who define what it is to be acceptably different (Husband 1998, p. 140). It is a counter to the safe and superficial multiculturalism lamented by Zygmunt Bauman (2011), where diversity masks inequality through a series of cultural expressions that have little recourse to actual political action. Differentiated citizenship is therefore based at the level of social structure, and involves institutional, financial and legal assurances for the rights of ethnic and religious minorities, including support for ethnic and religious practices and the presence of minority groups within the 'central institutions of the larger state' (Husband 1998, p. 14). Importantly, the market is unable to guarantee support for these rights and protections, which instead require the intervention of the state in the form of 'provision for media regulation and funding to address the specific needs of minority ethnic groups' (p. 141).

The right to be understood is directly related to the need for the discursive expression of subaltern publics to be heard, recognised and acknowledged. It reflects aspects of an ideal speech situation and emphasises the commitment to 'seek comprehension of the other' and to recognise the legitimacy and value of the voices of other communities (Husband 1998, p. 139). The importance of this notion is articulated by Dreher (2010, p. 98), who has argued for the importance of 'questions of "listening" as well as "speaking"' when it comes to mediated interactions between minority and majority public spheres. This right to be understood can be seen as a safeguard against a monological media system that discourages debate and dialogue and systematically silences or misrepresents minority voices (Husband 1998; Jakubowicz et al. 1994).

At the systemic level, then, the multi-ethnic public sphere as an ideal goes some way to highlighting the limits of the current role of ethnic minority media in conceptualisations of multiple public spheres. Without some form of institutionalised avenues for cross-cultural dialogue, the role of ethnic media is unlikely to expand beyond the articulation of discursive subaltern publics, contributing to an image of cultural diversity with little political substance, sans some select public issues that gain prominence amongst the majority public sphere. As Husband has suggested,

> [c]onsequently a balanced multi-ethnic public sphere must also possess well-developed media systems which are capable of *sustaining* ethnically diverse agendas and which *promote dialogue across ethnic boundaries*. The multi-ethnic public sphere must articulate the differing interests of national minorities and minority ethnic groups ... (1998, p. 143, emphases added)

In Australia, both the community and, by extension, ethnic minority broadcasting sectors have had to fiercely defend their small slice of funding in an increasingly market-oriented media system. Although state intervention is antithetical to the original public sphere, it is necessitated by the rise of multinational media corporations with a monopoly on the media environment (Fraser 1990). At the same time, the limits of a publicly funded system can be seen in the historical analysis of Graham Murdock (1992), who points to the largely paternalistic and exclusory nature of the early BBC's broadcasting charter under Lord Reith. Such critiques have been echoed in analyses of Australia's multicultural broadcaster, SBS (Roose & Akbarzadeh 2013). Thus, as Graham Murdock (1992, p. 18) suggested almost a quarter of a century ago,

> [t]he crucial choice is not, as so many commentators suppose, between state licensing and control on one side and minimally regulated market mechanisms on the other. It is between policies designed to reinvigorate public communications systems which are relatively independent of both the state and the market, and policies which aim to marginalise or eradicate them.

The role of ethnic media in contributing to cross-public dialogue and political efficacy for marginalised public spheres is also limited by institutionalised communicative norms and standards in several Western countries. The dominant public discourse around communicative ethics, for example, has as its basis individual rights to speech and expression, with scant attention paid to the obligation to listen and comprehend (Husband 1998). The Western ideal of professionalism, particularly when it comes to journalism (Waisbord 2013), also limits the extent to which ethnic minority media are able to cross into the mainstream without abandoning their representative status vis-à-vis the minority community (Husband 2005; Sreberny 2005). Journalistic ideals of objectivity and impartiality are often applied pejoratively to ethnic minority journalists, who are expected to abandon their community aims if they desire acceptance into mainstream media institutions. As Husband (2005, p. 468) suggests, '[t]he moral concerns of identity politics with cultural viability and survival do not sit comfortably with the economic logic of media production and distribution'.

While these issues do not necessarily reduce the power of ethnic media in giving voice to minority ethnic public spheres, they certainly raise questions as to how to best think about the relationship between subaltern and dominant publics. As Couldry and Dreher (2007) suggest, it is perhaps more fruitful to approach the media of ethnic minorities as bridging systems, neither forming separate counterpublics nor being subsumed into the dominant public spheres. Their analysis of the Forum for Australia's Islamic Relations [FAIR] in Sydney suggests that this organisation sits outside of the mainstream public sphere, and yet is not completely separate from it, engaging as it does in a series of attempts to provide 'deliberation and activism that seeks to reform the mainstream public sphere, but from a position at present outside it' (p. 82).

Such an approach has several advantages. It captures the practices undertaken by ethnic media producers in order to reach beyond their own communities and have an impact on wider social discourses — practices that are present amongst media producers in Australia (Budarick & Han 2015). It also acknowledges the inevitable rigidness of any approach that neatly divides complex social actors into separate publics, and it recognises the potentially fluid nature of both marginal and dominant public spheres. Perhaps most importantly, this approach draws more attention to the nature of bridging. How is it that certain ethnic minority organisations are able to more or less effectively perform this function? What are the structural conditions necessary for such a role to be played in a sustainable manner? Answering these questions would go a long way to both clarifying and deepening our understanding of the relationship between ethnic media, public spheres and public opinion.

A transnational public sphere

The shifting contours of the public sphere have also expanded beyond the nation-state to incorporate transnational and even global public spheres. It is again useful to draw on Fraser (2014) as a starting point. Writing in the context of a recent explosion of literature on transnational communities, diasporas and media, Fraser points to the emergence of writing suggesting that the public sphere, once bound to the nation-state, has been expanded to account for transnational communities and movements. There is a rich history of work upon which such a changing view of the public sphere is able to draw. Studies of diasporas and transnationalism have challenged the equation of community and society with the Westphalian nation-state, demonstrating instead the existence of transnational communities held together over time and space by a series of processes, beliefs and organisations (Vertovec 2009).

Depending on which literature one reads, these processes and structures include the formation and maintenance of a shared history, destiny and collective identity by dispersed groups, supported by primordial claims to belonging, as when a transnational group sustains a collective identity through an adherence to a lost homeland they hope to one day reclaim (Safran 1991). They include transnational social and political movements and organisations that centralise dispersed communities, giving some of them more or less stable political formations and representative bodies to whom to turn for the reification of a recognised political identity. Then there is the role played by physical travel and interaction, with the material exchange of people, products and money across borders reaffirming a specific, transnational cultural identity (Vertovec 2009).

Underpinning much of this, however, are transnational communications networks — satellite television, digital communications technologies, telecommunications — which have the ability to transcend time and space and overcome the specificities of dispersed people living in different sociopolitical spaces. For example, in Steven Vertovec's (2009) detailed review of transnationalism, media and communications networks are a constant presence. In discussions of 'What's new?' about current trends in transnationalisation, modern media technologies — from satellite to Skype — offer a point of distinction from older forms of transnationalism, increasing the speed, intensity and sustainability of transnational processes. Such is the power of disembedded and re-embedded symbols and narratives, and the synchronicity afforded by media that can connect geographically dispersed migrants into a transnationally connected community. When discussing transnationalism as a site of political engagement, a definition that brings it directly into line with discussions of the public sphere, Vertovec (p. 9) has suggested that 'such a transnational framework — a global public space or forum — has been actualized largely through technology'.

Media and communication are also central to recent definitions of diasporas, themselves considered by some to be 'the exemplary communities of the transnational moment' (Tololyan 1991, p. 5). Floya Anthias (1998) has helpfully engaged with the changing understandings of diasporas, including their constitutive elements. She outlines a shift away from *descriptive typological* approaches that sought to define diaspora based on a set of criteria, most famously provided by William Safran in 1991, and based heavily on the classical Greek definition of diaspora as (forced) dispersal from the homeland with a longing and commitment to one day return. The homeland itself was central to such definitions, and the diasporic group was often seen as a unified ethnic community with primordial ties to a collectively recognisable home (Anthias 1998). Critics argued that such rigid definitions were unable to appreciate the diversity within and between diasporas, and solidified what were in fact changing, hybrid and imagined communities into monolithic ethnic groups.

Understandings of diaspora as a *social condition* focus less on testable definitions based on origin and the nature of dispersal, and instead focus on diaspora as being formulated and sustained through a transnational imagination that encompasses multiple transnational linkages, identities and communicative practices. The approach captures the changing understandings of diaspora that emerged largely from work in cultural studies and the influence of postmodern social theory. Identity was detached from ethnicity, and the homeland was no longer seen as a stable point of collective nostalgia, but rather as something imagined differently by different diasporic agents (Budarick 2014). What emerged was an 'understanding of diaspora that makes central culture — its formation, transformation, multiplicity, and complexity — rather than place' (Field & Kapadia 2011, p. xiii). Werbner (2002, p. 2) thus defined diasporas as 'deterritorialised imagined communities which conceive of themselves … as sharing a collective past and common destiny … existing beyond the nation state with its fixed boundaries'. Diaspora thus shifted from a categorical descriptor applied to certain populations, to a fluid, multifarious way of being, formed through imagination, connection and identity.

Like transnationalism, ideas of connectivity and communication are central to understandings of diaspora as a social condition. Cross-border media facilitate the transnational imagined community of diaspora (Karim 2003). These media overcome the tyranny of time and distance and construct an overarching 'space' in which diasporas can imagine themselves as part of an evolving and changing community. Transnational community is facilitated, then, through a mediated process of 'suppressing or neutralising internal differences, of establishing the context in which common experiences can be developed and past experiences can be interpreted in similar ways' (Sofos 1996 in Tsagarousianou 2004, p. 60).

Understanding the role of media in discussions of transnationalism and diaspora is an important foundation for identifying some of the pressing questions in considerations of a transnational public sphere, particularly as those questions relate to media. As the above discussion attests to, transnational communities are thought to be built, to a large degree, on the framework of transnational communications networks. However, the question remains as to what extent transnational media — satellite television, digital communication, telecommunications and the physical trade in older analogue forms — can be considered to be sustaining a transnational community or public. Furthermore, at what moments can people be said to belong to such a public, or to feel themselves as part of a transnational public?

The formation of publics

As with the formation of so-called transnational communities, the formation of a transnational public requires sustained political debate across borders and a common consensus over issues of public importance across different sociopolitical landscapes (Vertovec 2009; Cammaerts & van Audenhove 2005). In other words, people must share some idea as to what the political and social events that affect them are, despite living in potentially diverse social and political environments. And they must share an open and accessible forum through which to debate such issues using a shared language and non-exclusive cultural modes of interaction (Crack 2008; Fraser 2014).

In regards to the first issue, there is ample evidence to suggest that transnational media, in their old and new forms, struggle to provide a framework through which experiences of commonly held concerns and issues can be sustained. Rather, these media are part of a process in which watching satellite television or accessing digital technology facilitate and challenge allegiances, identities and belongings that are fluid and malleable (Budarick 2013). In some cases, this malleability leads to the exacerbation of differences in political, social and cultural experiences. Aksoy and Robins (2000, 2003; Robins & Aksoy 2001, 2004), for instance, question the assumption that transnational and diasporic media provide a sense of synchronicity to dispersed groups. In a study of Turks in Europe, they find that the use of transnational media can result in reminders of difference based on the local context of reception (2000). They describe the problem as one of a continuing fixity on the imagined community, even in its transnational forms:

> The analysis of transnational media remains grounded in the conventional idea of community bonding and the sharing of a common culture. For, in the end, in spite of all the evocations of the possibilities inherent in global flows and mobilities, there seems to be a basic inability to move on from the core ideas and concepts of the national imagination. In the discussion of transnational futures, the fundamental reference point continues to be the stubborn and insistent idea of 'imagined community'. (Robins & Aksoy 2004, p. 183)

Transnational media do not necessarily provide a resource for a transnational public of interest, one in which there is at least a basic level of acceptance that members are each affected by similar social and political issues. Further, they are seldom used in isolation, free from the pulls of localised media directing the attention of even the most transnational social agent to their local environment and to issues not shared with others in the supposedly transnational public (Budarick 2013). Migrants, as the archetypal dispersed citizens, are particularly diverse in their media consumption habits (Gillespie 2007). Much of this diversity stems from a lack of trust in any one source of information. It also comes from a need to be informed about a variety of geographical, political and cultural areas, and an epistiphilic desire for information built from the insecurity of movement and exile (Naficy 1993; Budarick 2013). What it means, however, is that the use of transnational media is always contextualised by more local, embedded forms, which potentially call on different incarnations of public and community.

However, transnational public spheres are increasingly being seen in terms of specific global issues, those that cannot be said to be attributable to, or resolvable by, a single nation-state (Cammaerts & van Audenhove 2005; Loader 2014). Cammaerts and van Audenhove (2005) describe these public spheres as being linked to changes in forms of citizenship, from *communities of birth* to *communities of interest*. Thus there are seemingly more and more instances of shared issues of interest and debate across borders, from global environmentalism to trade, foreign policy and free market capitalism. Even if the transnational media of diaspora and migration are unable to facilitate a transnational agenda of pressing social and political issues, isolated from and prioritised ahead of localised concerns, the prevalence of identity politics, organic social movements and alternative discursive communities ensures the formation of publics around global issues (Cammaerts & van Audenhove 2005).

But what of the mechanism for cross-border debate? If the issues can be said to exist individually of media, in terms of coming from concerned 'global citizens' rather than through media discourses, what forms of transnational media can truly support public deliberation transnationally? Digital media networks, including the internet and social media, are often held up as the archetypes of such media (Loader 2014). Aligned as they are with global social movements, from the Occupy movement to the anonymous and so-called Arab Spring, social media are giving rise to a new form of community of interest in which geographical dispersion is no impediment to collective debate and action.

As work on the relationship of digital media to transnational public spheres attests, however, class-, gender- and ethnicity-based exclusions from a public are still a reality. In her work on the relationship between transnational public spheres and media networks, Crack (2008, p. 70) cautioned against conflating the technological ability of digital media, and the utopian discourses that surround it, with the ability to support cross-border public spheres in all their complexity:

> A transnational public sphere rests on the ability of interlocutors to communicate across state borders with ease. It could be said that this requirement has already been met in terms of material capability. ICT [Information and Communications Technology] has eradicated temporal and spatial barriers to distanced communication. However, the prerequisites of public debate are more demanding than this.

These prerequisites include issues familiar to all who have critically engaged with the public sphere at the nation-state level: inclusiveness, accessibility and freedom from government and market interference. Just as they have been shown to be problematic ideals in Habermas's original theory, so, too, are they yet to be demonstrated as anything else at the transnational scale. This is recognised by Loader (2014), who suggested that the same weaknesses in the original bourgeois public sphere are in all likelihood replicated in digital publics based on social media and internet communication. As well as issues of gender and race, class is still a determining factor when thinking about the nature of a transnational public facilitated by digital networks (Loader 2014).

Such ambivalence to the potential of the internet was expressed by Habermas in the late 1990s, with a nod to contemporary debates around the democratic substance of many digitally formed social movements, as well as the potential fragmentation of social and political positions into ideological bubbles:

> The publics produced by the Internet remain closed off from one another like global villages. For the present it remains unclear whether an expanding public consciousness, though centered in the lifeworld, nevertheless has the ability to span systematically differentiated contexts, or whether the systemic processes, having become independent, have long since severed their ties with all contexts produced by political communication. (Habermas 1998 in Downey & Fenton 2003, p. 189)

As Papacharissi has suggested (2015, p. 8), 'the internet pluralizes but does not inherently democratize spheres of social, cultural, political, or economic activity'. The individualisation of much online content and the blurring of public and private through online expression problematise any neat connection between transnational digital networks and global public spheres (Papacharissi 2009). What is needed is a commitment to the recognition of the realities of the use and production of transnational media (as well as their content), which take place in specific locales, influenced but not over-determined by transnational and global factors. Transnational media — whether diasporic and exilic satellite television, issue-based global chat rooms online, or products from mainstream commercial media corporations — are produced with some combination of ideological, financial and political aims (some less than democratic), and with a more or less broadly defined audience in mind. As well as potentially transcending difference to the point of sustaining shared public debate across borders, these media are involved in the creation of networked and symbolic borders, wherein inclusion and belonging are based upon exclusion and division (Morley 2000; Shields 2014).

In both articulating issues of common public concern amongst dispersed communities, and providing the framework for debate across borders, transnational media are limited. Acknowledging and understanding these limitations is an important aspect of discussions of the public sphere. In order to avoid traversing old ground, discussions of transnational or global public spheres need to take seriously the empirical realities of transnational media and not be seduced by the technological capabilities of transborder technologies.

Conclusion

In this chapter I have critically analysed the role of ethnic, transnational and diasporic media in conceptualisations of multiple and transnational public spheres. I have demonstrated that these different forms of media are important to the changing parameters of the public sphere. Each allows for new forms of social interaction, provides new platforms for political debate and facilitates a framework for the emergence of new types of communities and publics. However, important limitations on the role of media in sub- and transnational public spheres have been raised. While ethnic media are undoubtedly a central part of the emergence and sustenance of subaltern and counterpublics, their ability to foster dialogue between different publics is less clear. While the public nature of discourse would seem to contribute to cross-public dialogue, without underlying structural and ethical conditions there is no guarantee that counterpublics will not simply be relegated to marginal voices with little political effect (Fraser 1990; Husband 1998).

Evidence for the emergence of a transnational public sphere can be seen in the growth of communities of interest around issues that are truly transnational, if not global, in their causes and impacts. While transnational media in no way guarantee that such issues are articulated and interpreted in a way that provides for deliberation across borders, the prevalence of global social movements 'from below', and their use of social and digital networks, would seem to reduce the reliance on media. However, as empirical studies demonstrate, even such open communicative environments as the World Wide Web come with their own problems of access and use, favouring an already privileged white, Western, urban elite whose central place online is perhaps foreshadowed by the dominance of their fathers and grandfathers in the physical political spaces on the global stage (Loader 2014; Cammaerts & van Audenhove 2005).

As the work of several authors explicitly and implicitly points out, the public sphere can be thought of as a 'horizon for the organization of social experience', and counter- or subaltern publics can never be completely separate from this overarching framework (Downey & Fenton 2003, p. 194). In this chapter I have attempted to contribute to an understanding of how 'non-mainstream' media may contribute to the interactions between public spheres in modern societies. The structures and systems that support or preclude more effective interpublic dialogue and debate are worthy of close academic attention.

References

Aksoy, A & Robins, K 2000, 'Thinking across spaces: Transnational television from Turkey', *European Journal of Cultural Studies*, vol. 3, no. 3, pp. 343-365.

Aksoy, A & Robins, K 2003, 'Banal transnationalism: The difference that television makes', in KH Karim (ed.), *The media of diaspora*, Routledge, London, pp. 89-104.

Anthias, F 1998, 'Evaluating diaspora: Beyond ethnicity', *Sociology*, vol. 32, no. 3, pp. 557-580.

Bauman, Z 2011, *Culture in a liquid modern world*, Polity, Cambridge.

Browne, D 2005, *Ethnic minorities, electronic media and the public sphere: A comparative study*, Hampton Press, Cresskill, NJ.

Budarick, J 2013, 'Localised audiences and transnational media: Media use by Iranian-Australians', *Media International Australia*, vol. 148, pp. 70-78.

Budarick, J 2014, 'Media and the limits of transnational solidarity: Unanswered questions in the relationship between diaspora, communication and community', *Global Media and Communication*, vol. 10, no. 2, pp. 139-153.

Budarick, J & Han, GS 2015, 'Towards a multi-ethnic public sphere? African-Australian media and minority-majority relations', *Media, Culture and Society*, vol. 37, no. 8, pp. 1254-1265.

Butsch, R (ed.) 2007, *Media and public spheres*, Palgrave MacMillan, Houndmills.

Calhoun, C 1992, *Habermas and the public sphere*, MIT Press, Cambridge, MA.

Cammaerts, B & van Audenhove, LV 2005, 'Online political debate, unbounded citizenship, and the problematic nature of a transnational public sphere', *Political Communication*, vol. 22, no. 2, pp. 147-162.

Couldry, N & Dreher, T 2007, 'Globalization and the public sphere: Exploring the space of community media in Sydney', *Global Media and Communication*, vol. 3, no. 1, pp. 79-100.

Crack, A 2008, *Global communication and transnational public spheres*, Palgrave Macmillan, US.

Cunningham, S 2001, 'Popular media as public "sphericules" for diasporic communities', *International Journal of Cultural Studies*, vol. 4, no. 2, pp. 131-147.

Dahlgren, P 2000, *Television and the public sphere: Citizenship, democracy and the media*, Sage, London.

Deuze, M 2006, 'Ethnic media, community media and participatory culture', *Journalism*, vol. 7, no. 3, pp. 262-280.

Downey, J & Fenton, N. 2003, 'New media, counter publicity and the public sphere', *New Media and Society*, vol. 5, no. 2, pp. 185-202.

Dreher, T 2010, 'Speaking up or being heard? Community media interventions and the politics of listening', *Media, Culture and Society*, vol. 32, no. 1, pp. 1-19.

Eley, G 1990, *Nations, publics and political cultures: Placing Habermas in the nineteenth century*, CCST Working Papers, The University of Michigan, Ann Arbor.

Field, RE & Kapadia, P 2011, *Transforming diaspora: Communities beyond national boundaries*, Fairleigh Dickinson University Press, Madison, NJ.

Fraser, N 1990, 'Rethinking the public sphere: A contribution to the critique of actually existing democracy', *Social Text*, vol. 25/26, pp. 56-80.

Fraser, N 2014, 'Transnationalizing the public sphere: On the legitimacy and efficacy of public opinion in a post-Westphalian world', in K Nash (ed.), *Transnationalizing the public sphere*, Polity, Cambridge, pp. 8-42.

Gillespie, M 2007, 'Security, media and multicultural citizenship: A collaborative ethnography', *European Journal of Cultural Studies*, vol. 10, no. 3, pp. 275-293.

Gitlin, T 1998, 'Media sphericules', in T Liebes & J Curran (eds.), *Media, ritual and identity*. Routledge, London, pp. 79-88.

Habermas, J 1989, *The structural transformation of the public sphere*, Polity, Cambridge.

Habermas, J 1996, *Between facts and norms: Contributions to a discourse theory of law and democracy*, Polity, Cambridge.

Hallin, D 2008, 'Neoliberalism, social movements and change in media systems in the late twentieth century', in D Hesmondhalgh & J Toynbee (eds.), *The media and social theory*, Routledge, Oxon, pp. 43-58.

Hartley, J & McKee, A 2000, *The Indigenous public sphere: The reporting and reception of Aboriginal issues in the Australian media*, Oxford University Press, Oxford.

Husband, C 1998, 'Differentiated citizenship and the multi-ethnic public sphere', *Journal of International Communication*, vol. 5, no. 1-2, pp. 134-148.

Husband, C 2005, 'Minority ethnic media as communities of practice: Professionalism and identity politics in interaction', *Journal of Ethnic and Migration Studies*, vol. 3, no. 3, pp. 461-479.

Jakubowicz, A, Goodall, H, Martin, J, Mitchell, T, Randall, L & Seneviratne K 1994, *Racism, ethnicity and the media*, Allan and Unwin, Sydney.

Karim, KH (ed.) 2003, *The media of diaspora*, Routledge, London.

Loader, B 2014, 'A transnational public sphere for a digital generation?', *E-International Relations*, viewed 21 August 2016, <http://www.e-ir.info/2014/08/15/a-transnational-public-sphere-for-a-digital-generation/>.

Morley, D 2000, *Home territories: Media, mobility and identity*, Routledge, London & New York.

Murdock, G 1992, 'Citizens, consumers and public culture', in M Skovmand & K Christian Schroder (eds.), *Media Cultures: Reappraising transnational media*, Routledge, London, pp. 17-41.

Naficy, H 1993, *The making of exile cultures: Iranian television in Los Angeles*, University of Minnesota Press, Minnesota.

Papacharissi, Z 2009, 'The virtual sphere 2.0: The internet, the public sphere, and beyond', in A Chadwick & PN Howard (eds.), *Routledge handbook of internet politics*, Routledge, London and New York, pp. 230-245.

Papacharissi, Z 2015, *Affective publics: Sentiment, technology, and politics*, Oxford University Press, New York.

Robins, K & Aksoy, A 2001, 'From spaces of identity to mental spaces: Lessons from Turkish-Cypriot cultural experience in Britain', *Journal of Ethnic and Migration Studies*, vol. 27, no. 4, pp. 685-711.

Robins, K & Aksoy, A, 2004, 'Parting from phantoms: What is at issue in the development of transnational television from Turkey?', in J Friedman & S Randeria (eds.), *Worlds on the move*, IB Taurus, London, pp. 179-206.

Roose, JM & Akbarzadeh, S 2013, 'The special broadcasting service and the future of multiculturalism: An insight into contemporary challenges and future directions', *Communication, Politics and Culture*, vol. 46, no. 1, pp. 93-115.

Safran, W 1991, 'Diasporas in modern societies: Myths of homeland and return', *Diaspora*, vol. 1, no. 1, pp. 83-99.

Shields, P 2014, 'Borders and information flows and transnational networks', *Global Media and Communication*, vol. 10, no. 1, pp. 3-33.

Sreberny, A 2005, 'Not only, but also: Mixedness and media', *Journal of Ethnic and Migration Studies*, vol. 31, no. 1, pp. 443-459.

Tololyan, K 1991, 'Nation state and its others: In lieu of a preface', *Diaspora: Journal of Transnational Affairs*, vol. 1, no. 1, pp. 4-5.

Tsagarousianou, R 2004, 'Rethinking the concept of diaspora: Mobility, connectivity and communication in a globalised world', *Westminster Papers in Communication and Culture*, vol. 1, no. 1, pp. 52-65.

Vertovec, S 2009, *Transnationalism*, Routledge, Oxon.

Waisbord, S 2013, *Reinventing professionalism*, Polity, London.

Werbner, P 2002, 'The place which is diaspora: Citizenship, religion and gender in the making of chaordic transnationalism', *Journal of Ethnic and Migration Studies*, vol. 28, no. 1, pp. 119-133.

'Imagine if our cities talked to us': Questions about the making of 'responsive' places and urban publics

3

Mary Griffiths

> The digital world is converging with the physical world, and this phenomenon, known as the Internet of Things, represents the next era of computing. It is one where just about anything can be connected, through sensors and data to other objects, environments, people and, of course, the Internet. (Altimeter Group 2015)

The range of technical, social, environmental and political issues raised by the possibility of 'just about anything' being invisibly connected is overwhelming in breadth, scale and depth. The seamlessness of the connectivity predicted is unprecedented in human history and there are as yet few convincing full-scale examples in connected buildings, or in consumer supply chains enabled by the Internet of Things [IoT], or in smart cities, to illustrate how it works in practice. Critical issues already identified include a controversial means of data collection, which makes new forms of urban planning and placemaking as a 'whole-of-city' enterprise possible; and related governmental techniques through which city populations (and specific publics) can be involved in designing their own governance. Yet initiatives exist (some of which will be used to illustrate this chapter's arguments) which cast light on the ways that smart technologies are starting to shape everyday experiences of the material world, and generate new relations of power.

In this chapter, the making of places and publics is addressed through the prism offered by the nascent Internet of Things and locative technologies in the 'smart city'. The smart city can be defined as an urban digital infrastructure supporting, amongst other activities, technologically-enabled responsive environments. These spaces are governed by big data collected by various means, which allow 'the city' to talk back to its inhabitants by offering real time information and a range of choices designed to alter behaviour or encourage different relationships to place. The chapter aims firstly to identify the drivers of the rapid adoption of 'smartification' by cities and users, and then to canvass the democratic and participatory factors involved in implementing radical change, noting the risks which may occur in the rush to connect on such a global scale.

My argument is that the democratic governance of data which allows a city to 'talk' to its inhabitants requires the adoption of participatory, inclusive practices from those designing responsive places. As the big data collected represents a 'collective enterprise' (Ruppert 2015), the 'makers' of the urban space include all those from whom information is collected, those who extract it and analyse it, and those to whom it is returned, as well as the urban designers of the smart city. Speaking politically in Latour's sense of having no preconceptions about how things work (2003), but a sense of how they *could* serve populations democratically, I argue that a critical gap in awareness of, and ambitions for, the urban IoT may be emerging between, on the one hand, municipal governments and their technology partners and, on the other, the urban inhabitants whose everyday experiences are directly affected by smart design. Users are already being familiarised to the IoT by their experience of smart consumer products, and made subjects of the IoT in different contexts such as work and home. The provable accountability and success of 'responsive' urban placemaking, and even the inclusiveness of rights to the city for all, could be affected if planners do not engage with existing publics, or accurately reconceptualise the new publics made by 'smartification' processes. At this early stage of the IoT, smart city planning requires contextualisation and democratic scrutiny.

Placemaking in cities

Placemaking has a civic, aesthetic and communitarian history which long precedes the arrival of digital technologies, emerging from urban planning, citizen activism and built practices. It is described as a 'crucial and deeply valued process for those who feel intimately connected to places in their lives', one which helps them 'to reimagine everyday spaces, and see anew the potential of parks, downtowns, waterfronts, plazas, neighbourhood, streets, markets, campuses and public buildings' (Project for Public Spaces, n.d.). Placemaking as a practice generates the participatory publics who help shape traditions of mutuality, as well as feelings of neighbourhood belonging and community membership. Large-scale civic placemaking often has a recognisably aesthetic or public art component. The allusive poetic texts embedded into the surfaces of Federation Square in Melbourne, and the arts community's curation of the Victorian Arts Projects 'Testing Grounds' on City Road, Southbank, are Australian examples. Both shape participation by prompting mindfulness of civic issues beyond individuals' immediate experience of their physical surroundings.

Striking international examples of placemaking include botanist Patrick Blanc's creation of the vertical garden for museums in Paris, and on corporate buildings in downtown Sydney and Toronto (Blanc, n.d.). The spectator is encouraged to ponder the meanings generated by the exotic plant colonisation of spaces from Qantas lounges to concrete towers. These and art-based revivifications of urban 'dead spaces' attract mutable publics, an assembly of individuals with no prior attachment, hailed by an external prompt and, in the sense Warner (2002) describes them, made through their visibility to each other before dispersal. One such public, reminiscent of a Rheingold flash mob, comprises passersby around a digital pop-up installation under Manhattan Bridge in Chinatown, New York (Jaffe 2012). The pop-up is unlikely to sustain a collective sense of place, but the installation's continued material presence has the potential to remake these transient publics. Placemaking like this is confined to specific areas of a city, and produced by adding a piece of art or an engaging activity to an environment or by redesigning its physical attributes.

Beyond beautification projects and spectacles originated by individual makers, institutions, corporations and governments, a distinctive placemaking practice is emerging, characterised by the element of participatory design with a broader set of stakeholders. The movement for collectively remaking a city's spaces, and reclaiming them for inhabitants, has been gaining traction since the late 1960s. The Project for Public Spaces [PPS], a US nonprofit planning, design and educational organisation operating since 1975, has worked on over 3000 placemaking projects in forty-three countries and in all fifty states, with the participatory approach indicated by its logo: 'It takes a place to create a community, and a community to create a place'. The practice emphasises a collective working for common ground in shared values and assumptions about places and their meanings, and a commitment to the extensive consultative processes and inclusivity needed to achieve, animate and sustain them. Considering the renewal of the wastelands typical of cities established during the first industrial revolution, an urban photographer writes, 'Any truly meaningful reinterpretation or reinvention of a site's history must take its context and future into account; it must be woven thoughtfully into the contemporary urban fabric, and animated by its inhabitants' (Lister in Project for Public Spaces, n.d).

A contemporary movement which acts on this philosophy is 'creative placemaking', a professional practice often represented by the work of design companies invited to generate projects with communities for government and corporate clientele. For example, the redesign of urban mobilities in the Boston-Washington mega-metropolis refers to older ideas about supercities and 'Boswash', but uses contemporary digital mapping tools to shape intersecting transit systems and hubs, significantly elaborating on the concept of mobility by envisioning a flexible timeshare basis for areas once seen as separate: private homes and public spaces (Rubin 2012). Another project, successful and on a smaller scale, places multiple swings attached to musical chords into an urban 'dead zone' of Montreal so that, as people participate physically, they can make music together (Fadden 2013).

'Smart' placemaking

With the arrival of the IoT and its adoption by municipal planning departments, the convergence of the digital and the physical worlds means that placemaking imperatives will both speed up and change fundamentally, whether they are grassroots-based or the objects of patronage by corporations and governments. Smartification encompasses the oversight of the distributed physical networks, digital data and human agencies which together will co-produce the ubiquitous information flows, and the ambient digital experiences of the future information ecologies. Placemaking becomes a central pillar of urban planning as municipal agencies work with digital infrastructure staff and external partners to develop 'liveability', economic sustainability and tourism potential by deploying all their resources, within the overall framework provided by a city's strategic technology plans and its inventories of data resources. More genuine attempts at co-production of place may result than was evident in the initial stages of the creative industries push (Kent & Nikitin 2013). The new approach is also underpinned by reuse of a city's data, and by opening access for citizens' use. The European Union has early prize-winning examples in Spain's Aporto portal, and Helsinki's Infoshare (European Commission 2013).

However, comprehensive governance of smart systems goes beyond offering citizens open information access and designing portals for information sharing and placemaking. Smart placemaking, developed alongside the current forms, will be a challenging, strategic and integrated project, one where the informating of city spaces will take Australian populations and their municipalities into uncharted technology development, participation and governance territory. Will inhabitants feel a sense of belonging and feel empowered to participate in city-wide placemaking? Citizen awareness, education, understanding and consent to data-driven experiences enabled by the IoT are being seen as critical to a city's success. As Scholl and Scholl (2014) argue, 'open, transparent and participatory government' is the key to establishing the 'new models' of democratic response to smart technologies and practices. Smart norms, protocols, procedures and considerations could develop which limit access or deny urban participation to stakeholders, if they are developed conceptually, democratically and empirically unexamined, without priority attention being paid to investigating project 'failures'.

Cities as pressure points: A driver of systems thinking

Understanding the non-civic externalities which drive trends in smart uptake by municipalities is important, as it explains its speed and comprehensive nature. The exponential global growth of urban populations is the major reason that municipalities are favouring systems thinking and smart solutions. The United Nations' Department of Economic and Social Affairs predicts that up to 66 per cent of the world's population will live in cities by 2030, with 2.5 billion extra people by 2050. The UN's original estimates have been revised as population graphs show steeper recent rises, indicating that cities will be the pressure points for 'sustainable development challenges' (United Nations, Department of Economic and Social Affairs, Population Division 2014).

All aspects of cities can be a specific cause for concern — their size, amenities, resources, geography, legacy of built environment, and global footprint — as well as the equity with which their inhabitants are treated and the extent to which city-dwellers feel they belong. Mexico City and Hong Kong struggle to deal with waste disposal effectively. Beijing has air pollution levels considered dangerous enough that government advice is to stay indoors on 'orange alert' days. Non-stop influxes of people into Tokyo, predicted to remain the world's biggest city, create problems for the capital itself, and also a loss of human resources, business and revenue for the cities from which internal migrants are drawn (Johnson 2015b). Infrastructure and resource problems faced by European cities have multiplied with increased numbers of refugees and migrants seeking immediate help and accommodation. The collapse of car manufacturing centres in the United States has led to population loss, and to the 'post-apocalyptic' wasteland of Detroit documented in the work of many photographers, most evocatively perhaps in 'The Ruins of Detroit' (Marchand & Meffre 2012).

Newly constructed cities — say, in China — do not have the post-industrial legacy common in Western cities but they are not without serious governance as well as rights issues. 'Apple City', the aerotropolis designed around a hub of economic smart activity in Zhengzhou Airport Economic Zone, is home to Foxconn iPhone manufacturing. Over a quarter of a million workers assemble parts flown in from around the world, and oversee the iPhone units flown out. A business report on the human cost claims that, despite their virtual entrapment in the aerotropolis, Foxconn workers are required to register as living in their hometown. There is no management imperative to make 'Apple City' liveable or responsive to individuals' needs, nor do employees necessarily have the right to residency in nearby Zhengzhou. They are 'citizens in transit' (Pedroletti 2014), without the means or power to make a more amenable place of the aerotropolis. Worker protection, an achievement of democracies embedded in cumulative legislation for over a century and enforced through collective actions, is missing. Photographs of suicide prevention nets outside accommodation buildings exist, which attest to the desperation caused by exclusions. They are suggestive of what Bauman calls the 'collateral damage' of liquid modernity (2011).

Turning closer to home, Australian residents' experience of place, sense of attachment and entitlement to participate is equally affected by location-specific factors, by access to the city and by socioeconomic status. Under-serviced suburbs impose disadvantages on families, youth, the sick and disabled, the poor and the old, restricting the benefits of living in cities — such as employment opportunities or access to fast broadband, medical and educational facilities — and therefore affecting the right to participate fully in urban life. Distance in Australia has always been a major factor in effective urban planning, governance and placemaking. For example, Canberra, the 'bush' capital, is disposed over a large area relative to its population. The plan for a small light-rail development, to ease traffic flows into the city from a new northern suburb and lessen the need for central parking, has been controversial not simply because of the expected charge on the public purse but also, some argue, because of its inevitable obsolescence as the city grows (McIlroy 2015). Canberrans argue through *The Canberra Times* about inner city property development, and the squeezing out of the young from home ownership, with the resultant impact on social inclusivity. The concentration of vulnerable, high-risk populations in an outlying housing estate, 'the suburb where the only business is a liquor store, and no buses run' (Ellery 2016), particularly animates public debate. The Canberra Centre, a well-appointed shopping mall in the city centre, nevertheless has many 'dead spaces' that divide those with rights from those who are excluded. Surveilled walkways run between buildings where cars and pedestrians share access, and the homeless beg. Inside the mall, Salvation Army collectors are able to sit down, and an attractive illumination, 'A Light Touch', on the wall opposite a major retail outlet amuses consumers' children (Figure 3.2).

Conventional assumptions about people, uses and values are embedded in these examples, but the practice of placemaking can unexpectedly open up. Canberra traders outside the mall recently announced a new revivification fund for small community projects for the city's 'dead heart', Garema Place, because, according to the fund's director, 'No single citizen should curate the city' (MacDonald 2016).

Although cities' specific problems differ, large-scale, complex and individual problems are shared across cities. Planners' attention is justifiably attracted to the smart technologies thought capable of capturing the data necessary for more efficient designs — data which promise to provide timely whole-of-city information and can be used to model future population movements, to predict whole-of-city priorities, and

Figure 3.1: Dead space.
Source: M Griffiths, 28 May 2016.

Figure 3.2: 'A Light Touch', Responsive Mural.
Source: M Griffiths, 23 April 2016.

to avoid the backlash from publics disappointed by unmet needs. Multiple examples of controversial placemaking, and a growing awareness of public connectedness or the lack of it, exist everywhere in Australia. Youth and children's interests and rights, particularly, require careful deliberation. It is rare to find these groups self-represented in planning discussions, though Melbourne has implemented some strategies of inclusion (Corkey & Bishop 2015). An example, at the building level, is 'Play Up' at the Museum of Australian Democracy, a child-oriented place at the heart of Old Parliament House, popularly visited at weekends. It was designed 'for and by children with the help of adults', according to video signage.

The panoptic gaze of UN Urban Renewal expert panels has resulted in endorsement of a charter of guiding principles on 'rights to the city' for global and local adaptation and implementation. Participatory approaches to urban governance have become the paramount consideration in urban renewal discussions. UN panels determined that, given the complexity of issues and problems that governments face, preserving inclusive 'rights to the city' will need a particular governance: 'Above all, new urban governance should be democratic, inclusive, multi-scale and multi-level' (Habitat 111 2016, p. 3).

Technology is to be put to use democratically in administrative and governance functions for populations, and with populations. A governance approach is useful for analysis of responsive space, where technology may inflict collateral damage by unforeseen exclusions. Data streams 'place' people physically in a city square, and simultaneously locate them as nodes in the IoT, interacting with, and changing, the environment around them. Primary modes of data collection are through mobile usage, beacons and locative devices. The ways that rights are currently conceptualised will need to be supplemented in future by consideration of the limitations imposed by access to and use of technology, and the smart literacies and practices of city populations. Smart phone possession, knowledge of functionalities and app uses, and the ability to navigate data flows will be necessary to fully participate in urban life.

The second driver: Consumer familiarisation with 'enhanced experiences'

Across industrial and commercial sectors, IoT innovation and uptake is becoming substantial enough for the German government to name the revolution Industry 4.0 — the next stage in the information revolutions that are, as in the past, formative elements in the dynamics of cities. Others name it the Industrial IoT, but it is also social. Characterised by timely data measurement and machines acting without intervention, 4.0 goes beyond automated product assembly to altering a company's relationships with employees and consumers, and it acts as a proxy for the civic domain in both the efficiencies that municipalities hope to gain through smartification, and in concerns about big data's capacity for consumer profiling and invasions of privacy.

4.0 illustrates how new relationships and value chains are made possible: sensors are deployed to protect workers in hazardous conditions, whether they are in mines or on the shop floor; embedded devices extend a manufacturer's engagement with customers by tracking products after sale and returning information to original producers and third parties.

For corporations, adopting the IoT has a consumer-based inflection: Ford, for example, talks about what these technologies can do less in terms of the design of 'product-based interactions', and more in terms of a connectivity which offers the driver 'end-to-end experiences' — and how the changes these technologies bring will play out in everyday smart city planning (Cameron 2016). Thus, after years of machine-to-machine industrial and commercial uses, connectivity now includes people and things in extended consumer relationships. Smart developments may seem singular and dispersed but, scaled up, they signify radical social change.

The discourse of 'enhanced experiences' has been a significant marker of the debate about technology-enabled urban modernity. Pew research based on over 2558 expert predictions of the likely impact of the Internet of Things in 2025 found that the majority framed it positively, with one participant likening it to the way electricity now works seamlessly in everyday life (Anderson & Rainnie 2014). Smart features are increasingly familiar additions to consumer goods (from Mimo's baby-monitoring devices, to Safewise's wearable child and pet tracker, to Nintendo's sleep monitor). These products are all marketed as 'experiences': the first two, promising greater security for children, offer an enhanced parenting experience. The third sells an experience of personal health management. All have the potential to change behaviour patterns and relationships. Such products so rapidly familiarise consumers with the 'smart' functionalities of a range of ordinary goods that the process of data collection and reuse could seem merely part of a seamless continuum of technological advancements to improve individuals' everyday life.

Marketed this way, the changes look beneficial. Though dependent on individual choices, they signify a more technologically invasive future. Manuel Castells argues that 'technology itself does not produce anything', and also that 'power relations are the DNA of society' (2012). The IoT, with human-machine actors, presents a different challenge from broadcast media and prior networks, and complicates a ready dismissal of technological determinism. Rapid migration of the IoT, from its main drivers in consumer and then civic domains, means that tracking the exact points of agency in each adaptation or new use of technology is complex. In the mass uptake of each smart device, and in each new value chain created, there are many individual and collaborative makers, interfaces, algorithmic designs, and evolving and automated connections between specialist businesses and platforms. Such chains disrupt established relationships, as well as generating and anchoring new ones.

In a city, as big data is collected and reused from a vast array of scarcely noticeable sensors, and information ecosystems are formed, the agents involved in helping a city 'talk' become invisible. Their invisibility and pervasiveness and the seamlessness of their operations means that inhabitants have less choice than when they are consumers of individual products. Pre-existing familiarisation with smart devices shapes and possibly restricts municipal approaches to 'experience'-driven civic relationships. Civil liberties groups rightly point to concerns about privacy and surveillance, governmental issues reminiscent of Foucault's disciplinary panopticon, and to the need to preserve the integrity of human agency and data security in these automated, non-transparent processes. The question of how consent is gained for the reuse of personal information, and all the (as yet) opaque affordances of smart technology, animates pessimistic discussions about smart technologies in the consumer domain and amongst privacy watchdogs such as the Electric Freedom Foundation, which tracks technological intrusions into the private domain and gives advice about the protective measures individuals can make to opt out of data collection or internet tracking (Budington 2015; Eckersley, Reitman & Toner 2015).

'Open' and 'closed' loops in the city that talks

Industry and commerce have also taken on a significant role as 'explainers' of the smart city for the public and, significantly, for journalists mediating the information in ways they judge appropriate for their particular news publics. The concept of eliminating human error is a much-used trope in introductory explanations about responsive environments. Cisco Australia's explanation of the scale of the change is that people 'can start expecting a more responsive environment', mitigating its novelty by noting that people are already monitoring real time traffic flows on Google Maps. Kevin Bloch, a spokesperson, explains in an interview published in *The Guardian* (Yoo 2016):

> It's responsive because we're measuring and collecting data then making decisions on that data to change the actual city itself ... With computers integrated into every piece of physical infrastructure, machines adapt to human behaviour and physical conditions to provide convenience, feedback and efficiency.

Bloch (in Yoo 2016) uses 'open' and 'closed' communication loops to further describe responsive environments. He suggests that the IoT is a closed loop, with predictive benefits:

> Today we're in very much an open loop — something happens, a human makes a decision and that's it. In the future, we're moving to what I call a closed loop environment, where the human will have data coming to it telling you — don't go this way, go that way, or panic, somebody's just died over here — all sorts of things can start coming to you without actually humans intervening in it.

Illustrating the way in which one closed loop might operate, he privileges data-driven mobility over human interventions (in Yoo 2016):

You go to watch a sports game. Because there are 70 000 people all going to the one stadium, the cost of parking will dynamically go up. At the end of that afternoon, because it knows that people are leaving, the cost of parking will dynamically drop. The actual city itself starts telling you [how to optimise that] rather than you just blindly doing what you've been doing for the last 100 years. That's what they call cognitive systems, autonomous intelligence or artificial intelligence, which starts making the city even smarter than, perhaps, humans are.

The activities described rely on real time information derived from big data, collected, stewarded, narrativised and reused by municipal agencies or corporations. Whether such data serve the demos depends on the level of granularity in the answers to questions about matters such as who collects the data, and why; what the alternative narratives are which can be told from data; who reuses the data, according to what kinds of protocols; and what the overall municipal governance objectives are. If the 'city' is 'talking' to its population, it is imperative to ask about both the premises of IoT scenography designers, and how they conceptualise the civic.

The scenarios and subjects of the IoT

Contemporary examples of the experimental design of responsive spaces, as represented by news reports or municipal websites, are useful for insights into the social and power relationships they anchor. A fully realised IoT experiment is said to exist at the building level in The Edge, Amsterdam, where 28 000 sensors capture real time, usable data for achieving energy efficiencies and the best use of the building, at the same time as they micromap employee activities. New ways of working, interacting and living are demonstrated in this contemporary panopticon — a vision of a 'smart future' in its transparency, aesthetics and, for some observers, its menace. The Edge primarily houses Deloitte, whose employees are said to endorse its benefits as a 'living lab'. A Bloomberg journalist (Randall 2015) notes the disruption to an orthodox sense of personal space in routine business practices. Fixed locations are linked, in this formulation, to a rigidity in attitudes:

> Since workers don't have assigned desks, lockers serve as home base for a day. Find a locker with a green light, flash your badge and it's yours. Employees are discouraged from keeping a locker for days or weeks because the *het nieuwe werken* philosophy is to break people away from their fixed locations and rigid ways of thinking. (Randall 2015)

Sensors in The Edge allow for ambient personalisation of workspaces through mobile apps set for individual preferences. Surveillance is all-encompassing, beginning with the scanning of employees' licence plates and cross-checking staff numbers before parking access is granted.

Deloitte executives do not, reportedly, have inappropriate access to employees' information; nevertheless, a vast data pool exists and some of it can be accessed by staff via 'data dashboards'. These give real time collective information about the building's functionalities, which in turn triggers modifications to the physical environment and thus, imperceptibly, to inhabitants' behavioural patterns. In a reprise of the IoT thinking about 'closed loops' discussed earlier, the facilities' manager notes in a BBC interview: 'We want to predict how things will happen in the building, that will be the really smart thing' (Wakefield 2016). Predictive uses of data in the interests of greater energy or business efficiencies limit individual agency for some subjects of the IoT. Though The Edge is an example of smart, sustainable integrated design, what it represents in terms of governing worker communities is neither entirely new, nor innocent of the DNA of social power relations noted by Castells. The deployment of technology could be said to belong to an industrial governance tradition started by socially minded capitalist-reformers from the first industrial revolution. British industrialists, notably (but not always) from pacifist Quaker families, created worker communities around their mills and factories, by offering amenities (like healthcare and community facilities) in exchange for workers' adherence to a set of social rules. Scaled up, the connected communities in buildings like The Edge could represent the responsive spaces of cities: smart neighbourhoods, central business districts and public spaces. Their predictive features make them attractive to contemporary planners.

Santander, a civic usage scenario

Santander in northern Spain is a living lab which suggests that the smart revolution enabled by data-driven placemaking is achievable for civic and democratic deployment. Sensors installed over a four-year period measured energy outputs and waste levels, parking spaces, and pavement traffic (Newcombe 2014). SmartSantander was funded by the EU to test the kinds of 'big picture' information that smart technologies could give city governments. The project now has test bed facilities in Belgrade, Lübeck and Guilford. Working from organic metaphors, Santander developed a Cloud City Centre, a 'brain' for the city which provides a visual capture of real time information and a 'Platform': a 'spine' of sensors which include static (fixed sensors), dynamic (those in movement), and 'participatory' types. The latter are the smart phones through which citizens collect data themselves, or report an event (Smart City, n.d.). The council's website notes that citizens participate in multiple civic projects, and in an Innovation Forum for promoting neighbourhood input. Endorsed citizen-based activities, called 'CityScripts', provide workstations to users for access to data to create collaborative projects. One of these, 'Friends', is about selecting a friend who is a follower on Twitter, and revealing his/her shared things and services with others in the group. Data deployed to enhance social bonding work from assumptions about existing levels of 'friendship', and potentially generate new connectivity bonds (Smart City, n.d.)

The governing protocols for monitoring a convergence of humans and things differ in The Edge and SmartSantander, yet these two illustrations of IoT deployment demonstrate that living labs are essential for IoT experimentation, incorporating designs which reflect democratic and inclusive principles for civic domains. MIT regularly initiates applied IoT and big data research, partnered with Santander and other cities, and the civic-focused examples they promulgate on YouTube channels show how 'rights to the city' can be enhanced through making narratives out of data to help planning departments. Using the often prioritised 'efficiencies' discourse of smart planning, one experiment documented 'the cost of justice'. It maps criminal offending patterns by district in New York, against the costs of repeated incarceration of real but unnamed individuals. MIT researchers thus present big data as a prompt for rethinking the use of public funding in the neighbourhoods where offending is, through cross-referencing, shown to be the result of poverty and unemployment. In an example of responsive placemaking, researchers show that the right to safety in the city can be underpinned by smart technologies. A persuasive document, *Public Safety, Justice and the Internet of Everything*, is filled with case studies, from improved emergency response times through smart technology to providing police with enhanced connectivity on investigation sites (Cisco 2014b).

'Non-ideological' efficiencies and the publics they serve

IBM's initial concept of smartification, speedily conceived after the global financial crisis, was persuasive and 'non-ideological'. The company announced the 'Decade of Smart' in 2008 and its CEO gave an influential speech about the need to infuse intelligence into smarter systems and build smarter infrastructure. IBM followed it with a program of strategic engagement at a hundred forums in 2009. By 2010, it was documenting persuasive evidence about smart efficiencies. Then CEO Sam Palmisano highlighted the collective good, arguing that

> building a smarter planet is realistic because it is so refreshingly non-ideological. Yes, debates will continue to rage on contentious issues in our society … but no matter which viewpoint one shares — or which ultimately prevails in any given society or industry — the systems which prevail will need to be smarter — more transparent, more efficient, more accessible, more equitable, more resilient. (IBM, n.d.)

The success of that goal depends on a political consideration: the governance of smarter systems for the whole collective. In the responsive spaces of the smart city, places and publics will become inextricably linked because, if big data is deployed to govern inhabitants and visitors through the information they themselves provide sometimes without their knowledge or consent, it is indeed 'a collective achievement' (Ruppert 2015). Discussions of design principles are only now emerging as the smart city is being constructed from the top down through formal partnerships between municipalities, technology infrastructure corporations and start-ups. As new ways of working and living emerge and others are imagined, city governments will be expected to inform populations, and co-create place with them.

Barcelona is a Cisco 'Lighthouse City', its smart developments internationally followed (Cisco 2014a). A mayor linked to the smart city concept was defeated in 2014, on the commons-based renewal platform of activist Ada Colau. Barcelona is now crowdsourcing and co-curating placemaking, and downplaying smart development for its own sake. The mayor of Paris Anne Hidalgo, also a socialist, explains the ethics of participatory governance:

> To build a just, progressive and sustainable city, collective intelligence is our greatest strength. Exchange and debate are our most powerful tools. It was this conviction that led us to make citizen participation a cornerstone of the development of our public policies. Because Paris belongs to the Parisians, I want to put them at the center of reflection and municipal action. I want to give them the means to make their voices heard, practically and simply contribute to the design of large and small urban projects. That's the core purpose of democracy. (n.d.)

Hidalgo is the face of the effective 'co-constructing Paris' portal, *Mairie de Paris, J'ai une idée*, which crowdsources and, through citizen and expert panels, applies proof of concept tests to ideas registered by citizens for improving Paris.

Making an Australian 'smart' city and citizens

The city council in Adelaide governs only the central business district, but its power to shape the city as a whole derives from its close strategic relationship with the government of South Australia. Effectively, the two bodies engage in most city initiatives on built environment, including communications infrastructure. South Australia has specific challenges, compounded by its perceived geopolitical disadvantage as a state with only one major city, when every Australian city is in competition. The loss of the car manufacturing industries, the downturn in mining profitability, the drift of professional workers and the young to the eastern states, and a host of other difficulties imposed by distance are major reasons why city and state have together embarked on ambitious renewal plans, incorporating the IoT in placemaking.

The city describes its ambitions as beginning on a small scale, at street level, with a project called Splash Adelaide (Adelaide City Council 2012), encouraging start-ups and community activists to break city by-laws on closing times, and allowing street activities in arts and business projects aimed at revitalising the city's dead spaces. Organisers were not to infringe civil or criminal law, but people were allowed to fail so that the city council could learn from their mistakes (Johnson 2015b). From that point on, selected city neighbourhoods were seen as distinctive places with invisible boundaries, yet coherent identities. AdelaideFree, the city wifi, was in place before the IoT was adopted as an underpinning strategic enabler for future developments.

When Adelaide was declared a Cisco 'Lighthouse City' (Department of State Development 2015; Cisco, n.d.), a year after a Memorandum of Understanding was agreed between the state government and the technology provider, Mayor Martin Haese spoke in terms of increased liveability and economic benefits, and of the practical uses (in smart street lighting and traffic controls) which would make the city safe for residents and attractive to visitors (Corner 2015). A buzz around smartification followed: driverless car trials were announced and took place on state highways; the city's Smart Hub was launched in November 2015; air-monitoring has been piloted.

One approach to citizen education about the benefits of the IoT has been to experiment with storying the technology-enhanced experience of a young professional returning to Adelaide to set up a business. From her searches online to her access to information about data on pedestrian traffic flows and possible competitors, the city's IoT makes her return easy in a storyboard (Figure 3.6).

IoT developments are enabled globally by formal partnerships between governments and infrastructure providers like Cisco, as well as Hitachi and Microsoft. These entities possess big data on residents and different remits from government. The remits are not mutually exclusive, or irreconcilable. As yet there are no clear joint pathways for deploying what is learned from big data. User-informed consent or opt-out provisions have not yet been worked out. To date it seems that the missing municipal partnership is with the city's own publics. Every municipality has a plethora of end-users who may know little about the predicted benefits of the IoT and who already have concerns about the privacy and security of their data and the reuse of such data. An IoT report from the EU's DG Connect, addressing the social and ethical dimensions of the IoT, prioritises governance and trust as key issues (van der Hove 2015).

In early 2016, as part of a larger study ('Smart technologies and cultural heritage'), I ran Adelaide- and Canberra-based pilot studies on awareness of, and attitudes to, smart technologies (Griffiths 2016). It found that low numbers knew about the concept of a smart city, and even fewer people had a sense of what smart technologies might enable, or of their impact on everyday life. Even so, most participants were open to the concepts of responsive environments, while noting concerns about privacy, autonomy and questions about the curation of information. This suggests that the challenge for smart placemakers will be to create informed engagement with city populations through dynamic and repeated consultations with representative publics, and those most concerned in each development; and to find ways to deploy the power and imagination of the collective. Identifying shared 'place capital' will prove necessary (Johnson 2015b) as will ensuring citizen empowerment (Gurstein 2014). Participatory governance is local government's challenge (Aulich 2009).

Big data techniques could shape a civic governance infrastructure for multilevel collective decision making, beyond the consultative protocols already in place in

Figure 3.3: Smart Hub.
Source: M Griffiths, 25 February 2016.

Figure 3.4: Location of Smart Hub.
Source: M Griffiths, 25 February 2016.

Figure 3.5: Mapping connections, Smart Hub.

Source: M Griffiths, 25 February 2016.

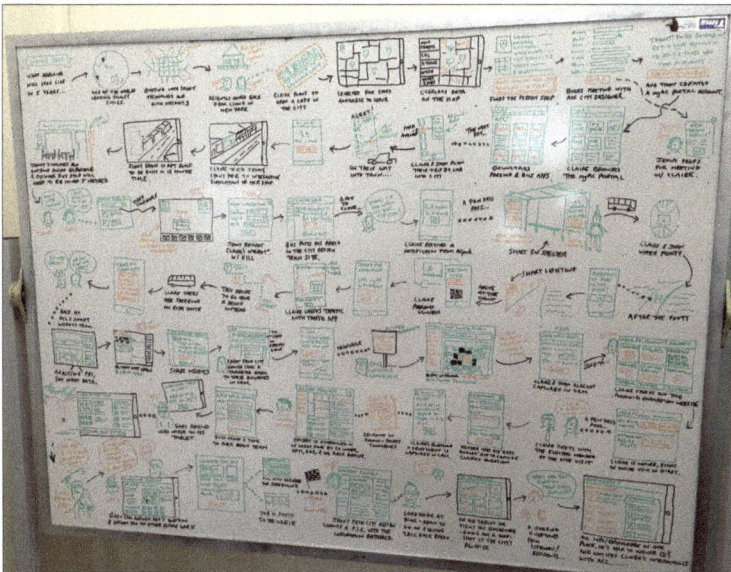

Figure 3.6: 'Smart' storyboard designed by Peter Auhl and the Information Management team, Adelaide City Council.

Source: S Ladd, 23 February 2016, published with the permission of Peter Auhl, CIO, Adelaide City Council.

South Australia. The record on Australian federal government consultations with citizens on digital policy has been patchy, even over the most successful period of e-government developments (2000-13), although the open-data movement advances e-government objectives of transparency, accountability, efficiency and effectiveness by, among other initiatives, advocating principles to help construct improvements in civic discourse, public welfare and public resources. South Australia's website data.sa.gov, Data Directory, Location SA and the spatial dataset Geocoded National Address File (G-NAF)[1] are examples of local implementation, and they illustrate the state's commitment to open government, to collaboration with other authorities, and to visualisation of data for citizen education and use. In October 2016, South Australia will launch OpenState, a festival with a focus on doing planning and consultation differently, more openly. At a preliminary event, state premier Jay Weatherill spoke in strong support of increased transparency and reversed the statement about people's diminishing trust in politicians, arguing that it is politicians who should trust people with participatory decision making. This bodes well for Adelaide developing as a citizen-oriented smart city.

Conclusion

Gartner forecasts in 2015 indicate that although smart cities will use 1.6 billion connected devices by 2016, the most rapid growth in smart uptake until 2018 will be in corporate buildings, after which uptake in smart homes will overtake them (Player 2015). Time spent in a smart home will accustom people to expect individuated responsive scenarios elsewhere, though user literacies will be needed to optimise experience (Tsukayama 2016). Participation practices such as those instituted in Santander may help populations appreciate improvements in shared civic experiences, but well-informed advocates for citizens' rights, and explainers, will be needed at all points of the city's 'smartification' processes. As IoT technologies are emergent, careful scrutiny and oversight protocols will be required to ascertain exactly how they are being used to make places and who they benefit. Smart sensors have the capacity to blur the distinction between humans and things as unique identifiers in the new ecosystems; municipalities are also likely to face difficulties in designing the inclusive consultative mechanisms for informed public deliberations, commensurate to the complexity and speed of IoT uptake. Smart governance systems will need to evolve to address these challenges (Griffiths 2016).

Whenever communication technologies offer innovative, socially generative forms of connecting people to place and through place to each other, anxiety and hope are typically expressed in equal measure about the human future enabled by each

---

1 Location SA: <http://www.location.sa.gov.au>. G-NAF: <https://www.psma.com.au/products/g-naf>.

advance. Philip Howard, writing of the IoT era from a global perspective, calls it the Pax Technica. One of its premises is that 'people use devices to govern', and though Howard envisions the civic potential of what he names 'the liberation technologies', he warns, '[y]ou are about to get many more such devices, and we need to think about what sort of world we're being liberated into' (2015, p. 256). This is the critical democratic question about placemaking which user advocates need to ask of smart city planners.

References

Adelaide City Council 2012, *Placemaking*, viewed 10 April 2014, <https://www.lga.sa.gov.au/webdata/resources/files/B7,b%20ACC%20LGA%20Presentation.pdf>.

Altimeter Group 2015, *Customer experience in the Internet of Things by Altimeter Group*, viewed 18 December 2015, <http://www.slideshare.net/Altimeter/report-customer-experience-in-the-internet-of-things-altimeter-group>.

Anderson, J & Rainnie, L 2014, *Digital life in 2025*, Pew Research Center, USA, viewed 10 March 2016, <http://www.pewinternet.org/files/2014/03/PIP_Report_Future_of_the_Internet_Predictions_031114.pdf>.

Aulich, C 2009, 'From citizen participation to participatory governance in Australian Local Government', *Commonwealth Journal of Local Governance*, no. 2, pp. 44-60.

Baumann, Z 2011, *Collateral damage: Social inequalities in a global age*, Press, Cambridge.

Blanc, P n.d., *Vertical gardens*, viewed 10 April 2016, <http://www.verticalgardenpatrickblanc.com/realisations/oceania>.

Budington, B 2015. 'Pantoptoclick 2.0 launches, featuring new tracker protection and finger printing tests', *Electric Frontier Foundation*, viewed 30 April 2016, <https://www.eff.org/deeplinks/2015/12/panopticlick-20-launches-featuring-new-tracker-protection-and-fingerprinting-tests>.

Cameron, N 2016, 'Why Ford is counting on the Internet of Things to drive customer engagement', *CMO*, viewed 29 March 2016, <http://www.cmo.com.au/article/596864/why-ford-counting-internet-thing>.

Castells, M 2012, 'Networks of outrage and hope: Social movements in the internet age', Library of Congress, viewed 20 May 2016, <https://www.youtube.com/watch?v=0lfPg_5iaGQ>.

Cisco n.d., *Smart + connected communities*, viewed 5 March 2016, <http://www.cisco.com/c/en/us/solutions/industries/smart-connected-communities.html>.

Cisco 2014a, *Cisco Smart + connected communities: Envisioning the future of cities now*, viewed 15 March 2016, <https://www.cisco.com/c/dam/en_us/solutions/industries/docs/smart-cities-expo-barcelona.pdf>.

Cisco 2014b, *Public safety, justice and the Internet of Everything*, viewed 10 March 2016, <http://www.nascio.org/events/sponsors/vrc/Public%20Safety%20Justice%20and%20the%20Internet%20of%20Everything.pdf>.

Clinton, N 2015, 'Smart cities: Opportunity for procurement innovation and a bright future for lamp posts', *Public spend: Matters Europe*, viewed 8 April 2015, <http://public.

spendmatters.eu/2015/04/08/smart-cities-opportunity-for-procurement-innovation-and-a-bright-future-for-lamp-posts>.

Corkey, L & Bishop, K 2015, 'Envisioning urban futures with children and young people', paper presented at the State of Australian Cities Conference, viewed 10 January 2016, <http://soacconference.com.au/wp-content/uploads/2016/02/Corkery..pdf>.

Corner, S 2015, 'Cisco elevates Adelaide to "Lighthouse City" status', *Tracking the Internet of Things for the Australasian IT community*, viewed 13 Februrary 2015, <http://www.iotaustralia.org.au/2015/02/09/iotnewanz/cisco-elevates-adelaide-lighthouse-city-status>.

Department of State Development (Government of South Australia) 2015, 'Adelaide named first "Lighthouse City" for innovation', viewed 30 January 2015, <http://www.statedevelopment.sa.gov.au/news-releases/all-news-updates/adelaide-named-australias-first-lighthouse-city-for-innovation>.

Eckersley, P, Reitman, R & Toner, A 2015, 'Clear rules of the road with the do not track policy', *Electronic Frontier Foundation [EFF]*, viewed 28 May 2016, <https://www.eff.org/deeplinks/2015/08/clear-rules-road-do-not-track-policy-0>.

Ellery, D 2016, 'Oaks Estate a de facto mental health detention centre, say residents', *The Canberra Times*, viewed 11 May 2016, <http://www.canberratimes.com.au/act-news/oaks-estate-a-de-facto-mental-health-detention-centre-say-residents-20160511-gos9lk.html>.

European Commission 2013, *Winners of the European Prize for Innovation in Public Administration*, memo, Brussels, 6 June, viewed 20 March 2016, <http://europa.eu/rapid/press-release_MEMO-13-503_en.htm >.

Fadden, R 2013, '21 Swings brings music to the Quartier de Spectacles', *Tourisme Montreal*, viewed 12 October 2016, <http://www.tourisme-montreal.org/blog/21-swings-brings-music-to-the-quartier-des-spectacles>.

Griffiths, M 2016, 'Smart governance', in *Draft proposal for an Australian Centre for Smart Cities*, University of Adelaide, August version, 2017, pp. 27-28.

Gurstein, M 2014, 'Smart cities vs. smart communities: Empowering citizens not market economies, *Journal of Community Informatics*, vol. 10, no. 3, viewed 20 March 2016, <http://www.cijournal.net/index.php/ciej/article/view/1172/1117>.

Habitat 111 2016, 'Rights to the city, and cities for all', Policy Unit 4: Urban governance, capacity and institutional development, Policy paper, viewed 3 May 2016, <https://files.lsecities.net/files/2016/03/Habitat-III-PU4-Urban-Governance-Capacity-and-Institutional-Development-Policy-Paper_Final.pdf>.

Hidalgo, A n.d., 'Co-constructing Paris', *Madame la Maire, j'ai une Idée*, viewed 10 January 2016, <https://idee.paris.fr/co-construisons-paris>.

Howard, PH 2015, *Pax Technica: How the Internet of Things may set us free or lock us up*, Yale University Press, New Haven & New York.

IBM n.d., 'Smarter planet', *IBM*, viewed 31 May 2016, <http://www.ibm.com/smarterplanet/us/en>.

Jaffe, E 2012, 'Reviving the dead spaces under elevated structures', *Citylab*, viewed 1 June 2016, <http://www.citylab.com/dsign/2015/06/bringing-the-dead-spaces-under-elevated-back-to-life/396236>.

Johnson, S 2015a, 'How Adelaide revitalised itself through "placemaking"', *Citiscope*, viewed

3 March 2016, <http://citiscope.org/story/2015/how-adelaide-revitalized-itself-through-placemaking>.

Johnson, S 2015b, 'Finding data to measure "place capital"', *Citiscope*, viewed 20 March 2016, <http://citiscope.org/story/2015/finding-data-measure-place-capital>.

Kent, F & Nikitin, C n.d., 'Collaborative, creative placemaking: Good public art depends on good public spaces', *Project for public spaces*, viewed 29 January 2016, <http://www.pps.org/reference/collaborative-creative-placemaking-good-public-art-depends-on-good-public-spaces>.

Latour, B 2003, 'What if we talked politics a little?', *Contemporary Political Theory*, no. 2, pp. 143-164.

MacDonald, E 2016, 'Civic's dead heart gets kickstarted with $340,000 in cultural and artistic grants', *The Canberra Times*, viewed 31 May 2016, <http://www.canberratimes.com.au/act-news/civics-dead-heart-gets-kickstarted-with-340000-in-cultural-and-artistic-grants-20160531-gp7vrr.html>.

Mapping the Cost of Justice 2014, Extract from television program *The Human Face of Big Data*, PBS Television, 24 February 2016, viewed 28 February 2016, <http://www.pbs.org/program/human-face-big-data>.

Marchand, Y & Meffre, R 2012, *The ruins of Detroit (2005-2010)*, Photo essays, viewed 3 March 2016, <http://www.marchandmeffre.com/detroit>.

McIlroy, T 2015, 'A disturbing lack of facts on Canberra's capital metro light rail: Experts', *The Canberra Times*, viewed 3 January 2016, <http://www.canberratimes.com.au/act-news/a-disturbing-lack-of-facts-on-canberras-capital-metro-light-rail-experts-20150416-1mm8ig.html>.

Nelson, SA & Metaxatos, P 2016, 'The Internet of Things needs design, not just technology', *Harvard Business Review*, viewed 1 June 2016, <https://hbr.org/2016/04/the-internet-of-things-needs-design-not-just-technology>.

Newcombe, T 2014, 'Santander: The smartest smart city', *Governing*, viewed 29 January 2016, <http://www.governing.com/topics/urban/gov-santander-spain-smart-city.html>.

Open Government Data 2015, *The annotated 8 principles of Open Government Data*, viewed 7 November 2016, <https://opengovdata.org>.

Pedroletti, B 2014, China's '"Apple City" — Assembling iPhones in the urban shadows', *World Crunch*, viewed 29 January 2016, <http://www.worldcrunch.com/business-finance/china-039-s-039-apple-city-039-assembling-iphones-in-the-urban-shadows/iphone-factory-boom-urbanization-poverty-foxconn/c2s15252>.

Player, C 2015, 'Smart cities will use 1.6 billion connected things in 2016: Gartner', *ARN*, viewed 21 December 2015, <http://www.arnnet.com.au/article/590451/smart-cities-will-use-1-6-billion-connected-things-2016-gartner>.

Project for Public Spaces n.d., 'What is placemaking?', *Project for public spaces*, viewed 3 March 2015, <http://www.pps.org/reference/what_is_placemaking>.

Randall, T 2015, 'The smartest building in the world', *Bloomberg Business Week*, viewed 30 December 2015, <http://www.bloomberg.com/features/2015-the-edge-the-worlds-greenest-building>.

Rubin, J 2012, 'The Boswash shareway', *Cool hunting*, viewed 1 June 2016, <http://www.coolhunting.com/design/howeler-yoon-boswash-shareway-aufi>.

Ruppert, E, 2015, 'Background: A social framework for big data', viewed 30 January 2016, pp. 1-5 <https://sloddo.files.wordpress.com/2015/09/sfbd-background3.pdf>.

Sadoway, D & Satyarupa Shekhar, S 2014, '(Re)prioritising citizens in smart cities governance: Examples of smart citizenship from urban India', *The Journal of Community Informatics*, vol. 10, no. 3, viewed 20 April 2016, <http://ci-journal.net/index.php/ciej/article/view/1179/1115>.

Scholl, HJ, & Scholl MC 2014, 'Smart governance: A roadmap for research and practice', in *iConference 2014 Proceedings*, pp. 163-176, DOI: http://dx.doi.org/10.9776/14060.

Scroxton, A 2015, 'Local government blind to Internet of Things savings', *Computer Weekly*, viewed 29 January 2016, <http://www.computerweekly.com/news/4500247803/Local-government-blind-to-internet-of-things-savings>.

Singapore-MIT Alliance for Research and Technology [SMART] n.d., 'The death of the traffic light', viewed 30 March 2016, <http://smart.mit.edu/news-a-events/press-room/article/56-the-death-of-the-traffic-light-.html>.

Smart City n.d., 'Santander SmartCity', viewed 10 March 2016, <http://www.redciudadesinteligentes.es/municipiosraiz/municipios/ampliar.php/Id_contenido/350>.

Tsukayama, H 2016, 'Devices are getting harder to operate. Get used to it', *The Washington Post*, reprinted in *The Age Green Guide*, Thursday 7 April, p. 11.

United Nations, Department of Economic and Social Affairs, Population Division 2014, *World urbanization prospects: The 2014 Revision, Highlights (ST/ESA/SER.A/352)*, viewed 30 January 2016, <https://esa.un.org/unpd/wup/Publications/Files/WUP2014-Highlights.pdf>.

van der Hove, J 2015, 'Fact Sheet Ethics Sub-Group IoT, Version 4', *Expert IoT, DG Connect*, viewed 30 January 2016, <http://digitalchampion.bg/uploads/agenda/en/filepath_85.pdf>.

Wakefield, J 2016, 'Tomorrow's buildings: Is world's greenest office smart?' BBC News: Technology, viewed 6 April 2016, <http://www.bbc.com/news/technology-35746647>.

Warner, M 2002, 'Publics and counter-publics', *Public Culture*, vol. 14, no. 1, pp. 49-90, DOI: http://dx.doi.org/10.1215/08992363-14-1-49.

Yoo, T 2016, 'Australia must catch up as industry 4.0 heralds fourth industrial revolution', *The Guardian*, viewed 3 February 2016, <http://www.theguardian.com/sustainable-business/2016/feb/01/australia-must-catch-up-as-industry-40-heralds-fourth-industrial-revolution>.

Picturing placelessness: Online graphic narratives and Australia's refugee detention centres

4

Aaron Humphrey

Introduction

This chapter will examine an online comic published by the *Global Mail*, 'At Work Inside our Detention Centres: A Guard's Story' (Olle & Wallman 2014), which documents the difficult situations faced by asylum seekers who have been detained by the Australian government. Asylum seekers face the dilemma of placelessness on political, psychological and phenomenological levels, and the comic affectively conveys this dilemma to its readers by employing elements of the visual language of online communication used in social networking. An analysis of the comic demonstrates how online communication can also be characterised as engendering placelessness, although in a significantly subtler and less perilous way than seeking political asylum.

This discussion is significant because the media that we use to communicate are strongly tied to our understanding of place as a political, physical and phenomenological experience. For example, the modern conception of national identities was shaped in part by the industries of print, particularly novels and newspapers (Anderson 1997), which were able to connect people across relatively long distances, while Marshall McLuhan suggested that broadcast technologies of radio and television helped to shape a 'global village' where physical boundaries could be largely transcended (1964).

Although advances in communication technologies have largely served to extend our political sense of place, theorists of place, such as Edward Relph and Melvin Webber, have argued that our phenomenological sense of place is being eroded by the industrial emphasis on accessibility and efficiency. Webber (1964) noted the rise of urban 'nonplaces' such as warehouses, loading docks and freeway overpasses crisscrossed with telephone wires, while Relph (1976, p. 143) described the alienation that humans experience in these kinds of 'anonymous spaces and exchangeable environments'. Although Relph and Webber were writing in the mid-twentieth century, their theories are even more applicable now. Digital technologies are further streamlining communication, and social media platforms are increasingly aggregating and decontextualising content.

This phenomenological collapse of place is exemplified in the way most social media platforms present an infinite scroll of standardised content drawn from disparate sources. The simultaneous expansion of place in a political sense can be seen in the way visual communication like emoji and memes are able to bypass language barriers that have historically played a crucial role in national identities. While online

Figure 4.1: Illustration from 'A Guard's Story'.
Source: S Wallman, 18 Feburary 2014, Global Mail. *Reproduced with permission.*

communication has made national and place-based identities more porous, there have also been retrenchments of national political boundaries, as seen particularly in the response of countries like Australia to the current refugee crisis. Users of social media may experience a phenomenological alienation from a sense of place, but refugees who are unable to find political asylum face a much more profound and potentially deadly alienation.

'A Guard's Story' conveyed the profound placelessness of asylum seekers in a way that resonated strongly with Australian readers, in part by leveraging the placeless qualities of online communication which Australian readers were deeply familiar with. To explore the implications of this kind of communication, this chapter will first discuss how 'A Guard's Story' can be understood in terms of the changing and increasingly placeless online media landscape. This will be followed by a discussion of the Australian government's asylum seeker policies, and a critique of how these policies have been reported by traditional text-based and broadcast news media. Finally, an analysis of 'A Guard's Story' will show how it departs from earlier representations of asylum seekers to present a different conception of citizenship, place and placelessness.

Placelessess of online communication

The way that the *Global Mail* published 'A Guard's Story' and how it was shared by readers exemplifies how online communication is changing, particularly in regards to journalism, both in terms of becoming more visually based and more reliant on audiences sharing content through social networks. The *Global Mail* was funded philanthropically by Graeme Wood, and received many awards for the quality of its journalism, but despite partnerships with larger commercial sites like the *Guardian* and *Time*, its audience remained relatively small. In 2014, after two years of operation, Wood withdrew his funding, despite having initially pledged support for five years, and the website subsequently closed in February of the same year.

As the *Global Mail*'s offices were being vacated, a handful of employees scrambled to get 'A Guard's Story' uploaded to the server. 'A Guard's Story' was not only the *Global Mail*'s first comic, it was also its last article in any form, published so late into the site's death throes that it was not even hyperlinked from anywhere else in the site. It existed like a ghost on the site: accessible if you had the URL, but otherwise unmentioned. At the last moment, a single link to the comic surfaced on the *Global Mail*'s Facebook account.

'A Guard's Story' represents both the visual shift in online content (as seen elsewhere in the growth of online comics journalism, along with the popular usage of GIFS, memes and emoji in all kinds of discourse) and the increasing use of social media platforms as a tool for publishing and sharing information. The main way that readers found 'A Guard's Story' was through sites like Facebook and Twitter, as it could not be accessed from anywhere else on the *Global Mail*'s website.

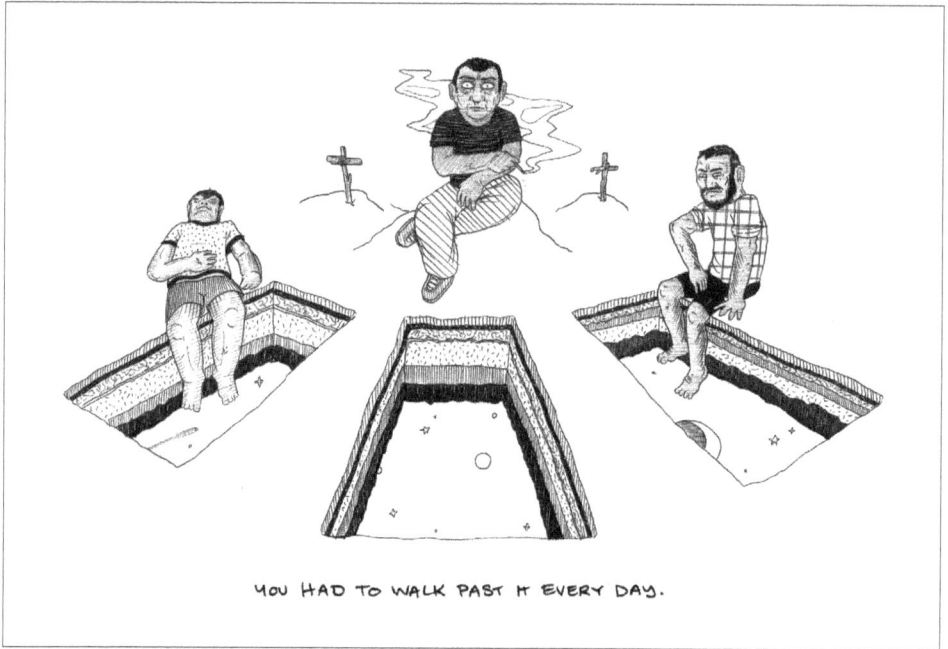

YOU HAD TO WALK PAST IT EVERY DAY.

Figure 4.2: Illustration from 'A Guard's Story'.
Source: S Wallman, 18 Feburary 2014, Global Mail. *Reproduced with permission.*

Through these platforms it attracted the kind of readership that the site had struggled to generate in its two years of operation. Thousands of readers found 'A Guard's Story' on Facebook, where it was shared more than 56 000 times. Even though the *Global Mail* soon stopped monitoring its Facebook page, comments from enthusiastic readers quickly piled up, like letters shoved under the door of a closed storefront. 'That moved me to tears', wrote one reader, while another seemed almost evangelical: 'Print it! Print 1,000s of them I'll hand them out on street corners!' (in Jeffrey 2012).

In some ways, sharing links on social media has become the digital version of handing out pamphlets on street corners. The use of the city streets as conduits for communication was enabled by what Melvin Webber (1964) characterised as urban 'nonplaces', the generic and standardised spaces of industrialisation where accessibility is prioritised over proximity and propinquity. Social networks like Facebook and Twitter have remediated these networks of 'nonplaces', building upon digital, networked technologies that have dramatically increased the accessibility of information beyond what Webber could have conceived. They have also increased the 'placelessness' of information and communication (for example, Aguirre & Davies 2015; Odom, Zimmerman & Forlizzi 2014; Ogawa et al. 2013), resulting in an erosion of what Mahyar Arefi has called 'the communal ties and bonds that were once considered the main characteristics of place-bound communities', as 'communities of interest' replace 'communities of place' (1999, p. 181).

The placeless quality of much online communication, and certainly of the sharing of articles like 'A Guard's Story' on Facebook, is paralleled in the way 'A Guard's Story' depicts detention centres themselves as floating in a placeless kind of limbo.

Placelessness can be understood through the theoretical framework developed by Edward Relph in *Place and Placelessness* (1976). Relph suggested that 'place' can be understood both in terms of how people create identities *of* places as unique and particular, and how people identify *with* those places and see themselves as either outside or inside them. For Relph, placelessness arises when the distinctive characteristics of places are removed and replaced with standardised features: 'a replacement of the diverse and significant places of the world with anonymous spaces and exchangeable environments' (p. 143). This process, often driven by 'the overriding concern with efficiency as an end in itself', undermines the abilities of both individuals and cultures to locate their identities in relation to a place (Seamon & Sowers 2008, p. 46). Of course, it bears repeating that the placelessness that asylum seekers face is much more immediate and life-threatening. The next section will discuss how government policies and media reporting have participated in the construction of this kind of placelessness.

Placelessness of asylum seekers

Since refugees are people who are fleeing from one place to another and who 'occupy the realm of the stateless' (Binaisa 2011, p. 523), the issue of asylum seekers is deeply connected to the conception of places as having physical, political and affective aspects. The Australian government has attempted to deter asylum seekers by denying them access to Australia on all three of these levels. An example of denying access to Australia as political space has been the erosion of Australia's 'Migration Zone', a space that granted particular political rights to those who crossed into its physical boundary. Established by the Migration Act 1958, the Migration Zone initially encompassed the entire physical territory of Australia. In 2001 the Howard government's 'Pacific solution' excised thousands of islands from the Migration Zone, meaning that refugees who reached these islands could not make a claim for asylum in Australia and would be transferred to detention centers in Papua New Guinea [PNG] and the Republic of Nauru (Phillips 2013) — further distancing refugees from Australia as a political and physical space. This alteration of the political meaning of Australia's physical boundaries was further extended in 2013, when Parliament excised the entire mainland of Australia from the Migration Zone (Barlow 2013).

Although the Migration Zone remained a political concept, the 2013 legislation rendered it unreachable, placeless. This was accompanied by a campaign called Operation Sovereign Borders that aimed to transform Australia into a place both physically and politically inaccessible to asylum seekers who travelled to Australia by boat. The use of offshore detention centres in PNG and Nauru, which cost the Australian government more than $400 000 per person each year (Australian Government 2014), has been an extremely costly way of maintaining this boundary between these refugees and any aspect of Australia as a place.

Finally, the detention centres themselves, even those on the mainland of Australia, serve to distance asylum seekers from the affective dimensions of place. They are 'un-places' — liminal, nationless spaces where the detainees are caught in a limbo between the country they have fled and the country where they hope to be resettled, engendering a phenomenological sense of placelessness. These centres, perfunctorily built to 'detain' and 'manage' people in transition (Seamon & Sowers 2008) are characterised by what a detainee in a writing workshop described as 'the deprivation of beauty, the absence of touch and limited sensory experiences', which leads to a 'starvation of the soul' (Galbraith 2015, p. 26).

Detention centres resemble prisons in many ways, but as David Isaacs has observed, unlike convicted prisoners who at least have a release date, asylum seekers may be held for indefinite periods, and they are often unsure of when, if ever, they will be released (2015a, p. 2). Isaacs also notes that, without a sense of place or of time, 'long-term immigration detention causes major mental health problems, is illegal in international law and arguably fulfils the recognised definition of torture' (p. 1). This amounts to not only the unmaking of places, but also the unmaking of people. Reports of life inside Australia's detention centres often describe mental and physical illness, sexual abuse, suicide and violence (Hamilton 2015, p. 55).

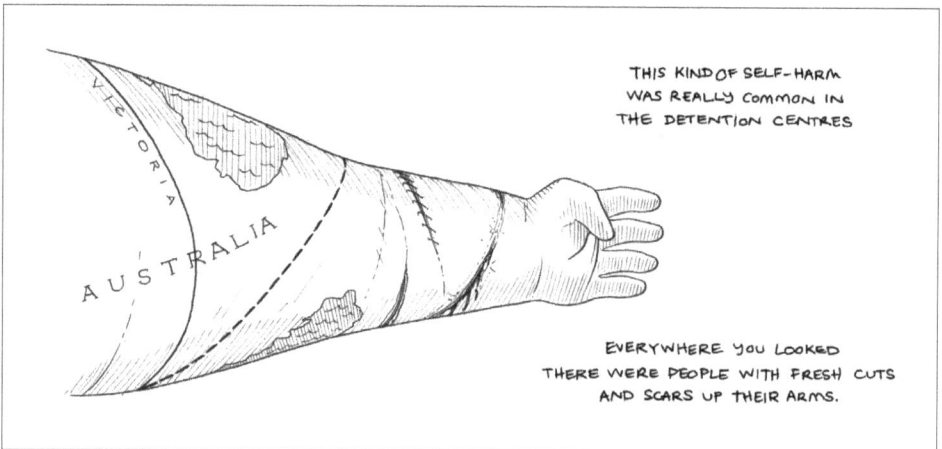

Figure 4.3: Illustration from 'A Guard's Story'.
Source: S Wallman, 18 Feburary 2014, Global Mail. Reproduced with permission.

The government's 'Detention Health Framework' maintains that 'all people in immigration detention have access to healthcare at a standard generally comparable to the healthcare available to the Australian community' (Department of Immigration and Border Protection 2016), but Ebony Birchall argues that 'it is highly likely that duties of care are being breached in immigration centres on a daily basis' (2015, pp. 49, 52). If detainees are not receiving healthcare of a comparable standard to that which the Australian community receives, it is clear that they are not considered part of the Australian community, even if they are detained within the country.

Relph has suggested that when people strongly identify themselves as 'inside' a place, they feel 'safe rather than threatened, enclosed rather than exposed, at ease rather than stressed' (Relph 1976 paraphrased in Seamon & Sowers 2008, p. 45), with feeling outside a place producing the opposite sensations: stress, strangeness and alienation. Australia's detention centres are designed to physically contain people inside a space but simultaneously engender a deep affective sense of 'outsideness' in people who have also been denied access to the political 'insideness' of citizenship or refugee status. In this way, these detention centres can be considered truly placeless spaces.

Perpetuating placelessness and isolation — Media reports and Australian understanding of detention centres

Both Relph and Webber considered placelessness/nonplaces to result from industrialisation, as byproducts of a system of mass culture which prioritises efficiency and access. Australia's immigration detention centres, though, are characterised by profound *lack* of access to, and communication with, the wider Australian community (as well as severe financial inefficiency). Commentators note that the issue of asylum seekers has been a 'vexed issue in Australian society since 1999' (Romano 2004, p. 43). Recently the issue has been 'a prominent theme in political and popular discourse' (Christie & Sidhu 2002, p. 11), as well as 'a central issue in recent federal elections' (Hugo & Napitupulu 2016, p. 213). Despite this national attention, the Australian government's policies toward asylum seekers have remained characterised by secrecy (Human Rights Law Centre 2014; Isaacs 2015a).

The Australian public has little access to information about this issue, since the detention centres are 'in secluded locations, some on offshore islands, and are subject to extreme secrecy, comparable with "black sites" elsewhere' (Isaacs 2015a, p. 1). Journalists must pay thousands of dollars for visas to visit the offshore centres, no unauthorised photographs may be taken, and the Border Force Bill of 2015 ('Australian Border Force Bill 2015') stipulates that healthcare workers may be imprisoned for up to two years if they reveal unauthorised information about the conditions inside detention centres, leading some to speculate that doctors and nurses may be jailed for reporting abuses of detainees (Hamilton 2015; Isaacs 2015b, p. 2; McCall 2015).

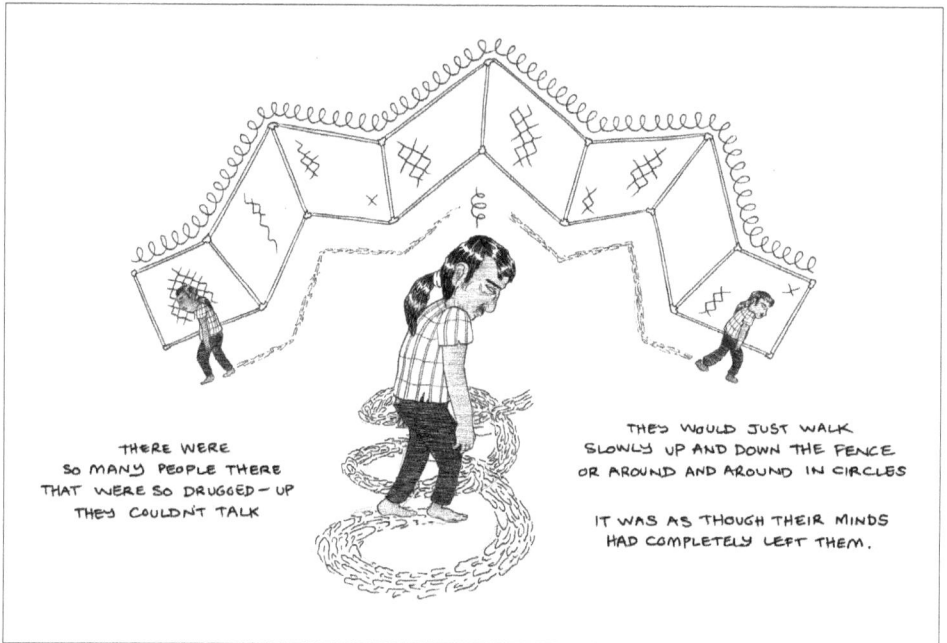

Figure 4.4: Illustration from 'A Guard's Story'.
Source: S Wallman, 18 Feburary 2014, Global Mail. *Reproduced with permission.*

Many of these policies have faced criticisms, but the government has routinely responded with silence. For example, a letter ninety-two pages long from fifteen doctors detailing their concerns about the medical care provided in detention centres was met with a single-page response (Laughland 2014), and Immigration Minister Scott Morrison, when faced with allegations that the Australian Navy had mistreated asylum seekers, has claimed that it is 'not for the government to disprove the negative, it's for those who have allegations to actually prove the positive' (in Farrell 2014).

Alongside treating asylum seekers in detention as fundamentally placeless and without the rights that are afforded to citizens of a place (such as a certain standard of healthcare), the Australian government has encouraged the public to view asylum seekers as less than human. According to Leach, this was part of a

> calculated manipulation of public opinion[;] the Government's selective and distorted release of information throughout this period promoted attitudes of fear and resentment towards asylum seekers. (2003, p. 26)

For example, during the debate over the fate of refugees stranded during the 'Tampa Affair', the Australian Navy was given specific instructions that 'no personalizing or humanizing images' were to be taken of the asylum seekers (p. 29). During this time, the government and media began the longstanding practice of referring to refugees using terms like 'floods' and 'waves' — the dehumanising language of natural disasters.

Media reporting

Much of the information that Australians receive about asylum seekers and immigration detention centres comes from the Australian news media. Although some journalists have done commendable investigative work to expose the poor conditions in detention centres, the government's policies of secrecy have served to limit the kinds of information that gets reported. In a recent analysis of articles published in three major Australian newspapers, Rebecca Dunn observed that the papers typically presented asylum seekers not as people but 'as a problem to be solved on the basis of their illegitimacy, immorality and criminality', an approach that was consistent with the narrative of both major political parties (2015, p. v). In this way, the major newspapers can be considered complicit in perpetuating both the portrayal of asylum seekers as non-people and the policies that render them placeless.

The work that news media have done to support the placelessness of asylum seekers should be considered in the light of the historical role that print media, especially newspapers, have played in 'the creation of nation as an imaginary community' (Doyle & Griffiths 2006, p. 6). Marshall McLuhan implicated print as a historical catalyst for modern systems of government, and, similarly, Benedict Anderson has argued that print, combined with capitalism, 'laid the bases for national consciousness' (1997, p. 62). Print is certainly a foundation of modern democracies, with their constitutions, bills, treaties and declarations. If this medium of printed text 'cried out for nationalism' as McLuhan has argued (1964, p. 49), then different responses are suggested by the digital, networked and increasingly visual forms of communication that flourish on social media platforms, such as memes, emoticons, animated GIFs and webcomics. As we move to a post-print society, I would argue that 'A Guard's Story' is one example of how our understandings of place, nationhood and community are subtly shifting. In order to understand how 'A Guard's Story' presented the issue of asylum seekers in a way that had not been possible in previous forms of media, and did so in a way that appealed to users of social media platforms, the next section will delve into how the comic was initially conceived, before providing an analysis of the comic itself.

Creation of 'A Guard's Story'

The *Global Mail* was lauded for publishing innovative and interactive pieces of journalism (Wake 2014), many of which could be described as fulfilling the remit of Simon Cottle's 'thick journalism' — stories that 'reveal something of the deep structures, contending perspectives and lived experiences' under the surface of typically 'thin' and superficial headlines and news reports (2005, p. 109). Cottle argues that 'thick journalism' often requires customised formats and technologies that may depart from prescribed reporting genres. This departure from standardised formats is easier to accomplish with online journalism, which is not bound by the space constraints of newsprint or the time constraints of television and radio program lengths. As an online-only site, the *Global Mail* was able to focus on a thick, project-based approach to journalism; its staff were encouraged to present their stories using unusual formats or technologies that would bring out the most depth of the material.

'A Guard's Story' developed from journalist Nick Olle's contact with an anonymous source who had worked in a detention centre, a story that could have been conceived of as a traditional news feature. However, the *Global Mail*'s interest in project-based journalism led to a discussion of how to best present it. The staff debated whether to use video, graphics or another format before settling on the style of a graphic novel, as suggested by Ella Rubeli. The burgeoning cultural authority of 'graphic novels' (see, for example, Humphrey 2014) helped sway the *Global Mail*'s decision to publish a comic (Fisher 2014).

'A Guard's Story' required the work of several people working in different modalities. Pat Grant, whose graphic novel *Blue* was published to critical regard in 2012 (Mills 2012; Scott 2012), was the first cartoonist the *Global Mail* approached. He drafted a visual structure for the article, and suggested Sam Wallman as the project's cartoonist. Olle, Grant and Wallman worked to develop the comic, with Grant and *Global Mail* designer Pat Armstrong providing the final design and editing (Fisher 2014; Grant 2015). All four are credited on the story, along with producer Sam Bungey, developer Mark Finger and editor Lauren Martin. The source of the interview, whose 'voice' narrates the comic, remains anonymous.

The comic tells the story of the anonymous narrator's employment at Serco, a multinational services company that runs Australia's mainland detention centres. Although the narrator is initially motivated by a desire to help detainees from inside the system, after witnessing their mistreatment and psychological distress, he finds that his own mental wellbeing and personal relationships begin to deteriorate. Eventually the narrator surrenders and gives up the job. The story ends on a note of ambiguous hope, with a silent sequence depicting the narrator encountering two former detainees at a shopping mall.

Within a fortnight, 'A Guard's Story' was shared on Facebook more than 50 000 times (Fisher 2014), a number that grew to more than 64 000 before the *Global Mail*'s website finally went offline in 2015. Considering that only a portion of readers would have shared the page, its actual readership must have been several times larger. This final missive from the *Global Mail*, their first foray into comics journalism, became their 'biggest story ever' (Fisher 2014). The comic became a nexus for a large community of readers — the number of readers who shared the comic on Facebook alone far exceeded the *Global Mail*'s estimated subscriber base of 17 000 readers, and would have caused a huge spike in the site's estimated average of 120 000 unique visitors per month (Reynolds 2014).

Analysis of the comic

The infinite canvas of placelessness

Doyle and Griffiths note that '[t]he cartoon has a long Western history as an aesthetic and political genre' (2006, p. 3), and comics that tackle serious subjects are not a new phenomenon. However, while comics printed in newspapers have generally been limited to single panels or short strips, online comics like 'A Guard's Story' are freed from the constraints of the page and are able to expand to longer, more complex narratives. In contrast to quick, humorous caricatures where 'deliberative space is occluded' (p. 3), the drawings in 'A Guard's Story' are surrounded by expanses of white space, encouraging readers to linger, pondering the words and images. These empty white spaces are also used to reinforce the feeling of floating placelessness that permeates the comic.

'A Guard's Story' is read by scrolling down through a long sequence of images, a form of digital comics dubbed an 'infinite canvas' by comics theorist Scott McCloud (2000b), which allows for 'sustained, uninterrupted sequences' (2000a) where time and space can be presented in ways that are 'far less fixed and rigid than is easily achievable in print' (Goodbrey 2013, p. 192).

In some 'infinite canvas' comics, the movement of scrolling down can be used to convey movement or travel (Miller 2015, p. 22). Although there is a narrative movement to 'A Guard's Story', there is no sense of moving through space while reading the comic. The same scenes are repeated multiple times from different angles, and some images are so large that they appear larger than the screen and must be scrolled through. This creates an affect of lack of movement and claustrophobia, which contributes to the placelessness of the comic.

The way that the comic is read also mirrors some aspects of the ways that social networks such as Twitter, Tumblr and Facebook are read, as the reader scrolls down a seemingly endless flow of content. Additionally, comics can be understood as a medium of 'gaps', in that each panel may depict different moments in time and space, and readers must mentally fill in the gaps and make connections between the panels (Freinkel 2006, p. 251; Refaie 2012, p. 206). The posts that fill social media feeds are similarly fragmented, each depicting different places and times. Of course, readers of comics expect that the fragmented panels can be connected, while readers of social media accept that each post is separate, but the sensation of scrolling through a vertical

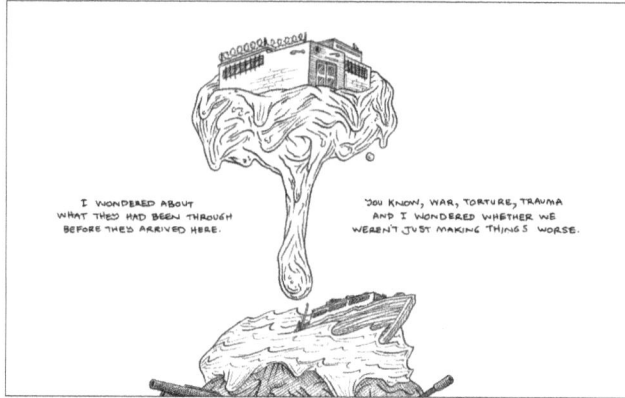

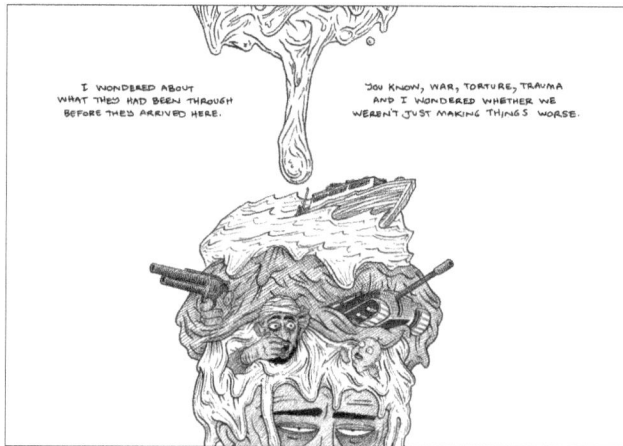

Figure 4.5: Scrolling down through a large image in 'A Guard's Story'.

Source: S Wallman, 18 Feburary 2014, Global Mail. Reproduced with permission.

feed of discrete moments in 'A Guard's Story' would be familiar to users of the social media sites where it was widely shared.

Emoji and universally accessible emotions

Another aspect that would be familiar is the way that some sections of 'A Guard's Story' are told almost entirely through abstracted facial expressions. The final, silent exchange between the narrator and two former detainees consists of little more than a short series of emotionally expressive heads floating against a white backdrop and reads almost like a conversation conducted with emoji or messaging app 'stickers'.

Wallman's illustrations for 'A Guard's Story' are iconic and symbolic, characteristics shared with emoji. McCabe writes that Wallman's drawings 'have immediate impact' and are 'instantly accessible' — or, in emoji terms, 👍💯 (2015, pp. 15-16). Emoji also have instantly accessible qualities that mean that they are 'recognizable across boundaries' (Skiba 2016, p. 56), and communicate meanings that extend beyond place-based communities. This is not to say that they are universal, as emoji reflect hegemonic Western cultural values that are largely white and highly gendered (Gay 2013; Kraus 2013), but that they have a quality of being untethered and rootless — able to semantically slide across cultures, platforms and devices in a way that makes them essentially placeless.

In fact, Stark and Crawford argue that emoji are a way of helping people to cope emotionally with the effects of placelessness wrought by 'the experience of building and maintaining social ties within hierarchical technological platforms and unjust economic systems that operate far outside of their control' (2015, p. 8). Emoji can help to foster a feeling of emotional 'insideness' which may sooth the alienation of an increasingly placeless environment.

In English the word 'emoji' is commonly understood to be related to the word 'emotion', as is the word 'emoticon' (emotion + icon). Although 'emoji is a loanword from Japanese, and comes from e "picture" + moji "letter, character"' (Oxford Dictionaries 2015), this etymological coincidence has helped shape the way emoji are used and understood in the English-speaking world, with researchers and businesses exploring the connections between emoji and emotion (Al Rashdi 2015; Sugiyama 2015; Vidal, Ares & Jaeger 2016; Yeole, Chavan & Nikose 2015).

One thread that has emerged from this research is, as Sternbergh notes, that 'emoji are not, it turns out, well designed to convey meanness … anger, derision, or hate' (2014). Additionally, as the emotional strength of messages increases, the use of emoticons decreases (Kato, Kato & Scott 2009). In 'A Guard's Story', however, Wallman's illustrations depict many negative, intense and complicated emotions, often using facial expressions and visual metaphors.

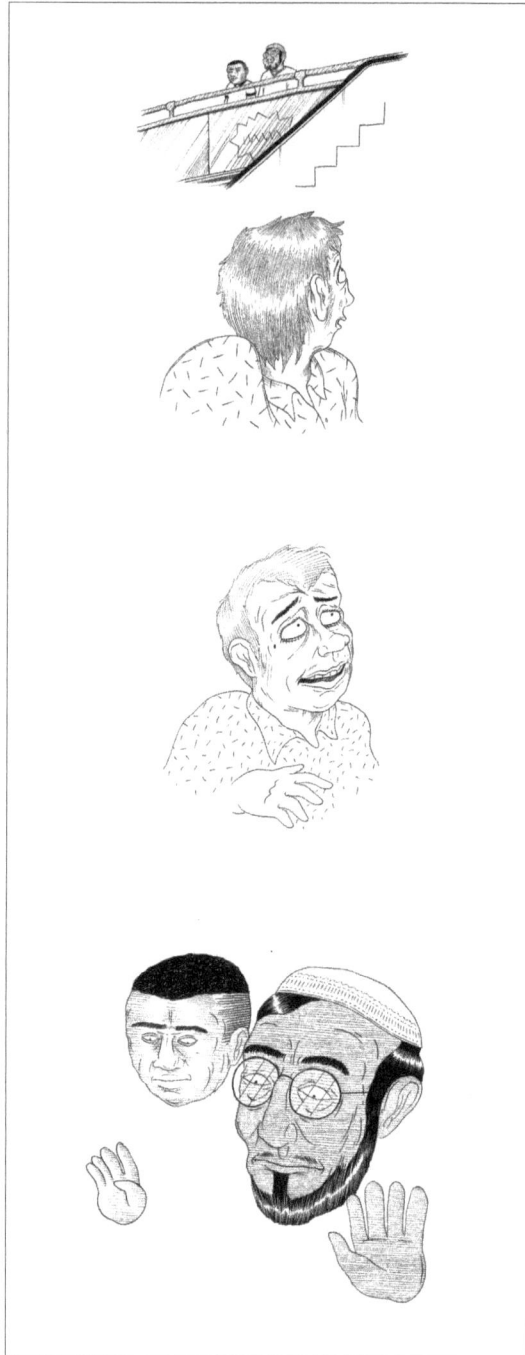

Figure 4.6: Illustrations from 'A Guard's Story'.
Source: S Wallman, 18 Feburary 2014, Global Mail. Reproduced with permission.

Masking and identification

The yellow emoji faces that represent emotions tend to resemble masks. Marshall and Barbour remind us that masks are detachable, and 'allow actors to play more than one role', while in Greek theatre 'the uniformity of some masks, such as those used by the Chorus, created a univocal identity' (2015, p. 2). The uniform and ubiquitous masks of emoji faces create the impression of emotions that are shareable, transferable and in some ways universal — while also being detachable, not tethered to any place individual.

Comics theorist Scott McCloud has used the term 'masking' to describe the use of abstracted faces in comics, and argues that this technique allows readers to imagine themselves in the place of a character. The simplified nature of these kinds of characters, like emoji, provides readers with avatars that are easy to identify with, and allows them to feel as if they are entering the space of the comic (1993).

Although Wallman's drawings are different from the standarised yellow-faced emoji in many ways, he chose to use a simplified cartoon language in 'A Guard's Story'. In an interview with Tim Fisher (2014), Wallman noted that this helped to make the story more universal, and relatable, since

> all the workers in the centre could be reduced to one character ... When you read kids' books, the characters' faces often have really simple, minimal features, they're just vessels so the kid reading the book can project onto this character. Not knowing a lot about the informant meant I could make it more about what they were going through, and the experiences of the asylum seekers.

As Wallman only had access to the ideas and emotions of the guard's story, he used the languages of facial expressions and visual metaphor to build his interpretation of the story. Faces and emotions are the strongest visual touchstones of 'A Guard's Story', while the backgrounds are either missing entirely, or surreal and abstract. This helps to further the impression of placelessness, since the masks that readers are encouraged to identify with are floating in the placeless prison of detention.

Placing the mark of the graphiateur

One way of highlighting the differences between Wallman's iconic style of drawing and the similarly iconic emoji that are common across social networking platforms is to examine how Wallman himself draws emoji. Wallman has extolled the virtue of emoji in a comic for The Wheeler Centre (2015), which included his version of 😂 , the 'Face with Tears of Joy' emoji that the Oxford Dictionary dubbed the Word of the Year for 2015.

Figure 4.7 bares the hallmarks of the style Wallman also uses in 'A Guard's Story'. The drawing is imperfect, with the circle of the head slightly misshapen, the lines wobbly, the shading idiosyncratic. Unlike most versions of the emoji, which have

Figure 4.7: Illustration from 'What implication does the emoji have for the future of linguistics?'
Source: S Wallman, 1 November, 2015, The Interrobang. Reproduced with permission.

a symmetrical, digital sheen, Wallman's drawing appears almost fleshy, even a little grotesque. His cartoons strike me as emphasising the imperfect humanness of both his subjects and his own style of drawing. There is a sense of embodied humanity in his work that is missing from emoji — the feeling that a particular human in a particular place and time created it.

Comics scholar Philippe Marion (1993) has argued that authorship in comics is largely determined by the handmade quality of the drawn line (in Groensteen 2012, p. 117). As Jared Gardner notes, readers don't consider the choice of font in a printed book to be connected to the 'labor involved in the scene of writing' (the same could be said about the design of a set of emoji, which differs slightly depending on which device or service the reader uses), but 'we cannot look at the graphic narrative and imagine that the line does not give us access to the labored making of the storyworld we are encountering' (2011, p. 64).

Both Sam Wallman and Pat Grant have backgrounds in producing zines, which are handmade, self-published publications with small print runs that are sold at low cost, part of a grassroots culture of publishing physical objects that can help to foster place-based communities and creativity. 'A Guard's Story' reflects some ethos of zine culture. Chidgey describes zines as 'personally crafted artifacts and sites of activist labor and connection', which are 'avenues for shared creativity and learning' and ways of 'enacting "cultural citizenship"' (2014, p. 105). The obvious and personalised labour that has gone into these hand-drawn comics is at odds with the anonymous, urbanised industrial efficiency that characterises Relph's placelessness and Webber's nonplaces, as well as the 'universal' and ubiquitous emoji.

The strangeness, awkwardness and humanness of Wallman's drawn lines manage to convey a sense of places where ink meets paper. This allows for a different, more varied kind of expression than the emoji 'normcore system of emotion' and 'grid menu of ideograms' (Crawford 2014).

In Figure 4.8, for example, the messy, interwoven jumble of thoughts has a certain impact because of its specificity and the obvious effort that went into drawing it. A glib emoji version, 😵🔯📧⁉️, could not carry the same weight. The drawing is also rich in specific details, from the man's facial expression, to his slouch, to his missing shoe, all of which assist in helping readers to picture the placeless limbo of detention.

Abstracted and unlabelled

Using a nonverbal language to depict the detainees also has other interesting effects that might apply more readily to emoji and other visual communication online. Perhaps most crucially, Wallman's drawings avoid both categorising individuals as 'refugees', 'asylum seekers', 'detainees', 'visa breakers', 'migrants', 'boat people', and using other nationalist political definitions that are difficult to avoid in written communication.

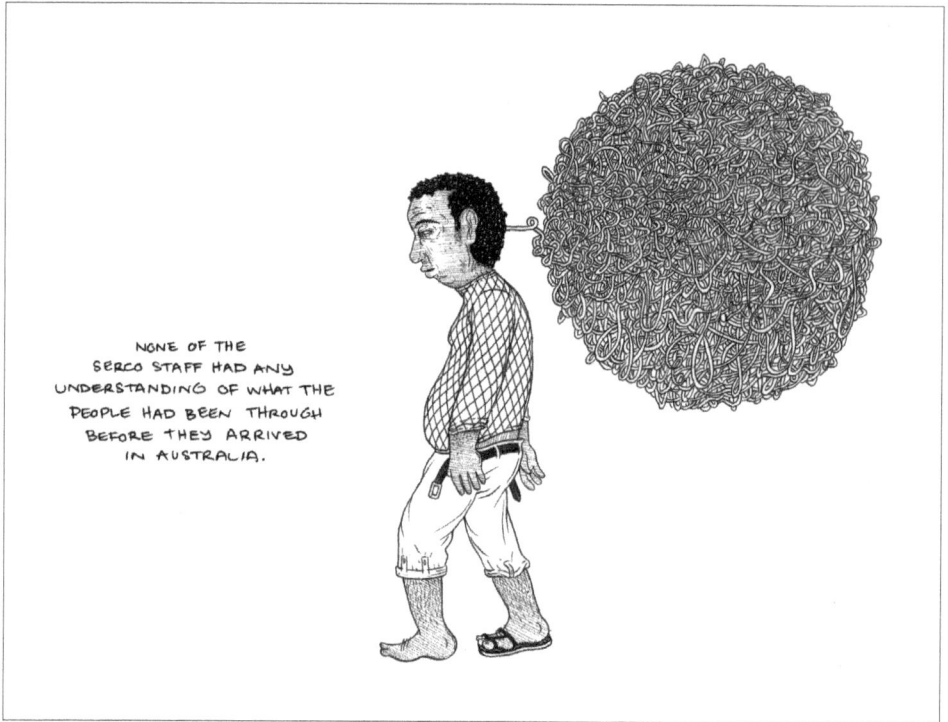

NONE OF THE SERCO STAFF HAD ANY UNDERSTANDING OF WHAT THE PEOPLE HAD BEEN THROUGH BEFORE THEY ARRIVED IN AUSTRALIA.

Figure 4.8: Illustration from 'A Guard's Story'.
Source: S Wallman, 18 Feburary 2014, Global Mail. *Reproduced with permission.*

Scalettaris has critiqued academic studies of refugees for using categories like these that are 'policy related labels, designed to meet the needs of policy rather than of scientific enquiry', and that reflect and reinforce the principles of those policies (2007, p. 37).

Cartoon images like emoji and comics have what Stark and Crawford call a 'conceptual plasticity' (2015, p. 5) that allows them to encompass a multiplicity of meanings, and to express things for 'which written language is often clumsy or awkward or problematic' (Sternbergh 2014), such as the fact that each individual may occupy a 'range of identity positions', including citizen, refugee, migrant and any number of other categories (Binaisa 2011, p. 522). This helps 'A Guard's Story' to counteract the dominant media narrative of detention centres as nonplaces full of non-people by describing the inhabitants of detention centres not through political labels, or numbers on a chart, or through the metaphorical language of 'floods' and 'waves', but by drawing pictures of human beings who may possess a range of identities and personas.

Wallman's drawings contain racial and religious cues, but they eschew binary characterisations and do not fit into neat categories. Unlike, for example, the different skin colours that are available to emoji — which fall into a scale, 'Type I for the "whitest" skin, Type VI for the "blackest,"' thus 'reflect[ing] established hierarchies of gendered and racialised authority and inequality', (Stark & Crawford 2015, p. 7) — Wallman's subtle use of shading and idiosyncratic drawing style make his characters feel like individuals.

As Ganguly-Scrase and Lahiri-Dutt argue, 'questions of culture and history, and the personal narratives of home and the everyday shaping of belonging must never be elided in framing migrants by simplistic discourses of documentation, status and integration' (2012, p. 4). Although 'A Guard's Story' does not detail the narratives

Figure 4.9: Illustration from 'A Guard's Story'.
Source: S Wallman, 18 Feburary 2014, Global Mail. *Reproduced with permission.*

of any individual detainees, Wallman's drawings imply that each has an individual culture and history, which the reader is able to reflect upon. Doyle and Griffiths argue that caricatures of 'the other' are often used by mainstream news as a way of appealing to audiences' nationalist sensibilities (2006, p. 4), but Wallman's illustrations appeal to a broader, more humanist sensibility.

Conclusion

The humanism that is at the heart of 'A Guard's Story' also underpins Article 14 of the United Nations Declaration of Human Rights, which was adopted by the UN General Assembly in 1948 and states: 'Everyone has the right to seek and to enjoy in other countries asylum from persecution'. The digital comic is different in many ways from that Declaration and the other print-based constitutions, bills, treaties and laws which form the foundation of modern democracy. The Australian government has used this print-based language of laws to exclude certain kinds of asylum seekers from the privileges granted by the UN Declaration of Human Rights, a stance that has been supported by the nationalism of most print-based news sources. This kind of language serves both to support policies and ways of thinking that make places into nations, and to make people without nations placeless. However, online comics like 'A Guard's Story' serve to disrupt this kind of dialogue in several ways.

The decentralised nature of social networking sites like Facebook and Twitter promotes communication that crosses political and place-based boundaries, and often privileges narratives that are personal, rather than nationalist. Dunn, for example, observed that stories about asylum seekers that were shared on Twitter 'directly opposed' many of the stories featured in mainstream news media: 'Rather than illegal or criminal, asylum seekers were innocent; rather than deserving of punishment, they were desperate for our mercy and aid' (2015, pp. 63-4). This is consistent with the prominence on social networks of emoji that are more suited to convey positive emotions, such as compassion, than negative emotions such as anger or fear. As a visual language, emoji also extend the way online communication can reach across borders and language barriers. If, as Anderson and McLuhan argued, the industries, technologies and cultures that developed around print technology were crucial in the development of national identities, then it is important to consider how online industries, technologies and cultures are unmaking nations. Online communication may be 'placeless' in many of the ways Relph and Webber described, but it may also provide ways of thinking about places beyond the framework of nations and nationality.

The visual language of comics used in 'A Guard's Story' suggests a way of picturing the dilemma of placelessness that asylum seekers face in Australia's detention centres. This chapter has examined the ways that this comic mimics some of the design elements that facilitate the placelessness of social media environments, while also departing from the standardised forms of expression commonly used in those environments. I would suggest that the drawn form of comics, which is rooted in the place where pen meets paper, can be a powerful tool for resisting the placelessness of much online communication.

'A Guard's Story' is not an isolated case. Comics journalism, reportage and memoir have blossomed online over the last five years, from dedicated portals like *Cartoon Movement* and *The Nib*, to features in major newspapers like the *Guardian* and academic journals like the *Annals of Internal Medicine*. 'A Guard's Story' inspired Safdar Ahmed's online comic 'Villawood: Notes from an Immigration Detention Centre', which won a Walkley Award in 2015. As 'A Guard's Story' demonstrates, digital publishing has expanded the ways that this kind of drawn visual language can be produced, read and shared, and the audience for these sorts of narratives is vast. Furthermore, readers are able to interact with these kinds of graphic narratives in ways that are different from the ways they interact with traditional print-based news stories. The effects of these differences are reshaping what it means to be placeless online, and what it means to be citizens of the places where we live.

References

Aguirre, AC & Davies, SG 2015, 'Imperfect strangers: Picturing place, family, and migrant identity on Facebook', *Discourse, Context & Media*, vol. 7, pp. 3-17.

Ahmed, S 2015, 'Villawood: Notes from an Immigration Detention Centre', *The Shipping News*, viewed 17 October 2016, <https://medium.com/shipping-news/villawood-9698183e114c#.ray9i4nl8>.

Al Rashdi, F 2015, 'Forms and functions of emojis in Whatsapp interaction among omanis', PhD thesis, Georgetown University, viewed 6 October 2016, <http://hdl.handle.net/10822/761502>.

Anderson, B 1997, 'The nation and the origins of national consciousness', in M Guibernau & J Rex (eds.), *The ethnicity reader: Nationalism, multiculturalism and migration*, Polity, Cambridge, pp. 43-51.

Arefi, M 1999, 'Non-place and placelessness as narratives of loss: Rethinking the notion of place', *Journal of Urban Design*, vol. 4, no. 2, pp. 179-193.

'Australian Border Force Bill 2015' 2015, viewed 5 October 2016, <www.aph.gov.au/Parliamentary_Business/Bills_Legislation/Bills_Search_Results/Result?bId=r5408>.

Australian Government 2014, *Appendices to the Report of the National Commission of Audit 2014 — Volume 2*, viewed 5 October 2016, <http://www.ncoa.gov.au/REPORT/appendix-vol-2/index.html>.

Barlow, K 2013, 'Parliament excises mainland from migration zone', *ABC News online*, viewed 6 October 2016, <http://www.abc.net.au/news/2013-05-16/parliament-excises-mainland-from-migration-zone/4693940>.

Binaisa, N 2011, 'Negotiating "Belonging" to the Ancestral "Homeland": Ugandan refugee descendents "return"', *Mobilities*, vol. 6, no. 4, pp. 519-534.

Birchall, E 2015, 'Regulation of healthcare practitioners in immigration detention centres', *Precedent (Sydney, NSW)*, no. 127, Mar/Apr 2015, pp. 48-52.

Chidgey, R 2014, 'Developing communities of resistance? Maker pedagogies, do-it-yourself feminism, and DIY citizenship', in M Ratto & M Boler (eds.), *DIY citizenship: Critical making and social media*, MIT Press, Cambridge, MA, pp. 101-114.

Christie, P & Sidhu, R 2002, 'Sticks and stones will break my bones — and words will harm too: Australia's provision of education for asylum seeker children in detention', *Social Alternatives*, vol. 21, no. 4, pp. 11-16.

Cottle, S 2005, 'In defence of "thick" journalism; or how television journalism can be good for us', in S Allan (ed.), *Journalism: Critical issues*, Open University Press, Maidenhead, pp. 109-124.

Crawford, K 2014, 'The anxieties of big data', *The New Inquiry*, viewed 6 October 2016, <http://thenewinquiry.com/essays/the-anxieties-of-big-data/>.

Department of Immigration and Border Protection (Australian Government) 2016, *About immigration detention*, viewed 6 October 2016, <https://www.border.gov.au/about/immigration-detention-in-australia>.

Doyle, W & Griffiths, M 2006, 'Caricature and an "ethics of discomfort"', *Southern Review: Communication, Politics & Culture*, vol. 39, no. 1, pp. 1-7.

Dunn, RM 2015, 'Twitter and the transformation of the public sphere: An analysis of asylum seeker narratives in the new media landscape', LLB (Hons) thesis, Macquarie University, Sydney, viewed 6 October 2016, <http://hdl.handle.net/1959.14/1055955>.

Farrell, P 2014, 'Australia's asylum policies repeatedly criticised by UN officials at conference', *The Guardian*, viewed 28 April 2014, <http://www.theguardian.com/world/2014/apr/23/australias-asylum-policies-repeatedly-criticised-by-un-officials-at-conference>.

Fisher, T 2014, 'Telling "A Guard's Story"', *Broadsheet Sydney*, viewed 6 October 2016, <https://www.broadsheet.com.au/sydney/art-and-design/article/global-mail-guards-story>.

Freinkel, LM 2006, 'Book review: Art Spiegelman, in the shadow of no towers', *Visual Communication Quarterly*, vol. 13, no. 4, pp. 248-255.

Galbraith, J 2015, 'Writing through fences: Writing and shared exchange in the process of re-membering', *Fine Print*, vol. 38, no. 1, pp. 25-28.

Ganguly-Scrase, R & Lahiri-Dutt, K 2012, 'Dispossession, placelessness, home and belonging: An outline of a research agenda', in K Lahiri-Dutt & R Ganguly-Scrase (eds.), *Rethinking displacement: Asia Pacific perspectives*, Routledge, London, pp. 3-30.

Gardner, J 2011, 'Storylines', *SubStance*, vol. 40, no. 1, pp. 53-69.

Gay, R 2013, 'The unbearable whiteness of emoji', *emoji*, WOMANZINE, Forced Meme Productions, pp. 26-27, viewed 6 October 2016, <https://issuu.com/lindseyweber5/docs/emoji_by_womanzine/13?e=11319660/7206264>.

Goodbrey, DM 2013, 'Digital comics — New tools and tropes', *Studies in Comics*, vol. 4, no. 1, pp. 185-197.

Grant, P 2012, *Blue*, Top Shelf Productions, Marietta, GA.

Grant, P 2015, 'The Serco story … short-circuited', *The Walkley Foundation*, viewed 20 March

2016, <http://www.walkleys.com/the-serco-story-short-circuited>.

Groensteen, T 2012, 'The current state of French comics theory', *Scandinavian Journal of Comic Art*, vol. 1, no. 1, pp. 111-122.

Hamilton, A 2015, 'The Border Force Act's disquieting parallels', *Eureka Street*, vol. 25, no. 13, viewed 6 October 2016, <http://www.eurekastreet.com.au/article.aspx?aeid=45107>.

Hugo, G & Napitupulu, CJ 2016, 'Boats, borders and ballot boxes: Asylum seekers on Australia's northern shore', in M van der Velde & T van Naerssen (eds.), *Mobility and migration choices: Thresholds to crossing borders*, Routledge, Abingdon-on-Thames, pp. 213-233.

Human Rights Law Centre 2014, *Can't flee, can't stay: Australia's interception and return of Sri Lankan asylum seekers*, Human Rights Law Centre, Melbourne.

Humphrey, AS 2014, 'Beyond graphic novels: Illustrated scholarly discourse and the history of educational comics', *Media International Australia*, no. 151, pp. 73-80.

Isaacs, D 2015a, 'Are healthcare professionals working in Australia's immigration detention centres condoning torture?', *Journal of Medical Ethics*, online first article, pp. 1-4, DOI: http://dx.doi.org/10.1136/medethics-2015-103066.

Isaacs, D 2015b, 'Doctors should boycott working in Australia's immigration centres and must continue to speak out on mistreatment of detainees — Despite the law', *BMJ*, vol. 350, DOI: http://dx.doi.org/10.1136/bmj.h3269.

Jeffrey, G 2012, *Martin Luther King Jr. and the march on Washington (Graphic history of the Civil Rights Movement)*, trans. N Spender, Gareth Stevens Publishing, New York.

Kato, S, Kato, Y & Scott, D 2009, 'Relationships between emotional states and emoticons in mobile phone email communication in Japan', *International journal on e-learning*, vol. 8, no. 3, pp. 385-401.

Kraus, M 2013, 'Speaking in picture-letters', *emoji*, WOMANZINE, Forced Meme Productions, p. 5, viewed 6 October 2016, <https://issuu.com/lindseyweber5/docs/emoji_by_womanzine/13?e=11319660/7206264>.

Laughland, O 2014, 'Doctors' litany of medical neglect of asylum seekers still "largely ignored"', *The Guardian*, viewed 14 April 2016, <http://www.theguardian.com/world/2014/may/27/doctors-litany-of-medical-neglect-of-asylum-seekers-still-largely-ignored>.

Leach, M 2003, '"Disturbing practices": Dehumanizing asylum seekers in the refugee "crisis" in Australia, 2001-2002', *Refuge*, vol. 21, no. 3, pp. 25-33.

Marshall, PD & Barbour, K 2015, 'Making intellectual room for persona studies: A new consciousness and a shifted perspective', *Persona Studies*, vol. 1, no. 1, pp. 1-12.

McCabe, M 2015, 'How do you figure? Engaging and teaching with comics in the VCAL English classroom', *Ethos*, vol. 23, no. 1, pp. 16-20.

McCall, C 2015, 'Doctors silenced over Australia's immigration centres', *The Lancet*, vol. 386, no. 10007, p. 1932, viewed 6 October 2016 <http://dx.doi.org/10.1016/S0140-6736(15)00960-5>.

McCloud, S 1993, *Understanding comics*, Paradox Press, New York.

McCloud, S 2000a, 'Follow that trail', *I Can't Stop Thinking*, no. 4, Fall/Winter, viewed 5 October 2016, <http://www.scottmccloud.com/1-webcomics/icst/icst-4/icst-4.html>.

McCloud, S 2000b, *Reinventing comics: How imagination and technology are revolutionizing an art form*, Perennial, New York.

McLuhan, M 1964, *Understanding media: The extensions of man*, Routledge & Kegan Paul, London.

Miller, A 2015, 'Over under sideways down: An interview with Karrie Fransman', *European Comic Art*, vol. 8, no. 1, pp. 15-24.

Mills, J 2012, 'Fiction: Blue', *Overland*, viewed 19 September 2014, <https://overland.org. au/2012/04/fiction-blue>.

Odom, W, Zimmerman, J & Forlizzi, J 2014, 'Placelessness, spacelessness, and formlessness: Experiential qualities of virtual possessions', in *Proceedings of the 2014 Conference on Designing Interactive Systems*, ACM, New York, pp. 985-994, viewed 6 October 2016, <http://dl.acm.org/citation.cfm?id=2598577>.

Ogawa, M, Jurmu, M, Ito, T, Yonezawa, T, Nakazawa, J, Takashio, K & Tokuda, H 2013, 'Reinforcing co-located communication practices through interactive public displays', in *Proceedings of the 2013 ACM Conference on Pervasive and Ubiquitous Computing Adjunct Publication*, ACM, New York, pp. 737-740, viewed 6 October 2016, <http://dl.acm.org/ citation.cfm?id=2495998>.

Olle, N & Wallman, S 2014, 'At work inside our dentention centres: A Guard's Story', *Global Mail*, viewed 5 October 2016, <http://tgm-serco.patarmstrong.net.au>.

Oxford Dictionaries 2015, 'Oxford Dictionaries word of the year 2015 is … ', *OxfordWords blog*, 16 November 2015, viewed 6 October 2016, <http://blog.oxforddictionaries. com/2015/11/word-of-the-year-2015-emoji/>.

Phillips, M 2013, 'Out of sight, out of mind: Excising Australia from the migration zone', *The Conversation*, viewed 3 May 2016, <https://theconversation.com/out-of-sight-out-of-mind-excising-australia-from-the-migration-zone-14387>.

Refaie, EE 2012, *Autobiographical comics: Life writing in pictures*, University Press of Mississippi, Jackson.

Relph, E 1976, *Place and placelessness*, Pion, London.

Reynolds, M 2014, 'The *Global Mail* faces closure after Wood withdraws funding', *Mumbrella*, viewed 5 October 2016, <https://mumbrella.com.au/global-mail-close-203061>.

Romano, A 2004, 'Journalism's role in mediating public conversation on asylum seekers and refugees in Australia', *Australian Journalism Review*, vol. 26, no. 2, pp. 43-62.

Scalettaris, G 2007, 'Refugee studies and the international refugee regime: A reflection on a desirable separation', *Refugee Survey Quarterly*, vol. 26, no. 3, pp. 36-50.

Scott, R 2012, 'Pat Grant: Blue', *Australian Book Review*, viewed 19 September 2014, <https:// www.australianbookreview.com.au/component/k2/69-april-2012/861-pat-grant-blue>.

Seamon, D & Sowers, J 2008, 'Place and placelessness (1976): Edward Relph', in P Hubbard, R Kitchin & G Valentine (eds.), *Key texts in human geography*, SAGE Publications Ltd, Los Angeles & London, pp. 45-52.

Skiba, DJ 2016, 'Face with tears of joy is word of the year: Are emoji a sign of things to come in health care?', *Nursing Education Perspectives*, vol. 37, no. 1, pp. 56-57.

Stark, L & Crawford, K 2015, 'The conservatism of emoji: Work, affect, and communication', *Social Media + Society*, vol. 1, no. 2, pp. 1-11, viewed 6 October 2016, <http://sms. sagepub.com/content/1/2/2056305115604853>.

Sternbergh, A 2014, 'Smile, you're speaking emoji: The rapid evolution of a wordless tongue', *New*

York Magazine, viewed 5 October 2016, <http://nymag.com/daily/intelligencer/2014/11/emojis-rapid-evolution.html>.

Sugiyama, S 2015, '*Kawaii meiru* and *Maroyaka neko*: Mobile *emoji* for relationship maintenance and aesthetic expressions among Japanese teens', *First Monday*, vol. 20, no. 10, viewed 6 October 2016, <http://firstmonday.org/ojs/index.php/fm/article/view/5826/4997>.

United Nations General Assembly 1948, *Universal declaration of human rights*, Resolution 217 A (III), viewed 5 October 2016, <http://www.un.org/en/universal-declaration-human-rights/>.

Vidal, L, Ares, G & Jaeger, SR 2016, 'Use of emoticon and emoji in tweets for food-related emotional expression', *Food Quality and Preference*, vol. 49, pp. 119-128.

Wake, A 2014, 'Graeme Wood's *Global Mail* felled by financial reality', *The Conversation*, viewed 19 September 2014, <http://theconversation.com/graeme-woods-global-mail-felled-by-financial-reality-22581>.

Wallman, S 2015, ''What implication does the emoji have for the future of linguistics?'', *The Interrobang*, viewed 6 October 2016, <https://medium.com/the-interrobang/what-implication-does-the-emoji-have-for-the-future-of-linguistics-9320ebe88fba#.iuocj5n2k>.

Webber, MM 1964, 'The urban place and the nonplace urban realm', in MM Webber (ed.), *Explorations into urban structure*, University of Pennsylvania Press, Philadelphia, pp. 79-153.

Yeole, AV, Chavan, P & Nikose, M 2015, 'Opinion mining for emotions determination', in *Innovations in Information, Embedded and Communication Systems (ICIIECS), 2015 International Conference on*, IEEE, pp. 1-5, DOI: http://dx.doi.org/10.1109/ICIIECS.2015.7192931.

Reclaiming heritage for UNESCO: Discursive practices and community building in northern Italy[1]

5

Maria Cristina Paganoni

Study design

This research arises from an interest in heritage preservation in the public sector and, in particular, from the awareness of the key role heritage discourse can play as a tool for social inclusion in urban policy and planning. It reflects on the contribution of new media to what could be called 'the invention of heritage' in the line of Hobsbawm's 'invention of tradition' (1983), showing how heritage is discursively constructed to provide not just an objective historical truth, but collective memories. The selected area of analysis is the contribution of new media communication to the making and remaking of a UNESCO World Heritage site.

UNESCO's protection of World Heritage Sites was inaugurated by the *Convention Concerning the Protection of the World Cultural and Natural Heritage*, commonly known as the

---

1   This chapter mentions a number of websites, apps and other internet and social media platforms and sources. For those wishing to access such sources, they are listed at the end of the chapter under the heading 'Links'.

World Heritage Convention (UNESCO 1972), which elevated national symbols into items of 'outstanding universal value' and property of all mankind, thereby corroborating an essentialist view of the past (Paganoni 2015b). Since then the approach has changed, expanding the meaning of heritage from the protection of historic buildings and monuments towards a more general understanding of the wider context and preservation of tangible and intangible cultural forms. This wider approach was ratified first in 1992 by the World Heritage Committee's decision to include cultural landscapes in the World Heritage List (UNESCO 1992) and then by the *Convention for the Safeguarding of the Intangible Cultural Heritage* (UNESCO 2003). In particular, from what Article 1 of the 1972 Convention designated as 'the combined works of nature and man' (UNESCO 1972), the notion of 'cultural landscape' was deduced, a concept that embraces diverse possible interactions between people and the natural environment.

Against this background, the following analysis addresses the discursive practices leading to the inscription of a site on the World Heritage List, one of the most ambitious achievements for localities that aspire to global recognition of the symbolic value of their historic legacy. The time-consuming process of proposing a candidacy through its several steps of preparation can now benefit from the opportunity to promote the identity of a place via the internet, social networks and mobile technology (Webmoor 2008; Buescher & Urry 2009). The potential of new media to both generate community involvement by collapsing the boundaries between the private and the public and to make responsive publics coalesce around projects has attracted scholarly attention not only to the power of networks but also to the 'affective formations' these networks produce, their affiliations, activities and political expressions (Papacharissi 2015, p. 24).

In other words, the efforts required of a UNESCO World Heritage Site [WHS] may help gauge the potential of new media in the invention and reinvention of heritage, an activity whose political implications have been firmly established in the scholarly investigations dedicated to this subject (Tunbridge & Ashworth 1996; Smith 2006; Graham & Howard 2008). As Smith claims (2006, p. 13), 'the discursive construction of heritage is itself part of the cultural and social processes that are heritage'. If heritage can be dissonant and divisive — for example, when its preservation becomes a pretext for gentrifying historic districts that favour social elites — it can nonetheless contribute to fostering a new sense of belonging at the local level, adding social value to both the material and the intangible heritage of a region as a driver of cultural creativity and urban regeneration. This culture-inclusive and socially sensitive approach reflects a very recent trend in urban policy and planning, which aims to articulate heritage discourse with community involvement and economic development. This is spelt out by the '5Cs' strategic objectives reiterated in UNESCO's *Strategic Action Plan for the*

Implementation of the Convention 2012-2022 (2011): credibility, conservation, capacity building, communication and communities.[2]

The most populous region in Italy, a country that itself boasts more UNESCO World Heritage Sites than any other country (fifty-one as of 2016), Lombardy alone hosts nine. They include prehistoric rock art, Renaissance towns, the church of Santa Maria delle Grazie with Leonardo da Vinci's *Last Supper*, religious architecture of the sixteenth and seventeenth centuries, and industrial archaeology in Crespi d'Adda. Other Italian localities have been placed on UNESCO's tentative list — an inventory of those properties that each state party intends to consider for nomination.

For the purpose of this analysis, a virtual trajectory has been traced to connect three relatively close places in Lombardy which are involved with UNESCO world heritage. Each place — the town of Crespi d'Adda in the province of Bergamo, the city of Bergamo itself, and the city of Sesto San Giovanni in the province of Milan — is involved differently by reason of its different status. While Bergamo is included for its built historic environment dating back to the sixteenth century and Venetian domination inland and along the Adriatic coasts, Crespi and Sesto are powerful expressions of the industrial heritage of the last two centuries. Despite the evident differences between them, all three locations ultimately chime in with the kind of mainstream heritage discourse that is deployed at the European level to favour the construction of a pan-European identity — for example, prioritising transnational projects, or highlighting the legacy of industrialisation all over the continent. It is worth noting here that the Council of Europe declared 2015 as European Industrial and Technical Heritage Year, while recent scholarly research has underlined the rediscovery of the industrial culture in Italy in the 1980s and 1990s, with the birth of a remarkable number of both corporate and collective industrial museums focusing on local economic and manufacturing cultures (Martino 2015).

Crespi d'Adda is located on the Adda river, a geographical divide between the provinces of Milan and Bergamo; it is halfway between the two, alongside the A4 highway and within the administrative boundaries of the municipality of Capriate San Gervasio. It was named after its founder, Cristoforo Benigno Crespi, and became a World Heritage Site in 1995, when its textile factory was still operational. Crespi is a well-preserved model workers' housing settlement that dates back to 1878. The village housed the cotton factory workers and their supervisors and is still inhabited to

---

2   Credibility describes what should be a general consensus on the outstanding universal value of inscribed places. Conservation has to do with safeguarding and management. Meanwhile, capacity building involves the role of state parties; communication affects information sharing and awareness raising; and communities play a central role in the implementation of the World Heritage Convention.

this day[3], even after the company ceased manufacturing in 2003. The adjacent factory building, however, is dilapidated and needs massive regeneration interventions, with current stakeholders struggling to find a viable project that will satisfy the private investors who purchased the factory site in 2013 as well as local citizens and tourists. As a result, the regeneration plan seemed to come to a dead end in 2015, threatening the survival of the abandoned manufacturing areas, which became neglected and plundered, though the plan has recently been taken up again. While demanding major renovation of the site, a non-profit citizen association, Associazione Crespi d'Adda, nicknamed CrespiLove, is meanwhile committed to counteracting further deterioration and obsolescence in several ways, leading guided walks, organising evening tours with open-air performances of what life was like in the village, and promoting the use of an app to discover the surrounding natural areas. The case of Crespi d'Adda clearly illustrates both how being a World Heritage Site does not prevent the place from damage and how communication of the historical and cultural meanings of heritage needs to be constantly reinvented in order to warrant its protection.

The Venetian walls of Bergamo were listed on UNESCO's tentative list in 2006. Other Venetian fortifications built between the fifteenth and the seventeenth centuries under the Republic of Venice's rule, located in the Italian regions of Veneto and Friuli and in the two Eastern Adriatic countries of Montenegro and Croatia, were later added to the candidacy, while Greece and Cyprus did not join it.[4] Though the project may seem incomplete from a strictly historical point of view, its outcome is a transnational site along a journey of over 1000 kilometres, from the hills of Bergamo to the coast of the Balkans. In January 2016 the Italian National Commission for UNESCO submitted the nomination file of the site to the World Heritage Centre [WHC] in Paris, with Bergamo as the leading city. The nominated property is now awaiting review by the advisory bodies in charge of its evaluation. Since 2012, the City Council of Bergamo has joined with other public and private stakeholders to found the 'Terra di San Marco'[5] association, whose aim is to raise awareness of the candidacy and promote cultural events to seek citizen engagement.

Finally, on the outskirts of Milan, Sesto San Giovanni is a former heavy-industry district of the twentieth century which has shifted to a post-Fordist development model and aims to promote socially inclusive knowledge economy patterns. Sesto was once imaginatively nicknamed Italy's 'little Manchester' or 'former Stalingrad', after its

---

3   Gasparoli and Ronchi (2013) reported 'a community of about 400 people, mostly former workers or their descendants' (p. 362).

4   Greece backed out of the project for economic reasons; as for Cyprus, the island's divisive political situation, which involves the Greek and Turkish Cypriot communities, is presumably hardly conducive to the making of a common heritage.

5   That is, 'St Mark's land', from the patron saint of Venice.

working-class culture and political identity. Somewhat in the wake of Crespi d'Adda, which is only thirty kilometres away, it is applying to be recognised by UNESCO as an organically evolved cultural landscape for its tangible and intangible heritage; however, it is not yet on the tentative list. The municipality can be taken as an exemplary case study of a city committed to enhancing its industrial heritage, which saw the localisation of five major made-in-Italy companies in the last century — Breda, Campari, Ercole Marelli, Falck and Magneti Marelli — without neglecting the working-class and collective ethos of its material and intangible heritage. For Sesto San Giovanni, the UNESCO candidacy may act as the catalyst for an overall reassessment of its heritage. For this purpose, the city brand for the twenty-first century will hopefully combine corporate narratives into new forms of participatory storytelling from multiple urban stakeholders, addressing the potentialities for cultural heritage tourism against evolving European and global cultural action frameworks (Kaminski, Benson & Arnold 2014; Panzini 2015).

Study design methodology

The contribution of new media to the opening of social spaces can be explored through different perspectives that address social imaginaries, discourses and practices in turn (Langlois 2013; Georgakopolou & Spilioti 2016). While attentive to all interdisciplinary insights, this research nonetheless prioritises the impact that new media have on the discursive interpretation of heritage, exploring how they can innovate its understanding and uses in the social, political, economic and cultural life of communities. For this reason it draws on both discourse analysis and heritage studies (Harrison 2013), keeping an eye on the declared values of the UNESCO World Heritage Site. Qualitative analysis is applied to the types of linguistic evidence that can be retrieved on the digital platforms on which a given location is described and experienced, from institutional websites and tourist information sites to social media and mobile apps.

The textual selection is mostly comprised of website material, social media status updates (like Facebook posts and tweets) and mobile app content. Only part of it is translated into English since the main publics are local communities of Italian native speakers. In this context the main function of digital platforms, and especially of both Facebook and Twitter, seems to be that of keeping up interest in a place by engaging local stakeholders in an ongoing, co-constructed conversation. We can regard social media as bulletin boards on which events are announced and media content circulated and, simultaneously, as resonance boxes of largely affective and mercurial publics (Papacharissi 2015).

As for storytelling in the heritage sector as a means of cultural transference (Giovagnoli 2013), it is not hard to see how (re)scripting narratives across media platforms may turn into an opportunity for local communities to regain the *genius loci* from a more demotic and inclusive historical perspective that will hopefully surpass the scope of mere informative descriptions. Precious memories (a part, in themselves, of intangible heritage) and creative insights into the uses of heritage in the present can be shared across different groups (for example, cultural heritage tourists), who are thus invited to participate in the discursive making and remaking of a locality (Paganoni 2015a) and in its preservation. The emergence of these new social formations and networks has an impact on real communities and on how they interpret their material and intangible heritage to the world and future generations (Kalay, Kvan & Affleck 2008). Finally, engaging stakeholders in heritage protection and promotion gives rise to 'new civic vernaculars' (Papacharissi 2012), in which the renewal of communicative practices should mirror the delisting of heritage as an elitist form of cultural consumption and, thanks to the appeal of a vital notion of what heritage means for the present, reach much wider publics than previously.

Whenever necessary, this chapter provides the relevant translation from the original Italian. The textual selection is nonetheless indicative not only of the bilingualism that characterises the institutional arena of a non-English speaking European country but also, at a deeper level, of a discrepancy between different social imaginaries as this manifests itself in discourse. Local administrators are required to use English to communicate with supranational bodies like UNESCO, and to connect with global networks and brand cities for international tourists, investors, talent, sports and cultural events. However, civic interaction with, and within, local communities takes place in Italian and pursues intents that need to be connected or reconnected with the official urban management discourse. The influence of these intended publics on the ways in which the meanings of heritage are discursively constructed and negotiated with global and local stakeholders will be illustrated in what follows.

Cultural heritage and new media communication

The analysis in this chapter will concentrate on the ways in which the three selected locations in Lombardy — Crespi d'Adda, Bergamo and Sesto San Giovanni — promote their heritage through new media, with a special focus on the linguistic devices, discursive strategies and rhetorical patterns being employed. While UNESCO's assumptions about the timeless value of world heritage and cultural landscape form the most consistent and conventional rhetorical refrain, this chapter will also pay attention to the theme of economic development and social inclusion. This theme, which is often incorporated in heritage discourse, seems to provide a reality check on the 'aestheticisation' of the past. It is also important to be aware of the financial burden that heritage preservation represents today for local administrations constantly struggling with dwindling budgets.

On the UNESCO website, the World Heritage Site of Crespi d'Adda 'has conserved much of its integrity as all aspects of the industrial town remain well preserved including factories, housing and services' (UNESCO World Heritage Centre, n.d.). The visitor's appreciation of its beauty is enhanced by the grid pattern of tidy streets and the modular architecture of buildings. Hierarchical roles are clearly inscribed in the spatial organisation: the workers' detached houses are identical, all with a garden and an orchard, while supervisors and the director were assigned creatively designed villas in a more elevated position and the Crespi family lived in a castle-like mansion. Current residents and occasional tourists seem to appreciate the site's layout, which does not generate the panopticon effect of surveillance but rather a sense of nostalgia for bygone days. At the far end of the village we find the cemetery, dominated by the mausoleum of the Crespi family in the shape of a pyramid decorated with the three statues of Faith, Hope and Charity, thus ideally embracing all the deceased. At the entrance of the cotton textile factory, the clock over the door was stopped when the last work shift ended on 20 December 2003.

Whenever the incompatibility between timelessness and disruptive change cannot be reconciled, the narrative, almost reluctantly avowing the inevitability of history, adroitly conjures up positive change to counteract dereliction:

> Although the village remains *intact, changing economic and social conditions*, particularly a declining population, pose *a potential threat* to its continued survival. This *threat* might be contained and mitigated by *recent positive changes* with a demographic and socio-economic plan. (UNESCO World Heritage Centre, n.d., emphases added)

Unlike other company towns that were closer to big cities, Crespi d'Adda's surprising stability as a time capsule throughout history was warranted by its 'isolated setting', its geographical encapsulation at the confluence of the Adda and Brembo rivers. Nonetheless, 'some change has occurred' and 'the alteration in industrial practice has resulted in a change of use for many buildings' (UNESCO World Heritage Centre, n.d.). By replacing subject + transitive verb constructions with abstract nouns ('change', 'alteration') in the subject position followed by intransitive verbs ('occur', 'result'), the narrative glosses over a more detailed account of the site's recent history and elides agency, especially on the workers' part. Ultimately, the main actors are Crespi's enlightened founder, Cristoforo Benigno Crespi, and his son Silvio — a role as protagonists that the UNESCO WHC website makes explicit by indexing them as agent complements in passive constructions or subjects in active sentences.

> The village was founded *by Cristoforo Benigno Crespi*, to house the workers in his textile factory and its final form was developed *by Cristoforo's son, Silvio Benigno Crespi, who* had studied the functioning of German and English cotton mills. *He* developed the town to provide comfortable housing and services in order to maintain a stable workforce and prevent industrial strife. (UNESCO World Heritage Centre, n.d., emphases added)

The celebration of the founder's exceptional personality is echoed in a blog post on a local tourism website only partially translated into English: 'Il genio dell'industria cotoniera, probabilmente fattore genetico [The genius of the cotton industry, probably a genetic factor]' (Milano da Vedere, n.d.).

A more complex presentation of the Crespi owners is provided by Crespi d'Adda UNESCO, the institutional website managed by the municipality of Capriate San Gervasio, of which Crespi d'Adda is a neighbourhood.[6] Despite the less cursory historical recounts that the website offers, the dominant place narrative nonetheless continues to minimise not only historical change but also the 'decline' of the site and the current controversies as to regeneration plans, which risk compromising the promise of its 'rebirth'. The narrative perhaps aims to sound consensual, but the overall effect is not totally convincing. The rhetoric of timelessness would seem to imply a lack of bitter social conflict which does not reflect the true scenario.

> Crespi d'Adda is the most complete and *best-preserved* company town in Europe. It has a soul of its own, *essentially untouched by time. A visit can transport you out of the boundaries of time and space.* Crespi d'Adda *hasn't changed* from the 1930s — the houses, the urban structure, the boundaries are *all the same.* (Villaggio Crespi, n.d., emphases added)

The same discursive stance, realised by an impersonal voice addressing a general 'you', is apparent on *Villaggio Crespi*, a website maintained by the Crespi Cultura Association, which runs guided tours of the site for international tourists and is translated into French, German and Spanish, besides English, with the addition of Portuguese and Japanese.

> The Crespi Village was effectively a *complete and self-sufficient microcosm.* (Villaggio Crespi, n.d., emphasis added)

> The Crespi Village is *a place where time has stopped*: in fact, Crespi d'Adda has perfectly preserved many signs of its past. A careful visitor will notice how *this place* — together with its history, its houses, its factory and its river — *can bring you back in time*: to the times when the founders of the village — the Crespi family — succeeded to give birth to an ideal company town, where they combined the workers' needs with the entrepreneur's needs. The factory, which ceased to operate in 2003, is closed for public [*sic*]. Today the building that used to be a cotton mill is not equipped as a *museum*, but it has kept its *fascinating architecture*, which *you can admire* from the main street. (Villaggio Crespi, n.d., emphases added)

This kind of language sounds oblivious not only to the passing of time but also to the class divide that connoted the organisation of factory work and the ways in which contemporary publics experience Crespi today, impressed by its beauty but also aware

---

6 The municipality of Capriate San Gervasio runs the information point open inside the village, from Thursday to Sunday.

of its decline.[7] The choice of words and phrases such as 'museum' and 'fascinating architecture' (and elsewhere, 'enchanting', 'extraordinary', 'ideal', 'idyllic', 'superb') promotes the characteristic disembodied tourist gaze ('you can admire') which is recurrent throughout. In fact, navigating the website allows users to retrieve a few pages (in Italian) that illustrate meetings and cultural activities carried out with local residents in order to breathe new life into the village, but the predominant impression is that of a kind of storytelling deeply steeped in the past. Crespi Cultura has no Facebook page, while Crespi d'Adda UNESCO publishes status updates on its Facebook and Twitter pages which mostly proceed from, or include the participation of, institutional sources and the mainstream press. The main actors in this top-down narrative are the municipality of Capriate San Gervasio, the Lombardy regional government, the Italian Minister for Culture, politicians, artists, art critics and journalists. Crespi d'Adda UNESCO also has an official channel on YouTube, where a few educational videos in Italian and in English are uploaded. However, traffic on all these social media is still very low.

By contrast, the communicative exchanges on CrespiLove's website and social media pages are intended to align themselves with a different audience, made up of ordinary, mostly young citizens. The official CrespiLovers are all people with very close links to the region, mostly though not exclusively in their twenties or early thirties, whose motto is: 'We don't recount history, we live it!' The first-person-plural narrator is a collective fictive subject whose outspoken commitment reveals that the debate about the future fate of the site concerns the citizens of the area and looks beyond the maintenance of the place as an open-air heritage museum towards the 'sustainable tourist and economic development' of Crespi.

The association, which is painfully aware of the frail beauty of the village as well as of its current decline despite its WHS status, is networked with the most significant transnational heritage bodies — the European Federation of Associations of Industrial and Technical Heritage [E-FAITH], the European Route of Industrial Heritage [ERIH], the International Committee for the Conservation of the Industrial Heritage [TICCIH]. Through a well-designed website and social media pages, it promotes events but also gives space to the memories and voices of the village's citizens, especially older ones. The videos of these interviews are uploaded to a playlist on YouTube. Subscription to an e-newsletter is available and the use of a state-of-

---

7   This post, published on 16 November 2014 on *Italian Notes*, a travel blog kept by a Danish couple (see http://italiannotes.com/unesco-world-heritage-lombardy), is quite frank in its perception of the place: 'We had gone out of our way to visit this "remarkably intact" shrine for industrial history, and were more than a little disappointed to find the place half dead and deserted. Company owners caring for their employers by providing housing, shops, doctors and child care is obviously a thing of the past'.

the-art downloadable app[8] is recommended to explore the surrounding areas along the Adda river. Quite understandably, social media traffic is higher for CrespiLove than for Crespi d'Adda UNESCO. Of special interest are the updates on the ongoing negotiation between the municipality and the private investing group that bought the factory ground and has drafted a regeneration plan. The project still lacks general consensus but is nonetheless regarded as a vital infusion of money, creativity and opportunities into the Crespi community which local powers alone would be unable to provide.

Turning now to the transnational site that sees Bergamo as the leading city of the UNESCO nomination project, it can be observed that communication via new media is still very limited. Though the Terra di San Marco association's website introduces all the localities involved in the nomination, content is only partly translated into English, while the association's Facebook page does not seem to attract a lot of users and is not even networked to the website. A Twitter profile has not yet been opened. Besides other city-related blogs (for example, 'The City Hub'), mention of the UNESCO nomination is also found on the city's official tourism website, which uses mildly ironic language about Bergamo's pronounced Catholic identity to date: 'Building them caused eight excommunications by the local clergy, but it was worth it: today the massive defensive Walls of Bergamo were nominated to become a UNESCO World Heritage site' (VisitBergamo, n.d.).

The entire discursive construction of the nominated property is quite interesting, in the sense that the amount of knowledge it demonstrates about local history, with its interregional and transnational connections over the centuries, vastly exceeds the ordinary citizen's competence. It also challenges parochialism, in particular a kind of self-complacency with the city's heritage which is too often the dominant discourse on VisitBergamo.

> Bergamo wouldn't be the same without its *impressive* Venetian Walls. This *spectacular* circuit is over six km long: it's the *perfect* place to take a romantic walk and enjoy *wonderful* sunsets, and it has been enclosing the beauties of the Upper Town for more than four centuries. (VisitBergamo, n.d., emphases added)

Much more daring in its scope, the UNESCO candidacy is better articulated but also complex and sophisticated, especially for its involvement with Croatia, a recent European Union acquisition (1 July 2013), and Montenegro, a country which is currently applying for EU membership and is somehow off the beaten track of mass

---

8   The name of the app, 'Addentrarsi', plays with the name of the Adda river and the meaning of the verb 'addentrarsi', which is 'to go deeply into'. Images were acquired by drones and combined with 3D modelling of historical buildings, appropriately georeferenced and inserted in an orthophoto map. In this way, app users are able to take georeferenced pictures of anything within the natural and historic area and report problems, thus actively contributing to heritage and environmental preservation.

tourism. The network is 'the focus of a project of transnational integration' (Comune di Bergamo 2016, p. 322), announced by all the mayors involved in the candidacy in the very first pages of the nomination dossier, where the theme of European integration is foregrounded.

> The distinctive feature of the Serenissima was the organization of a multinational state, made up of several varied peoples united in their diversity. A preview of Europe to come? We like to think so. (p. 3)

Invented by a local web design agency, the logo aims to provide a visual equivalent of the making of this transnational set of localities.

> A *trait d'union* that ideally combines the Venetian fortifications built between the 15th and the 17th century in nine cities between Italy, Croatia and Montenegro. An application that tracks an invisible line from Bergamo to Kotor, connecting these states united by the presence of the precious works of defence of the Republic of Venice. (Woodoo Studio, n.d.)

At a thematic level we can observe that, throughout the nomination dossier and with respect to the variables of each locality, cultural heritage is related to key concepts like sustainable tourism, economic development and investment. In urban management parlance and in the policy discourse of the European Union, it is common to regard heritage as a driver for the economy, which is still recovering from the aftermath of the 2008 global financial crisis. In the case of Bergamo, the contribution of new media to the effective implementation of the project's goals through actions of citizen empowerment will need to be tested by time and in the plurality of geographical, social and political contexts connected by the UNESCO nomination. At the time of writing, the municipality is still enjoying the success of the 'Abbraccio delle Mura' ('Embracing on the Walls') initiative on Sunday 3 July 2016. This event called up 11 507 volunteers along the perimeter of the Venetian fortifications, a 4 kilometre-long human chain — a feat that set a new Guinness World Record. Social media were highly instrumental to the success of the effort.[9]

A dense and irregular settlement numbering 82 000 inhabitants, Sesto San Giovanni lies to the northeast of Milan, to which it is well connected thanks to major roads, railways and an underground train line that goes straight to Piazza Duomo (Cathedral Square), the heart of the Lombardy capital. At the beginning of the twentieth century, Sesto quickly became a major industrial centre in the steelmaking, mechanical engineering and electromechanical sectors, ranking as the fifth-largest manufacturing town by the end of the Second World War. Its landscape of sprawling factories was nonetheless interspersed with architectural attempts to provide some kind of urban

---

9   See 'L'Abbraccio delle Mura — Bergamo è nel Guinness dei Primati', the press release published on 6 July 2016, on the municipal website (https://www.comune.bergamo.it).

design and decent housing, like the Falck workers' village, the first example of a Fordist village in Italy, and the adjacent church, San Giorgio alle Ferriere (at the iron mills).

However, the industrial decline that took place during the second half of the century and led to the closing down or downsizing of its major factories by the mid-1990s forced the city to turn from a heavy-industry district into a postmodern network city, rooted in the global flows of information technology, knowledge and people. Though painful, this change has made Sesto aware of the tangible and intangible value of its industrial heritage, an increasingly mainstream trend in Europe where, for example, the Council of Europe designated 2015 the European Industrial and Technical Heritage Year. Now a part of the local government of Greater Milan, Sesto San Giovanni is an interesting embodiment of labour culture within yesterday's factories and today's service industries. The municipality is fully committed to urban regeneration; protected green and recreational areas; the creative reuse of industrial archaeology; and the creation of museums, libraries and archives documenting its past, without forgetting the connections with the present and the need to involve the local community in the remaking of the place and its recollections (Mah 2012). Memory becomes a resource to deploy when attempting both to heal the wounds of the past and, hopefully, to bridge the gap with the present:

> With the closure of the large factories, the idea of collecting, organizing, highlighting and handing down the memories of industrial and working-class Sesto began to make headway. Not just to preserve the history of the past, but to strengthen the community of Sesto San Giovanni's feeling of belonging to a cohesive body, so that the townspeople could share the stages covered, take new steps and reorganize themselves for the re-launch of their town and its area … The town has started to tell its story, its history and present-day relevance. A process of regeneration has thus been set in motion, the generation of a collective awareness, a highly vigilant, active and receptive awareness, as you will discover in the initiatives we describe in this section. (Sesto San Giovanni per l'UNESCO, n.d.)

The application process to become a UNESCO World Heritage Site in the 'Organically Evolved Landscape' category began in April 2006. As a result, the candidacy has greatly encouraged the municipality to improve its digital presence in order to raise awareness about the project.

Sesto San Giovanni's web portal is in Italian, with the exception of the pages dealing with the UNESCO candidacy, which are only partially available in English and are explicitly dedicated to the branding of its industrial heritage. 'Sesto San Giovanni per l'UNESCO' on Facebook is also only in Italian, but the descriptions of heritage places in the photo galleries have been translated into English. With the progress of the bid for World Heritage Site listing, the municipality intends to translate other sections of the promotional material. The Facebook page is an active platform, used to announce cultural and leisure events (for example, guided walking tours of the city's industrial heritage, group bike rides, photo contests and so on). However, at present, it addresses a mainly local public and does not reach international visitors and heritage tourists, who could help Sesto gain international visibility rather than continue to be included in descriptions of Greater Milan on tourism portals and guidebooks (Provincia di Milano 2008).

The interactive map of Sesto San Giovanni shows the five industrial areas the municipality can be divided into, based on the presence of the factories that were the backbone of the city throughout the twentieth century. These were: Breda, Falck (with two main sites) and Marelli (three industrial groups active in the mechanical engineering, steelmaking and electromechanical industries, respectively), as well as Campari, founded in 1860, a leading company in the global branded beverage industry. By clicking on each name, users have access to a more detailed map of that specific area, with its main heritage sites and a brief description of them. While this taxonomy mirrors the municipality's commitment to mapping and listing its heritage in view of the UNESCO bid, a more interactive and customisable version of Sesto San Giovanni's heritage can be experienced by downloading the free 'Sesto City of Factories' and 'North of Milan Urban Metropolitan Museum' apps. Users can also contribute to a participative geoblog ('MappaMI') or enjoy the psychogeographical map of the area, which is progressively growing.[10]

Among the initiatives to collect public memories to support Sesto San Giovanni's nomination as a World Heritage Site, special mention should be made of Sestopedia, a sort of municipal Wikipedia or online encyclopaedia (at present, only in Italian), which is co-authored by citizens willing to share their stories and memories. As with other rebranding initiatives launched by the municipality, the project intends to build a new identity for the city by giving voice to its citizenry, especially those ordinary people and workers that made Sesto what it is today, often through tragic periods in the history of the nation (like Fascism and the two World Wars). This is promoted as the true spirit of place branding versus mere urban marketing: 'authenticity versus image — basically, the content of collective memories and human work, not simply the preservation of the container' (Fossa 2015, p. 77).

---

10 'Psychogeography developed among European and American avant-garde revolutionary groups in the late 1950s and 1960s. It was later taken up in a range of cultural contexts and has come to be associated with creative, intimate and historically attuned explorations of hidden places and narratives of place. Its rediscovery in the 1980s has "continued into the 2000s with the emergence of Urban Explorations"' (Bonnett 2013). In June 2014, together with the board of PMVL, Parco Media Valle Lambro, a green corridor 6 billion square metres in area along the Lambro river, the municipality of Sesto San Giovanni joined the *Exercises in Psychogeography* (https://esercizidipsicogeografia.wordpress.com), whose participatory mapping could be found on GoogleMaps Engine before this web service was discontinued. The *Exercises*, with their explorations of land and water paths in the metropolitan city, were repeated on 1 and 2 October 2016.

A successful initiative in this direction was launched in December 2012 with the intriguing title of '16 no(n)ni per l'UNESCO' ('Sixteen grandparents for UNESCO', a title that also contains an allusion to '16:9', the common high-definition video size, as video production was a central part of the project). In a city where almost all of the inhabitants 'have elderly relatives who worked at the large factories that have since been abandoned' (Fossa 2015, p. 64), the project won a Lombardy Region grant for culture and social cohesion and succeeded in making the landscape of memories alive and meaningful for the young generation, building a bridge of empathy between real actors in the past and in the present (Paganoni 2015a). In 2016 a more recent project, entitled 'I racconti del villaggio Falck' ('The Falck village's tales'), also subsidised by the regional government, saw first the exhibition of the old photographs collected by female residents and then the publication of a booklet of memories and pictures. The project is now continuing with footage and interviews of the village's residents, involving Sesto's middle-school students.

Though the municipality also encourages citizen engagement through the use of participatory media like social networks, wikis, locative media and apps, the future of Sesto seems to be considerably beyond ordinary people's control. In May 2016 Renzo Piano, the world-famous Italian architect who designed one of London's iconic skyscrapers, the Shard, announced that he would withdraw from the regeneration plan of the former Falck area, one of the largest urban brownfields in Europe, located in Sesto but privately owned. Though the municipality has denied it, the national press has alleged that this is due, first, to the entrance of Saudi Arabian investors, the Fawaz brothers, into what was originally conceived of as a much praised 'City of Health and Research' and, second, to alterations to Piano's original project with the addition of a huge shopping and entertainment mall. The latest news (Bettoni 2016) has it that Piano is back in the project and in charge both of designing the train station that will provide access to the City of Health and of the regeneration plan of the nearby square. The political debate about the fate of heritage and heritage sites thus still remains open.

Concluding remarks

The description in this chapter of how three Italian localities in the Lombardy region — Crespi d'Adda, Bergamo and Sesto San Giovanni — promote their cultural landscape as present, future and potential World Heritage sites and communicate with local communities intends to exemplify the several ways in which new media can mobilise and engage networked publics (Papacharissi 2015). In the three cases here investigated, both institutional/public actors and private/third-party stakeholders have resorted to new media, especially to the social web and mobile technology, in order to gather publics around places that are being discursively reinvented in line with UNESCO's guidelines.

In the case of Crespi d'Adda, the analysis shows how new media communication could be used in more meaningful and participatory ways and how, instead, heritage promotion often falls back on the moves of Authorised Heritage Discourse (Smith 2006), which is an essentially expert-led and managerial kind of discourse. By contrast, we have seen that a local civic association, CrespiLove, has been able to breathe new life into the community, by means of effective communication on the internet and social networks. Having won the nomination process and now awaiting evaluation, the transnational site of the Venetian works of defence, which includes the city of Bergamo as the leading centre in the project, appears to be an 'invented place', still quite at a remove from ordinary citizens' experience of their region, thus obliging them to think of themselves as Europeans rather than as locals. The extent to which the project will effectively involve ordinary citizens from local communities, promote social inclusion and offer job opportunities to people (especially young ones) beyond the privileged niche of politicians, academics and professionals who traditionally control public discourse in what continues to be quite a conservative city, is still to be tested.

With the UNESCO nomination still underway and the several complexities that affect its urban regeneration plans, Sesto San Giovanni has nonetheless seriously invested in new media communication to promote citizen participation in the reinvention of the city's identity through its industrial heritage. Whether the recent turn of events with the announced infusion of Saudi Arabian capital will polarise the political debate is still to be seen, but it is a sobering reminder of the fact that the so-called collapse of the public and private spheres in new media communication still keeps the most important decisional processes in the city away from citizens.

References

'16 no(n)ni per l'UNESCO' ('Sixteen grandparents for UNESCO') 2012, *Il Portale del cittadino*, viewed 5 October 2016, <http://www.sestosg.net/sportelli/sestounesco/passidagigante/scheda/,3521>.

Bettoni, S 2016, 'Renzo Piano firmerà la nuova stazione di Sesto', *Corriere della Sera*, viewed 25 October 2016, <http://milano.corriere.it/notizie/cronaca/16_luglio_10/renzo-piano-firmera-nuova-stazione-sesto-area-falck-294f08ea-4684-11e6-991c-561dff04b946.shtml>.

Bonnett, A 2013, 'Psychogeography', *Oxford bibliographies*, viewed 30 April 2016, <http://www.oxfordbibliographies.com/view/document/obo-9780199874002/obo-9780199874002-0020.xml>.

Buescher, M & Urry, J 2009, 'Mobile methods and the empirical', *European Journal of Social Theory*, vol. 12, no. 1, pp. 99-116.

Comune di Bergamo n.d., website, viewed 19 October 2016, <https://www.comune.bergamo.it>.

Comune di Bergamo (ed.) 2016, *The Venetian works of defence between 15th and 17th centuries*, full nomination dossier, viewed 30 April 2016, <https://issuu.com/francescoalleva/docs/nomination_format.compressed-ilovep>.

Crespi d'Adda UNESCO n.d., website, viewed 19 October 2016, <http://crespidaddaunesco.org>.

Fossa, G 2015, 'Milan: Creative industries and the uses of heritage', in H Oevermann & HA Mieg (eds.), *Industrial heritage sites in transformation: Clash of discourses*, Routledge, New York and Abingdon, pp. 62-78.

Gasparoli, P & Ronchi, AT 2013, 'Crespi d'Adda. Beyond the management plan: Regulatory instruments for the management of built heritage transformations, in ' *Built Heritage 2013 Monitoring Conservation Management' Conference Proceedings*, Milan, Politecnico di Milano, pp. 361-369, viewed 30 April 2016, <http://www.bh2013.polimi.it/papers/bh2013_paper_70.pdf>.

Georgakopolou, A & Spilioti, T 2016, *The Routledge handbook of language and digital communication*, Routledge, Abingdon and New York.

Giovagnoli, M 2013, *Transmedia: Storytelling e comunicazione*, Apogeo/Feltrinelli, Milan.

Graham, B & Howard, P 2008, *The Ashgate research companion to heritage and identity*, Ashgate, Aldershot.

Harrison, R 2013, *Heritage: Critical approaches*, Routledge, Abingdon and New York.

Hobsbawm, E & Ranger, T (eds.) 1983, *The invention of tradition*, Cambridge University Press, Cambridge.

'I racconti del villaggio Falck' ('The Falck village's tales') 2016, viewed 25 October 2016, <http://www.sestosg.net/sportelli/sestounesco/passidagigante/>.

Italian Notes n.d., blog, viewed 19 October 2016, <http://italiannotes.com/unesco-world-heritage-lombardy>.

Kalay, Y, Kvan, T & Affleck, J (eds.) 2008, *New heritage: New media and cultural heritage*, Routledge, Abingdon and New York.

Kaminski, J, Benson, AM & Arnold, D 2014, *Contemporary issues in cultural heritage tourism*, Routledge, Abingdon and New York.

Langlois, G 2013, 'Participatory culture and the new governance of communication: The paradox of participatory media', *Television & New Media*, vol. 14, no. 2, pp. 91-105.

Lombardo, V & Damiano, R 2012, 'Storytelling on mobile devices for cultural heritage', *New Review of Hypermedia and Multimedia*, vol. 18, no. 1-2, pp. 11-35.

Mah, A 2012, *Industrial ruination, community, and place: Landscapes and legacies of urban decline*, University of Toronto Press, Toronto.

Martino, V 2015, 'Made in Italy museums: Some reflections on company heritage networking and communication', *Tafter Journal*, vol. 84, viewed 30 April 2016, <http://www.tafterjournal.it/2015/09/15/made-in-italy-museums-some-reflections-on-company-heritage-networking-and-communication/>.

Milano da Vedere n.d., website, viewed 19 October 2016, <http://www.milanodavedere.it>.

Paganoni, MC 2015a, *City branding and new media: Linguistic perspectives, discursive strategies and multimodality*, Palgrave Macmillan, Basingstoke and New York.

Paganoni, MC 2015b, 'Cultural heritage in the discourse of European institutions', *LCM*

Languages Cultures Mediation, vol. 2, no. 2, pp. 117-130, viewed 30 April 2016, <http://www.ledonline.it/index.php/LCM-Journal/article/view/948>.

Panzini, D 2015, 'Cultural policy making by networking: Local cooperation and global competition in small and medium-sized Italian cities', in S Hristova, M Dragićević Šešić & N Duxbury (eds.), *Culture and sustainability in European cities: Imagining Europolis*, Routledge, Abingdon and New York, pp. 100-111.

Papacharissi, Z 2012, *A private sphere: Democracy in a digital age*, Polity, Malden, MA.

Papacharissi, Z 2015, *Affective publics: Sentiment, technology, and politics*, Oxford University Press, Oxford.

Provincia di Milano 2008, *North of Milan, a tourist guidebook: Culture, enterprise and nature from Malpensa to Sesto San Giovanni*, viewed 30 April 2016, <http://www.visitamilano.it/export/sites/default/turismo_en/doc/guida_milano.pdf>.

Sesto San Giovanni per l'UNESCO n.d., Facebook post, viewed 19 October 2016, <https://www.facebook.com/Sesto-San-Giovanni-per-lUNESCO-650486915012297>.

Smith, L 2006, *The uses of heritage*, Routledge, Abingdon and New York.

Tunbridge, JE & Ashworth, GJ 1996, *Dissonant heritage: The management of the past as a resource in conflict*, John Wiley, Chichester.

UNESCO 1972, *Convention concerning the protection of the world cultural and natural heritage*, 17th Session of the General Conference, Paris, 16 November, viewed 30 April 2016, <http://whc.unesco.org/archive/convention-en.pdf>.

UNESCO 1992, *Operational guidelines for the implementation of the World Heritage Convention*, 16th Session of the World Heritage Committee, Santa Fe, USA, 7-14 December, viewed 30 April 2016, <http://whc.unesco.org/archive/1992/whc-92-conf002-12e.pdf>.

UNESCO 2002, *The Budapest declaration on world heritage*, document WHC-02/CONF.202/5, viewed 30 April 2016, <http://unesdoc.unesco.org/images/0012/001257/125796e.pdf>.

UNESCO 2003, *Convention for the safeguarding of the intangible cultural heritage*, document MISC/2003/CLT/CH/14, viewed 30 April 2016, <http://unesdoc.unesco.org/images//0013/001325/132540e.pdf>.

UNESCO 2007, *Proposal for a 'fifth C' to be added to the strategic objectives*, document WHC-07/31.COM/13B, viewed 30 April 2016, <http://whc.unesco.org/archive/2007/whc07-31com-13be.pdf>.

UNESCO 2011, *Strategic action plan for the implementation of the convention 2012-2022, Future of the World Heritage Convention*, document WHC-11/18.GA/11, viewed 30 April 2016, <http://whc.unesco.org/archive/2011/whc11-18ga-11-en.pdf>.

UNESCO World Heritage Centre [WHC] n.d., website, viewed 25 October 2016, <http://whc.unesco.org>.

UNESCO World Heritage List 2016, *The Venetian works of defence between 15th and 17th centuries: Nomination format*, viewed 30 April 2016, <https://issuu.com/francescoalleva/docs/nomination_format.compressed-ilovep>.

Villaggio Crespi n.d., website, viewed 19 October 2016, <http://www.villaggiocrespi.it/en>.

VisitBergamo n.d., website, viewed 19 October 2016, <http://www.visitbergamo.net/en/object-details/2979-le-mura-veneziane>.

Webmoor, T 2008, 'From Silicon Valley to the Valley of Teotihuacan: The "Yahoo!s" of new media and digital heritage', *Visual Anthropology Review*, vol. 24, no. 2, pp. 183-200.

Woodoo Studio n.d., *UNESCO World Heritage nomination: Logo design*, viewed 30 April 2016, <http://www.woodoostudio.com/en/portfolio/unesco-world-heritage-nomination>.

Links

World Heritage Sites and Industrial Heritage

European Federation of Associations of Industrial and Technical Heritage [E-FAITH], <http://www.e-faith.org>.

European Route of Industrial Heritage [ERIH], <http://www.erih.net>.

The International Committee for the Conservation of the Industrial Heritage [TICCIH], <http://ticcih.org>.

World Heritage Centre, <http://whc.unesco.org>.

Lombardy

In Lombardia (the region's official tourism website), <http://www.in-lombardia.com>.

Navigli Lombardi, <http://www.naviglilombardi.it>.

Crespi d'Adda

Associazione Crespi d'Adda [CrespiLove], <http://www.crespidadda.it>.

Crespi d'Adda UNESCO, <http://crespidaddaunesco.org>.

On Facebook: <https://www.facebook.com/CrespidaddaUNESCO>.

On Twitter: <https://twitter.com/CrespiUNESCO>.

On YouTube: <https://www.youtube.com/channel/UCpRuYFubCeTRlaBvrDEcdKQ>.

Italian Notes, <http://italiannotes.com/unesco-world-heritage-lombardy>.

Milano da Vedere, <http://www.milanodavedere.it>.

Crespi d'Adda on World Heritage List, <http://whc.unesco.org/en/list/730>.

The Workers' Utopia: Crespi d'Adda, <http://whc.unesco.org/en/list/730/video>.

Villaggio Crespi, <http://www.villaggiocrespi.it/en>.

The Venetian Walls of Bergamo

Associazione Terra di San Marco, <http://www.difeseveneziane.com>.

On Facebook: <https://www.facebook.com/AssociazioneTerradisanmarco-738134549633436>.

Comune di Bergamo, <https://www.comune.bergamo.it>.

The City Hub, <http://www.thecityhub.it>.

The Venetian Works of defence between 15th and 17th centuries, <http://whc.unesco.org/en/tentativelists/5844>.

VisitBergamo, <http://www.visitbergamo.net/en/object-details/2979-le-mura-veneziane>.

Sesto San Giovanni

City Council of Sesto San Giovanni, <http://www.sestosg.net>.

On Facebook: <https://www.facebook.com/Sesto-San-Giovanni-per-lUNESCO-650486915012297>.

Esercizi di Psicogeografia, <https://esercizidipsicogeografia.wordpress.com>.

Ecomuseo Urbano Metropolitano Milano Nord [EUMM] app ('North of Milan Urban Metropolitan Ecomuseum'), <http://www.jecoguides.it/en/portfolio_page/ecomuseo-urbano-metropolitano-milano-nord-en>.

MappaMI, <http://mappa-mi.eumm-nord.it>.

Sesto Città delle Fabbriche app ('Sesto City of Factories'), <http://www.jeco.biz/guidasestofabbriche>.

Sestopedia, <http://www.sestopedia.it>.

VisitaMilano, <http://www.visitamilano.it>.

Find your Adelaide: Digital placemaking with *Adelaide City Explorer*

6

Darren Peacock and Jill MacKenzie

A perfect storm of opportunity

Digital, mobile and social technologies are transforming the possibilities for place-based engagement and interaction. The rapid informating of public places and spaces offers many new ways to change how we encounter, explore and respond to place. A cluster of technology-based innovations — including smart phones, wireless connectivity, high speed broadband, GPS, cloud-based computing, mobile applications and social media platforms — bring into play many new potential combinations of content, interactivity and context of use. The emergence and co-mingling of these technologies create the conditions for a perfect storm of radical innovation, a step change in the relationship between people and place. For organisations and individuals interested in the interpretation of place, this creates vast opportunities and a complex conundrum of choices. The experience of place can now be mediated through a bewildering variety of digital content, devices and interactions that have enormous potential to change perceptions, interest and involvement.

For those with a commitment to the conservation of urban environments and their social and historical associations, the idea of heritage has been a guiding concept for advocating and promoting the preservation of our built and natural environments. Heritage and heritage places may be defined in different ways, but generally what distinguishes them in the environment is their recognised significance as sites of aesthetic, cultural, historical, scientific or technical interest. More simply, heritage may be defined broadly as those things that we preserve from the past for the future. For more than 120 years, organisations such as the National Trust have sought to raise awareness of the natural and built environment around us and to encourage an interest in conserving the physical fabric, natural systems, stories and cultural values of heritage places. The recent emergence and confluence of digital technologies and their rapid uptake present a unique opportunity to promote heritage conservation in the digital age.

Signifying significance

The recognition and documentation of places deemed to hold heritage significance is an ancient practice. In promoting significant places, we have also transcribed the stories of the past onto the landscape with memorials, monuments, markers and signage. In fact, it is fair to say that the heritage industry in its modern incarnation, dating from the mid-nineteenth century, has been particularly preoccupied with the challenges of connecting the past and present of places through information. Modern heritage informatics may be said to have begun with the attaching of plaques onto buildings in London 150 years ago in 1867, using the now famous ceramic blue-and-white plaques. Ever since, we have been attaching information to significant places, using text-based signage and, more recently, audio- and video-based material as a way to connect in situ with the past of a place or space and its cultural, historical, architectural and aesthetic significance.

The use of signage in heritage places has been strongly influenced by the work of people such as Freeman Tilden, a pioneer of natural heritage interpretation with the US National Parks Service. His seminal *Interpreting our Heritage* (1957) has shaped generations of practice in connecting people to place and, most importantly, in yoking interpretative practice to a heritage conservation agenda. Tilden's six principles earned him a leading role in the modern history of place-based interpretation.

Tilden's six principles (p. 34):

1. Any interpretation that does not somehow relate what is being displayed or described to something within the personality or experience of the visitor will be sterile.

2. Information, as such, is not interpretation. Interpretation is revelation based upon information. But they are entirely different things. However, all interpretation includes information.

3. Interpretation is an art, which combines many arts, whether the materials presented are scientific, historical or architectural. Any art is to some extent teachable.

4. The chief aim of interpretation is not instruction but provocation.

5. Interpretation should aim to present a whole rather than a part and must address itself to the whole man rather than any phase.

6. Interpretation addressed to children (say, up to the age of twelve) should not be a dilution of the presentation to adults but should follow a fundamentally different approach. To be at its best it will require a separate program.

Tilden's principles of interpretation are still widely advocated as guides to practice today. A new (fourth) edition of *Interpreting our Heritage* was published in 2007 to mark the fiftieth anniversary of the first. However, the world of communications has moved rapidly beyond the guidebooks and interpretive markers that were the focus of Tilden's attention. In today's digital, hyperconnected world, the physical limitations of signage and paper-based efforts to connect people to place through information are ever more apparent. Although Tilden's principles undoubtedly retain some of their currency, the digital revolution requires us to reconsider their relevance and application in twenty-first-century interpretation.

The argument for change: Digital, participatory narrative

Janet Murray has been most eloquent in suggesting just what these transformations in interpretive practice might be. Her *Inventing the Medium* (2012) — a reflection on the nature and impacts of digital media — proceeds from what she describes as three foundational principles (p. 2):

1. All things made with electronic bits and computer code belong to a single new medium, the digital medium, with its own unique affordances.

2. Designing any single artifact within this new medium is part of the broader collective effort of making meaning through the invention and refinement of digital media conventions.

3. When we expand the meaning-making conventions that make up human culture, we expand our ability to understand the world and to connect with one another.

These principles remind us of the need both to have a holistic understanding of digital media and to recognise the collective work of developing new practices of meaning-making with these technologies. It is essential to be attentive to the distinctive affordances of the digital medium and the opportunities and challenges they provide for new interpretive practice and experience.

According to Murray, digital media are differentiated from what has preceded it by four key affordances of media comprised of electronic bits. Those affordances mean digital media are potentially

- procedural (composed of executable rules)
- participatory (inviting human action and manipulation of the represented world)
- encyclopedic (containing very high capacity of information in multiple media formats)
- spatial (navigable as an information repository and/or a virtual place). (2012, p. 51)

In designing and deploying communications in digital spaces, we need to challenge ourselves to understand and make use of those affordances in order to engage contemporary publics immersed in increasingly participative digital cultures. Our designs need to make full and effective use of those affordances in moving beyond entrenched interpretive paradigms and technological forms. This is not simply a matter of technology, but of purpose and intent. As Murray (2011) suggests, the

new means of inscription and transmission (the bits and the computer network) are only part of what makes a medium: it is the systems of representation that we invent that allow us to turn mere transmitted signals into artifacts of human meaning.

Digital media suggest and support much more flexible, less didactic, more dialogic approaches to interpretation, without a predetermined cognitive destination for users. There is much greater freedom to explore, to construct and to configure different pathways through spaces, both mentally and physically. In exploring and describing heritage places in urban environments, the key affordances of digital media enable us to create new communications and relationships between people and the spaces they navigate, both physical and virtual.

Curating the city

In formulating a strategy for activating interest in our city's heritage, we sought out suitable tools for digital presentation and engagement. The National Trust, as the pioneering advocate for heritage conservation in the state of South Australia, has amassed, over more than sixty years, a remarkable dataset about heritage places, carefully and thoroughly documenting their history, features and significance. This unique archive includes photographs, news clippings and carefully researched reports on the oldest and most significant buildings in the city of Adelaide, including a substantial number that have now been demolished. This early documentation provided the basis for the first statutory register of heritage buildings in the city when legislative protection of heritage places was established in the late 1970s.

A decade earlier, two of the founding members of the National Trust in South Australia, Sir Edward Morgan and Stephen Gilbert, had prepared a book on Adelaide's most significant heritage buildings (1969). Even as they wrote that work, buildings from the colonial city included in their study were being demolished before their eyes.

The early research done by the National Trust pioneers and the work later undertaken by government agencies in the 1980s and 1990s created rich, well-documented records of the architectural heritage of the city and the state. However, with the exception of a few publications in that time, this information has remained largely inaccessible to the public. Nonetheless, whatever the changes in communications technology, the challenges of heritage conservation remain largely unchanged from the 1960s. The historic fabric of all modern cities is constantly under pressure from new developments and from the forces of decay and dilapidation.

Adelaide, like all Australian cities established in the colonial era, has sacrificed much of its architectural heritage from the nineteenth century to modern development. However, largely because of the visionary plan for the city laid out by Colonel William Light at its inception in 1837, Adelaide, despite many losses, retains much of its nineteenth-century form. Light's vision of a city wrapped within a figure-of-eight ring of parklands and laid out with elegantly proportioned streets and public squares is still readily discerned. Visitors to the city often comment with pleasure and surprise at the survival of many elegant nineteenth-century buildings, mostly crafted from local stone and produced with a high degree of skill in both design and construction. The boom decades from the 1860s to the 1880s furnished the city with a fine collection of public, commercial and religious buildings that would be impossible to replicate today. Adelaide is also, because of Light's design, an ideal walking city, because of the proportions of the city blocks he measured out, the human scale of its streetscapes, a generally flat topography carefully moulded to the contours of the Torrens River valley, and its benign Mediterranean climate.

Technological innovation and interpretation: Introducing *Curatescape*

Recognising that we are blessed with a wealth of unique heritage places and rich information about them, in a city designed for easy exploration, we were keen to put some of the thinking about digital placemaking into place. As we began our mission to increase engagement with the value and importance of Adelaide's heritage places and spaces, we sought out promising models for making the transition from the static, text-based interpretation of guidebooks and signage to an approach that made full use of contemporary digital technologies.

At the Centre for Public History and Digital Humanities at Cleveland State University, public historians Professors Mark Tebeau and Mark Souther had been considering similar issues. Over ten years, the pair had been grappling with the problem of how to curate a city in the digital era. From their work emerged a software platform now known as *Curatescape*, designed for the purpose of making the most of mobile digital technology in the interpretation of urban environments. The *Curatescape* platform is designed to harness the affordances of digital media through place-based storytelling that is delivered over mobile devices such as smart phones and tablets. The *Curatescape* team, also including Erin Bell, further aim to stretch the paradigm of humanities through 'an emphasis on storytelling through carefully constructed layers of text and multimedia digital artifacts' (Tebeau 2013).

The *Curatescape* framework is all about creating complex rich media objects as the core unit of interpretation. Tebeau (2013) argues:

> We believe that this building of cultural context, of telling stories, through the interplay of layered primary and secondary materials, provides a richer and more nuanced experience than simply displaying single archival images or objects. Additionally, by geo-locating stories, we emphasize that the richness of landscape itself becomes part of the interpretive frame — another layer of data with which audiences can interact. Finally, we allow for individual stories to have many strands whose elements are connected through a variety of meta-interpretive frames, including maps/location, tours, tags, subject, and search.

This is a significant paradigm shift from the place-based historic markers of the nineteenth century and Tilden's interpretive inscriptions. Stories, the units of interpretation employed within *Curatescape*, are more complex in themselves and also exist in more complex relationships to each other and to the places and experiences they describe. In this way, they deploy three of Murray's key affordances effectively — by having the qualities of the encyclopaedic and spatial, and by being intrinsically procedural (that is, the media follow executable rules via the use device). How they give rise to the fourth key affordance — that of being participatory — will be covered shortly.

These series of crucial breakthroughs, made by the *Curatescape* team in their framing of the interpretive challenge to create and share the significance of place in a digital medium, helped us to envisage how we could transform our own archival resources into rich user experiences connecting people to place.

Curating a city for conservation

The *Curatescape* concept of curating an urban environment using what Tebeau calls 'dynamic interpretive strategies' (2013) had a lot of appeal for our purpose, building awareness of the heritage of our city in a way which engendered interest and commitment to its preservation. In this regard, we concur with the famous tenet of Tilden's approach to interpretation (p. 65): 'Through interpretation, understanding; through understanding, appreciation; through appreciation, protection'. Where we began to diverge was in a more nuanced sense of how those connections between interpretation, understanding and appreciation might be made, and through a postmodern scepticism about linear narratives and monocultural interpretation. The rich palimpsest of our own urban environment — one born of an imperious act of European colonisation, with a complex history of human migration and a growing ambivalence in its commitment to heritage conservation — appeared far too fractured and fragmented to achieve Tilden's objectives easily, or perhaps at all. Moreover, the idea of curation is itself problematic. The curatorial eye omits as well as focuses. How, then, do we proceed to curate a city and connect inhabitants and visitors to the built and natural environment and to a collective memory of past people, places and events, their physical and cultural legacy?

The tools of curation used for collections and exhibitions were clearly inadequate to the task of navigating the piled up complexities of a city's past and present and the people who created it. We needed to find a way to both deconstruct and reassemble the connections of the city into coherent and, we hoped, illuminating and interesting patterns. It is here that we coined the idea of a kaleidoscopic view of the city, consciously shifting our perspectives so that new things came into view or combined in unanticipated ways. Kaleidoscopic curation suggests starting from the bottom up, from the smallest fragments, rather than imposing a top-down metanarrative on the city and its places. We noted a tendency in city walking guides to be driven by thematic constructs, using individual sites as illustrative examples for a bigger theme or argument. This top-down, theme-driven approach to urban interpretation seemed to us to remove much of what was joyful and serendipitous in exploring the city.

Theme-based approaches to place interpretation, championed most notably by Lewis (1980) and Ham (1992), follow on from Tilden's constructivist learning theory, and largely dominate the way in which cities are presented by human and print-based guides. The familiar tropes of architectural landmarks, historical periods and debates, ethnic or social groups provide an enduring framework for presenting and navigating the city by way of argument. (Phrases used in such a framework include, for example, 'This is the best collection of art deco buildings', 'the legacy of our pioneers', 'the struggle for emancipation of group x or y'.) At worst, such themed approaches can become little more than didactic manifestos; at best, they are forgettable classroom lessons.

We wondered also why the usual offerings of guided or self-guided walking trails left us largely uninspired. It was as if each were a curriculum of facts to be noted and digested, where the guided walk could be either a lesson or an examination of learning, or both; and the self-guided version was an uninspiring collecting of ephemeral factual information. The generally dispassionate, impersonal nature of the descriptive material in these presentations seemed to be a large part of the problem, delivered so often in the omniscient voice of an anonymous expert narrator. We yearned for an escape from the city as discursive argument to explore the city as adventure — surprising, mysterious and paradoxical.

As we have wrestled with new interpretive paradigms and come to understand the digital medium better through an ongoing process of trial and error, punctuated with epiphanies and disappointments, we have forged our own principles for interpreting and navigating urban environments:

- kaleidoscopic curation (that is, working from the fragment to the whole and back again)
- a focus on storytelling
- employing open-ended narratives with multiple pathways, entry and jumping-off points
- conscious, critical use of media
- blending activity and interaction modes to engage the senses and different modes of inquiry.

Adelaide City Explorer: An experiment in urban heritage curation

Adelaide City Explorer (http://www.adelaidecityexplorer.com.au) is a digital curation of an urban environment intended to promote physical, emotional and intellectual engagement with the city's architecture, open and natural spaces, environmental features, cultures, history and traditions. The promo 'Find your Adelaide' (https://youtu.be/ymgCBxcW43U) is an invitation to explore, discover and create by reading, relating and responding to the city in a new way.

We use place-based narratives constructed using multiple media formats to support a deepening awareness of how the city was planned and made, how people have lived and worked in it and to invite exploration of its special places and spaces.

In choosing Curatescape as our publishing tool, we became the first location outside of the United States to adopt the platform. We learned much from the storytelling strategies and techniques deployed on the Cleveland Historical implementation of *Curatescape*. There were good examples of both individual stories as well as connected narrative threads that combined different story nodes into extended elaborations of an idea, proposition, period, precinct or event.

This is one of the most important shifts at work in the new interpretive paradigm, enabled by a mobile app platform that connects information to place. Not only does each story stand in its own right as a digital enhancement to an experience of place, it also provides the building blocks for a larger narrative of connected places. This is where we also begin to transcend the linearity of traditional interpretative practice, making effective use of the much-vaunted capacity of hypertext to facilitate non-linear narrative progression with contingent navigation between story nodes offering the user a degree of autonomy. Individual stories can appear in multiple metanarratives, or what we call trails, which can be followed virtually or physically, using GPS guidance. The user, whether navigating hyperspace or walking the city streets, can pursue many different pathways from a single point.

Hypertextual narrative has long been hailed as offering the possibilities of infinite pathways for the user (Landow 1992, 2006; Murray 1997; Ryan 2001). '[H]ypertext changes the way narrative structures are encoded, how they come to the reader and how they are experienced in their dynamic unfolding' (Ryan, 2001). In *Adelaide City Explorer*, hypertext is used to reveal, signpost and connect the city within a web of potential pathways, memories and attachments.

Threading the stories

At the time of writing, the raw material of *Adelaide City Explorer* comprises more than 170 individual place-based stories and eighteen suggested walking trails, each consisting of ten to twenty individual stories which are connected thematically, spatially, or as narrative nodes. The connections that shape the suggested walking trails can be thematic or conceptual, architectural, biographical, historical or narrative driven. Examples of geographical constellations include the South West Corner (http://www.adelaidecityexplorer.com.au/tours/show/4), North Terrace: Cultural Boulevard (http://www.adelaidecityexplorer.com.au/tours/show/9) and East Terrace Promenade trails (http://www.adelaidecityexplorer.com.au/tours/show/15). Art Deco Delights (http://www.adelaidecityexplorer.com.au/tours/show/6) centres on a particular architectural style. Mary MacKillop's Adelaide (http://www.adelaidecityexplorer.com.au/tours/show/20) uses a biographical frame to explore the life in Adelaide of Australia's first Saint. East End Discovery (http://www.adelaidecityexplorer.com.au/tours/show/29) explores the identity of a single city precinct, Sacred Glass (http://www.adelaidecityexplorer.com.au/tours/show/30) explores the medium of stained glass and Cold Case: Mystery of the Somerton Man (http://www.adelaidecityexplorer.com.au/tours/show/26) unpacks an unsolved case of suspected murder.

In following the rigorous interpretive standards established by the *Curatescape* team for story and trail development, we worked hard both to redefine the elements of each story and to conceptualise potential threads connecting multiple stories into new metanarratives. Tebeau describes that challenge of shaping metanarratives as a search for narrative frames including thematic, geographical (proximate) temporal framcs:

> For us that process begins by identifying a broad theme, topic, or even collection
> of primary documents — an interpretive thread, if you will — that will tie

multiple stories together. This thematic, geographical, or temporal frame can be conceived as a frame for multiple stories that is tied together with tags, subjects, keywords, or as the basis for a tour. Alternately, this broader frame can become a story in its own right. In Cleveland Historical, the connecting threads have been defined thematically (crime and punishment, immigration, or the Civil War), by neighborhood (Tremont, Ohio City, Downtown), materials or architectural styles (statues, murals, art deco), or sources. (The Cleveland Heights series of entries uses a common historical collection of oral interviews and street photographs from the 1970s.) Most important though is finding that topic or theme, and making it specific enough that it can inform multiple stories, but also broad enough that those stories can find ways to complement one another analytically. (2013)

One of our most complex interpretive challenges to date has been to test and stretch unlikely connections within and between stories to create surprise and serendipity. The making of metanarratives combining individual stories allows for often surprising juxtapositions and connections. Connections may point to continuity or to change, telling stories through omissions (in the case of demolished buildings) as well as presence. By way of such connections an issue, event or individual life emerges in greater fullness through the different stories and perspectives of different places.

When it works well, it revives some of the lived, human connections between the different places. For example, one of the trails connects elaborate stained glass windows in the Brookman Building, named for its benefactor Sir George Brookman, with the William Morris stained glass windows donated by him in the old Stock Exchange making not just an aesthetic but an economic connection between the man, his work and his benefaction.

We have learned that enabling unexpected discoveries and connections can create the moment of surprise that supports a conceptual reconfiguration of the environment and a learning moment where understandings, attitudes and behaviour might be most amendable to shifting. Discovering the rich fabric of connections between people and places embedded in built and urban design can become a transformative moment in appreciating and valuing heritage.

New techniques for storymaking

The best digital platforms make thoughtful use of the capabilities of the medium with a clear purpose in mind. However, as has often been the case, the ultimate or most popular use for a platform or device may not have been anticipated by its creators. The evolution of the mobile phone is a case in point, as are social media platforms. When we design a platform and imagine its future use, no amount of scenario or use case design will anticipate all purposes or uses. The designers of *Curatescape* brought a strong humanities background to the task, which is most evident in the story-based structure that is at its heart. We have discussed the creation of stories above, but of equal interest are the navigational aids that are used to connect users to the stories, trails and the physical environment they represent.

Geospatial tagging of stories is a key feature and one that is a key affordance of contemporary mobile devices. The ability to instantly locate oneself in relation to points of interest, to map a trail sequence and to navigate there, is hugely empowering for people unfamiliar with a particular locale, whether they are residents or visitors. We appreciate the critical importance of this feature and believe it holds much further potential, perhaps by enabling users to filter items of interest by geographic range, or to choose their own start and end points to produce a suggested trail or sequence of sites on the fly.

Similarly, subject tagging of stories is another powerful technology integrated within *Curatescape*. This enables us to connect across stories easily by adding tags. We thought carefully about the kinds of tagging taxonomies we would use, making a clear differentiation between people, topics, locations and formal terms (for example, architectural). Through the use of the search facility, it is possible to pull up lists of sites by subject tag, a process which often reveals some of those latent and unanticipated connections suggestive of a new narrative arc or navigation pathway. The addition of user content tagging, as well as the usual social sharing and comment tools that are included, would add another way to include additional perspectives and open up new potential pathways. Other navigational aids such as Quick Response [QR] codes and Bluetooth beacons are also potential additions to the *Adelaide City Explorer* experience, by offering pull and push signals about the availability of digital content based on proximity. With these visible and invisible tools, users can be alerted or prompted to seek more information about their current location, or to pick up a trail.

However, not all digitally enabled technologies add significantly to the experience, and there is a risk of employing new technological functionality simply for its own sake. Tebeau (2013) is sceptical of some applications of technologies, such as augmented reality, to the interpretation of place:

> If these approaches provide a clever way of using technology to enhance our connection to place, they nonetheless emphasize the technical over the interpretive. Superimposing a present view of building over a past view does not reveal the full interpretive dimensions of place, unless it is accompanied by a further elucidation of some kind ….
>
> [S]uch an emphasis on technology over interpretation does not fully succeed in evoking landscape and place. In fact, one could argue for an alternative definition of augmented reality that is based not in technical wizardry but in interpretive rigor. Building a richer interpretive context for the landscapes being viewed — through imaginative images, oral history and other expressions from the past, and based in a theory and practice in the humanities — augments 'reality', and our experience of landscape in a much deeper fashion.

Always it is the narrative weave that makes for the compelling experience and connection, rather than the application of the latest fashionable technology. Technologies will come and go, and at an ever increasing rate. The *Pokémon Go* phenomenon that recently grabbed attention is a case in point of technological faddism. What will endure is good storytelling, using — but not beholden to — particular technological platforms or devices.

Sharing the story(making)

One of the key learnings in our development so far has been the power of working in collaboration with others as we plan and produce new stories and trails. We have followed the lead of the *Curatescape* team in seeking out a range of partners who bring to the project not only rich content for storymaking, but constituencies of their own, interested in representing and preserving particular aspects of the city's life. Our partners so far have included the Adelaide City Council and state government agencies, as well as cultural festivals and events, neighbourhood traders associations and an order of Catholic nuns. Each of these collaborations has produced new perspectives on the city and enabled our partners to experiment with a very new way of connecting digitally with a diverse range of publics. We have also engaged a number of university student interns in the task of researching and producing stories and in devising and creating trails. For them, it provides an opportunity to put to work the nascent digital literacies which they use effortlessly in their personal lives but which are seldom developed or recognised in their traditional academic work.

Taking it to the streets

Adelaide City Explorer was designed as a digital experiment, creating a smart, self-guiding platform for urban exploration. We have now begun to look at combining it with more guided experiences, with fascinating results.

One of the best established ways of connecting people to place has been the guided walking tour. The guided tour has been a mainstay of the tourism industry since the first European Grand Tours of the sixteenth century. Ubiquitous, but perhaps insufficiently analysed as an interpretive method and as a public experience, guided walks tend to place the guide at the centre of the interaction, generally consigning those being led to the role of followers. Often highly scripted, the linear narrative of most guided walks and their predetermined routes offer limited agency to participants. Dialogue with the guide/leader may be reduced to questions and answers pertaining to factual information. Seldom is debate allowed or encouraged, partly because of time constraints, but also because of the transactional nature of the exchange, with the guide as the dispenser of information that is largely prepackaged, making limited provision for the knowledge and experience brought by participants.

While there have been attempts to define the elements of the tour guide role (Holloway 1981; Cohen 1985), more recent work has dug further into some of the instrinsic problematics of the guided tour. A thoughtful analysis by Jonathan Wynne in *The Tour Guide* (2011) argues that there are deeply embedded tensions in the design and delivery of contemporary urban walking tours. He offers a heuristic framework for understanding guided walking tours in terms of 'seven constitutive struggles … between *profession* and *hobby*, *legitimacy* and *autonomy*, *independent freelancers* and *company employees*, *academic inclination* and *autodidacticism*, *education* and *entertainment*, *public* and *private* interests, and between *visitors* and *locals* (pp. 30-3, emphases in the original).

These points of tension shape the way in which tours are designed and delivered. Wynne argues that each of these tensions operates on a spectrum between two poles and that each tour and guide will fall along that spectrum at different points. Wynne's framework is a useful reminder of the complex interplays at work in the traditional guided walking tour.

What we found when we combined the digital experience of *Adelaide City Explorer* with a traditional guided tour delivery was that the guide played the role of conversational facilitator, encouraging a group to share and develop their own narratives of place. This social role was further enhanced by being able to integrate the affordances of digital media: oral histories, photographs, interviews and other video-based content. The mobile app enabled the guides to delve deeper on those items of particular interest to the group, introducing primary source material which was again reinterpreted by the group in a social interaction. In this way the guide is able to move from authority figure to enabler of group learning experience, which allows for a much more interactive and social experience.

The affordances of digital delivery both complement and transform the human interactions between guide and tour group. The hybrid digital/personal experience we are now exploring suggests many new possibilities for enabling and facilitating urban exploration.

Conclusion

Adelaide City Explorer has been a highly successful experiment in connecting people to place through the use of contemporary digital technologies. The *Curatescape* platform — with its web-based and mobile application user interfaces — has enabled us to formulate and test new paradigms for the creation, presentation and reuse of information and narratives about the history and significance of many aspects of the urban environment. We have made a start on 'curating a city' by identifying and connecting micro- and metanarratives of people, places and events.

In planning for the user experience, in creating and curating content, we have been able to question and remake our interpretive practice in order to make effective use of the key affordances of the new digital medium as defined by Murray: by being procedural, participatory, encyclopaedic and spatial. These affordances enable a new approach to reading, representing and navigating the city, which can be shared with residents and visitors as open-ended pathways to discover, explore and annotate buildings, spaces, streetscapes and natural environs. In this way, many opportunities for collective curation and inscription of information emerge, which hold great promise for fostering new forms of engagement with the significance and conservation of heritage places.

This was our starting point. However, our experience in observing how people create and make use of this information in their own emerging and evolving placemaking narratives suggests great potential for community-making around these memories and experiences. The obvious power of group discovery and exchange suggests that these narratives and connections can form, circulate and redistribute significant social capital.

Interpretation is both a verb and a noun, as is heritage — an active co-construction of meaning between environment, built form, artefact, cultural practice and contemporary people. It is not something simply passed down or given, but something that is actively made and remade in every interaction between people and place. The application of digital technologies to placemaking and heritage advocacy enables us to rethink heritage, not just as a collection of old stuff but as social connective tissue that binds us to the environment, to each other and to the people who have been here before us.

References

Cohen, E 1985, 'The tourist guide', *Annals of Tourism Research*, vol. 12, no. 1, pp. 5-29.

Ham, S 1992, *Environmental interpretation — A practical guide for people with big ideas and small budgets*, Fulcrum Publishing, Golden, CO.

Holloway, J 1981, 'The guided tour: A sociological approach', *Annals of Tourism Research*, vol. 8, no. 3, pp. 377-402.

Landow, GP 1992, *Hypertext 2.0: The convergence of contemporary critical theory and technology*, Johns Hopkins University Press, Baltimore, MD.

Landow, GP 2006, *Hypertext 3.0: Critical theory and new media in an era of globalization*, Johns Hopkins University Press, Baltimore, MD.

Lewis, W 1980, *Interpreting for park visitors*, Eastern National, Fort Washington, PA.

Morgan, EJR & Gilbert, SH 1969, *Early Adelaide architecture, 1836-1886*, Oxford University Press, Melbourne.

Murray, JH 1997, *Hamlet on the holodeck*, MIT Press, Cambridge, MA.

Murray, JH 2011, 'Lord of lisp', *Janet H Murray: Humanistic design for an emerging medium*, viewed 11 June 2016, <https://inventingthemedium.com/2011/10/31/lord-of-lisp/>.

Murray, JH 2012, *Inventing the medium: Principles of interaction design as a cultural practice*, MIT Press, Cambridge, MA.

National Trust of South Australia 2014, 'Find Your Adelaide', YouTube, viewed 18 November 2016, <https://www.youtube.com/embed/ymgCBxcW43U>.

Ryan, M-L 2001, 'Beyond myth and metaphor: The case of narrative in digital media', *Game Studies*, vol. 1, no. 1, viewed 8 December 2011, <http://www.gamestudies.org/0101/ryan/>.

Tebeau, M 2013, *Strategies for mobile interpretive projects for humanists and cultural organizations*, White paper submitted to the National Endowment for the Humanities, viewed 11 June 2016, <http://mobilehistorical.curatescape.org/>.

Tilden, F 1957, *Interpreting our heritage*, 4th edn, University of North Carolina Press, Chapel Hill, NC.

Wynne, JR 2011, *The tour guide: Walking and talking New York*, University of Chicago Press, Chicago.

Chinese films and the sense of place: Beijing as 'Thirdspace' from *In the Heat of the Sun* to *Mr Six*

7

Hongyan Zou and Peter C Pugsley

This chapter explores contemporary films set in Beijing, to examine how the city's protagonists are contextualised within the architecture and landscape of China's state capital, and how the city is spatially depicted and imagined amidst a time of immense technological change. Our investigation of *Mr Six* (*Lao Paoer*, directed by Guan Hu, 2015), illustrates how city-based films shape perceptions of a city beyond the glamourised images of technocratic metropoles designed to stimulate tourism found in international blockbusters such as *Skyfall* (directed by Sam Mendes, 2012). This chapter draws from Edward W Soja's discussions on the trialectical relation between space, social relations and history — particularly the 'Thirdspace' (based on Lefebvre's *Production of Space*), which combines material, physical and mental or cognitive spaces into a conceptual site that includes 'the knowable and the unimaginable and the unconscious, the disciplined and the transdisciplinary' (Soja 1996, p. 56). *Mr Six* serves as a postscript to an earlier Beijing-based film about disaffected youth, *In the Heat of the Sun* (*Yangguang can lan de rizi*, directed by Jiang Wen, 1994), enabling us to see how the cinematic view of the city has changed in the intervening decades.

The eponymous Mr Six (a.k.a. Zhang Xuejun, played by famed director and sometime actor Feng Xiaogang, who also appears in the earlier film as the central figure's teacher, the hapless Mr Hu) is a former youth gang member, now a revered fixture in his local community, well respected for his grassroots approach to justice. When his wayward son goes missing, presumed kidnapped, Mr Six wanders the streets and alleyways of Beijing looking for him. When he locates his son, Mr Six becomes entangled in a generational struggle between an organised group of wealthy young upstarts and his own band of ageing gang members.

Amidst a background of poverty, crime, corruption and violence a dystopian view emerges in *Mr Six*, where technologies (mostly mobile phones and the internet) permeate everyday life, but offer little respite from the harsh realities of the city. The constant street-level activities reflect Michel de Certeau's (1984) concept of walking as an effective way of conducting space practice, where walkers resist the rules and orders imposed by city planners, governments or other institutional bodies. The symbolic spaces of Beijing are depicted through its streetscapes in both *In the Heat of the Sun* and *Mr Six*, relative to a dramatically changing society where transforming economies and technologies can be presumed to increasingly impact on the day-to-day lives of the contemporary Chinese public. These cinematic places mirror the complexities of urbanisation and globalisation, and demonstrate how the production of space in the cinematic world reflects a changing public.

When *Mr Six* was first screened in Venice, Feng Xiaogang received critical acclaim for his portrayal of Mr Six. Some Chinese members of the press and movie-goers argued that Feng (as one of the most well-known mainland directors and now an actor) was just playing himself, for Feng is notorious for his quick temper and low tolerance of injustice. He denied that the role was a self-representation, but agreed that *Mr Six* could be regarded as an unofficial sequel to Jiang Wen's debut *In the Heat of the Sun*, due to the cohesive stories strung together by a similar group of Beijing local gangsters as main film characters. According to Feng, when Ma Xiaojun (Yu Xia), the protagonist of *In the Heat of the Sun*, grows up and becomes an old man, he naturally develops into the man known as Mr Six.

The slight name change from Xiaojun to Xuejun interrupts the direct line between the two films, but is an ingenious linguistic play — the *Xiao* part of the name means small or young, whereas *Xue* means educated, indicative that Zhang Xuejun, or Mr Six, is a wiser man than the naïve youth of the earlier film. The Chinese title of the film also makes reference to a second nickname for Mr Six, *Lao Paoer* (the name Mr Six refers to his ranking in his former gang, although this is not formally spelt out in the film). The use of *Lao Paoer* refers to a specific alley in Beijing known as *Pao* [Bomb] Alley, the site of a former police lockup. Anyone who had run afoul of the law became known as a *Paoer* ['er' used here as a suffix, as in English], or, in Mr Six's case, an old [*lao*] *paoer*. The director, Guan Hu, also underscores the close relationship between the two films regarding the main character's life experience amidst the dramatic temporal-spatial transformation of Beijing over the last several decades. Mr Six spends much of his time moodily reminiscing about his youth and about the sense of loyalty and trust which permeated his Beijing neighbourhood as he grew up.

Theorising place

In 'The Spatiality of Social Life' (1985), Edward W Soja begins a discussion on the dialectic relation between space and social relations. He further extends this discussion in *Thirdspace* (1996), reflecting on the social significance of space and 'those related concepts that compose and comprise the inherent spatiality of human life: place, location, locality, landscape, environment, home, city, region, territory, and geography' (1996, p. 1). Soja's spatial theory is greatly inspired by Henri Lefebvre's far-reaching volume *Production of Space* (1991), in which Lefebvre perceives human beings' spatial experience from different layers: perceived space, conceived space and lived space. In *Thirdspace*, Soja explicitly interprets and develops an alternative approach to Lefebvre by suggesting a 'Firstspace', which is seen to 'privilege objectivity and materiality', and which can be mapped and measured (1996, p. 75); a 'Secondspace', partially overlapping with Firstspace, which is 'entirely ideational, made up of projections into the empirical world from conceived or imagined geographies' (p. 79); and a 'Thirdspace', where

> everything comes together … subjectivity and objectivity, the abstract and the concrete, the real and the imagined, the knowable and the unimaginable and the unconscious, the disciplined and the transdisciplinary, everyday life and unending history. (p. 56)

This Thirdspace is a 'space of radical openness', which is not simply an additive combination of the objective material space and the subjective mental spaces, but rather a concept that extends these spaces, 'comprised of all three spatialities — perceived, conceived, and lived — with no one inherently privileged a priori' (p. 68). Thirdspace furthers Lefebvre's idea that the city has become the 'possibilities machine' (p. 81), by incorporating a wider conceptual base as an intellectual space with multifaceted discourses such as feminism, postcolonial theory, cultural studies and archaeology. Drawing extensively upon established authors in these fields, Soja orchestrates different voices into his unified concept of 'Thirdspace'. Our choice of the medium of film allows us to utilise Soja's approach to examine film as a technological production that projects the material space as well as the mental space. It is this amalgamation of sound, light, images and stories that produces the infinite possibilities within the Thirdspace as conceived by the audience.

Filmic Beijing as a Thirdspace scrutinises every aspect of the city amidst the transformation of an ideological, economic and technological (media) milieu, and ponders each characters' alternative experience of place so as to record and recover their minor history or personal memory of the old Beijing and envision their city as characterised by grand historical narratives and its infinite possibilities. Therefore, we approach films according to the three spaces proposed by Soja. First, we examine the physical spaces presented in films — specifically, the home, the neighbourhood and the city in which people dwell or which they desire to access, and people's way of living in certain city spaces. Second, we investigate the mental space of film characters — that is, how they may perceive and interpret the city spaces where their lives play out, and how they manage to adjust to changing situations during the social and economic upheavals of this rapidly developing urban space. Third, by comparing the urban arrangements and space practices reflected in two Chinese films both set in Beijing, but distanced by a period of two decades, we explore issues specific to China and the Chinese audience. These include the reality of 'disappearing' places, lost as rampant urban development tears through the city, which act as a trope of city memory and as an individual's personal memory. We also explore how these disappearances are presented in (state-funded or approved) films, which may act as ideological vehicles reflecting dialectic relations with the material space.

Despite the rapid technological changes taking place in China in areas such as communications (wi-fi connectivity) and transport (Maglev trains), for many people these technologies play only a minimal role in their lives, where their day-to-day existence is still dependent on street-level activities around transport, shopping and employment. Although written at the dawn of China's reform period, Michel de Certeau's observations of the modern city in *The Practice of Everyday Life* (1984) switch focus from earlier city-based studies that privileged the 'producers' (institutions or organisational power) and their role in the city, to examine more closely the role played by 'consumers' (individuals). In the seminal chapter 'Walking in the City', de Certeau asserts that the action of 'walking' is an effective way of conducting space practice. It is a way to 'repeat the joyful and silent experience of childhood … in a place, to be other and to move toward the other' (p. 110). It is a poetic journey to engage in walking through the same street time after time, pondering on the past, the present and the future in order to acquire a new self-knowledge as well as a new cognition of the city. By walking through the city street tactically, walkers rebel or resist the enforced rules and orders maintained and imposed by strategies of city planners, governments or other institutional bodies.

De Certeau declares that individuals always follow daily routes using clever 'tactics' (with or without being conscious of their actions), rather than allowing themselves to be wholly controlled or determined by 'strategies' imposed by institutional bodies. Cinematic figures in city-set films are often the kind of walkers described by de

Certeau. When it comes to a film and its protagonist, it is through a protagonist's walking that a cinema lens is able to catch the trivial details of urban life. Through carefully structured tracking and follow shots, the audience accompanies the 'walker' on their journey. Audiences thus observe a city not only from a panoramic view but also from a particular individual's view, allowing the hidden façades and subjective perceptions of the city to be uncovered.

Generative technologies and the city

A number of academic works over the past decade have begun to explore the dramatic changes to China's urban landscapes. Collections such as *The Urban Generation* (Zhang 2007), examine various aspects of contemporary Chinese cinemas through chapters providing comprehensive insights into individual filmmakers such as Jia Zhangke, Zhang Yuan and Ning Ying and their works. The authors in Zhang's collection draw on critical paradigms proposed by Walter Benjamin, Michel de Certeau or Gilles Deleuze to investigate the vastly different social, economic and cultural configurations in contemporary China's cities. While Zhang's volume articulates the distinctive aesthetic features of China's post-1980s films, Jason McGrath's *Postsocialist Modernity* (2008) defines China's alternative modernisation as a form of 'postsocialist modernity' in order to help describe mainland China's marketisation, pluralisation and individualisation under the unique political vision called 'Socialism with Chinese characteristics' (p. 7). By juxtaposing films such as Jia Zhangke's hometown trilogy *Xiao Wu* (1997), *Platform* (2000) and *Unknown Pleasures* (2002) with Feng Xiaogang's popular New Year's films (a name which refers to their date of release, rather than to their content), McGrath offers an alternative scenario of Chinese cinematic aestheticism and its narrative of the commercialised and profit-driven society.

An alternative cinematic memory of Beijing

Beijing has long been depicted differently in film from Shanghai, which, according to Li Zeng, is because 'conventional models of urban space tend to use the feminine to symbolise the pleasure and danger of the cityscape … Shanghai has been particularly, even excessively, sexualised' (2011, p. 104). In comparison, Beijing has been portrayed steadfastly in a more masculinised, workmanlike pose, dowdy and functional and lacking in style. There seems to be less focus on the multilingual, cosmopolitan lifestyle in Beijing films (one of the few to show this is Jia Zhangke's 2004 film *The World* — in Chinese, *Shijie* — which parodies the insularity of Beijing through its replica-theme-park view of the rest of the world). In *Mr Six*, any hints of cosmopolitanism seem to highlight the disparities between everyday Beijing and the extreme wealth of the Ferrari-driving youth, Kris (Wu Yifan). Li's article more accurately captures contemporary China in her class-based description of the 'spatial unevenness and conflicted coexistence of the low and the high', where the rich populate the city as 'a place of fashion, consumption and pleasure' (2011, p. 109).

Filmic depictions of Beijing from the 1980s and 1990s offered a fairly bleak view of the city. Chen Kaige's *Farewell My Concubine* (1993), for instance, is a grand epic narrative of Chinese history spanning over half a century. Beijing, as the filmic setting, witnessed the ups and downs of both the nation and the people, who went through a series of social and political upheavals. *Farewell My Concubine* 'commemorates old Beijing, makes urban spaces into places of post-traumatic recall, and works through the director's unsolved memories of growing up in the capital during the Cultural Revolution' (Braester 2003, p. 90). Most directors of the Fifth Generation (the first generation to graduate from the Beijing Film Academy following the Cultural Revolution) were dispatched to remote areas, sent 'down to the villages and up the mountains' [*shangshan xiaxiang*] (Clark 2005, p. 28) in order to be re-educated by living as peasants or soldiers during the Cultural Revolution.

The Fifth Generation is therefore prone to ponder on the grief and agony brought by these political events and to look back on this period with sentimentalism, representing the national trauma either realistically or metaphorically. Tian Zhuangzhuang's *Blue Kite* (1993) similarly reiterates the political persecution and average people's fear and agony during that special historical period in Beijing. Because of the citizens' miserable personal experiences, filmic Beijing often appears as a space of trauma. In addition to the 'scar literature' that emerged in the aftermath of the Mao era and reflected the far-reaching disastrous effects of the Cultural Revolution, it became common for Chinese people to perceive the whole period as a tragedy.

Perhaps surprisingly, Jiang's *In the Heat of the Sun* shows Beijing in a utopian light, depicting a group of listless, bored adolescents who are too young to be sent to the remote places and too privileged to be influenced by the political turmoil. For these disaffected youth, 'the family housing is a haven, almost a heaven, for the military brats' (Howard 2008, p. 163). Across the city, gangs of adolescents formed, as a way of killing time and harnessing their rebellious spirit. Those found in *In the Heat of the Sun* are known as the 'sons of the compound', in reference to the military complex where they live. Such compounds were an alternative urban space, hastily constructed after the establishment of the new nation in the Mao era.

According to Wang Shuo, the author of the book *Wild Beasts* from which the film was adapted, the military compound is a new and special urban space in Beijing, a city traditionally defined by the Forbidden City, narrow alleys (*hutong*), and courtyard-style housing. In his partly autobiographical novel, *Could be Beautiful,* Wang comprehensively describes this spatial existence:

> the over-ten-mile radius around the Fuxing ring road was called 'New Beijing', and
> was located on the west side of the city. The district was established after 1949, and

its residents were purely people who came from different places across China; none of them were Beijing natives. Therefore, their everyday lifestyles — including their diet, rituals, ways of thinking and residential architecture — were all markedly different from the old style of life in the alley and courtyard housing which had existed in Beijing for hundreds of years. (2006, p. 6)[1]

Compounds were constructed for officers of government departments, professors of universities or professionals from diverse kinds of institutional bodies, and were arranged around Tiananmen Square and Zhong Nanhai — the core area of the central political space of the new nation. The area centering on the Forbidden City is traditionally regarded as a space of imperial power, the home and administrative workplace of emperors across a succession of three dynasties. When Chairman Mao declared the foundation of a new China in 1949 on the Tiananmen Rostrum, the new nation inherited the tradition of making the area a space symbolising political power.

The new China saw urgent urban planning and infrastructure construction, which allocated the compounds to different institutional bodies in order to become an integral part of the massive urban redevelopment. As Xu Min points out:

[i]n this area, places for national rituals and the conducting of power, specifically Tiananmen Square and the nearby buildings and spaces, are sites for national ceremony and symbolic national power, with Zhong Nanhai, the space where political power is conducted, standing alongside. Buildings serving different departments of the superstructure are arranged from the east to the west along Changan Street according to a rigid hierarchy of power … as the capital of the new political body, the form of buildings, their aesthetic style and even the overall urban layout all work in concert with the space of national power. Moreover, they form the concrete and material base of the ideology of the nation, representing the political function of the area and the city. (2010, p. 96)[2]

Thus, compounds were built to be superior to the alley (*hutong*) spaces in Beijing, since the former were emblematic of the strengthening national myths and authority, while the latter stood for the vernacular and for locality.

Within this new urban environment, the military compound possesses much more significance than all the other compounds for its political and military significance in the new state. As Zheng Yiran observes,

[i]t is the site of central civil and military organs which are defining and protecting the state. It symbolizes the sovereignty of Communist China and represents its official ideology. Here, military compound residents work directly for the state and consider themselves as '*guojia de ren*' (people of the state)'. (2016, p. 21)

In the Heat of the Sun accurately depicts the military compounds, surrounded by high walls and guarded by police, as self-sufficient spaces encompassing dwellings, workplaces,

---

1   Translated from the Chinese by the authors of this chapter.
2   Translated from the Chinese by the authors of this chapter.

education (schools) and even recreation places (movie theatres or playgrounds). The compound is depicted like a park surrounded by trees and flowers, with classic-style pavilions and corridors, showing the privileged military and social rank of its residents. The distinction of housing conditions of various military compounds concisely corresponds to the residents' social status/military rank. Zheng Yiran (2016) notes that that '[d]ifferent buildings within certain areas with their corresponding living conditions act as spatial signifiers of social rank … [T]he notable distinction of housing also engenders an invisible psychological hierarchy among the residents' (p. 27). The military compound is at once an abstract space of power, an emblem of social rank and a concrete space of everyday routine life. The meaning of the reconstructed urban space, according to Yomi Braester, is 'to signal their [the political authorities'] hegemony and instill in the citizens the desired ideology' (2007, p. 168). The realist nature of *In the Heat of the Sun* reiterates the sense that the dwellers of the military compound belong to the privileged class as a result of their past sacrifices and contributions to the newly established nation, and they are still pioneers engaging in various social and political or military events during this period. As military officers, they are often sent to remote areas to lead the reconstruction or reform of that place or commit to military missions, and accordingly, their families are granted more material distributions and bonuses than those who inhabit the austere courtyard houses (Xu 2010, p. 98).

But Jiang's *In the Heat of the Sun* reflects on the generational change occurring at the time, and the shifting relationship with the space, which sees the young people brought up in such compounds only vaguely adhering to the socialist values and political movements of their elders. No matter how unreasonable or unjust the state's policies might be, the youth are too young to know the hidden powers that affect the older generation's life or career. For the youth, the most obvious difference lies in the residential spaces, which separate them from those in the alleyways where their parents grew up. When the boys in *In the Heat of the Sun* get involved in a brawl, the sons of the military compound come equipped with guns, sticks, bricks and two military trucks, while the sons of the alleys come with mere sticks and bicycles. Where they come from decides what type of, and how much, weaponry they can appropriate. The compound sets up a wall dividing the world — one side belongs to its privileged sons; the other side keeps out the young from the alleys. By fighting with other gangs and wandering around the city, each group aims to affirm their superior social status and constantly create new spaces for self-articulation.

As former 'sons' of the military compounds, director Jiang Wen and novelist Wang Shuo share similar boyhood memories of Beijing during the turbulent decades following 1949. Denied the opportunity to participate in the political movements, they were seen not as victims but merely as idle children left at home without parental supervision. As Cui Shuqin points out, 'with the fathers absent from view, the street and the city become a stage where adolescents inscribe their sense of history and experiment with the excitement of youthful impulses' (2001, p. 92). Jiang and Wang project their life experiences into their works, literature and film respectively. Thus *In the Heat of the Sun* unveils a very personalised, highly spatial memory of Beijing during the Cultural Revolution, which seems to have neither catastrophic political struggles nor personal traumas. Instead, the film

> draws a portrait of private lives in their naked and natural forms. Free from direct repression by the political power, the protagonists are a carefree, reckless gang who experience the Cultural Revolution only as playful, carnivalesque bright sunny days, not as gloomy, disastrous nightmares. (Chen 1997, p. 135)

Therefore, the adventurous and passionate days are represented with bright colours and lights. Beijing bathes in eternally bright sunshine, and it is a paradise for its young protagonist, Ma Xiaojun, to linger around, discover and explore.

Media and the city

At the beginning of *In the Heat of the Sun*, an audio 'flashback' from the now adult protagonist nostalgically reflects:

> [I]n only twenty years, Beijing has already turned into a modern city. It transformed so much that I can hardly find anything identical in my memory. Actually, the great transformation has disfigured my memory of the city so that I could not tell the illusion from the reality.

The film was produced in the 1990s, an age characterised by the massive numbers of old buildings torn down, by new modern constructions that were hastily erected across the capital city, and by commercialisation and consumption driven by the new market economy. The final scene of *In the Heat of the Sun* thus echoes the most recent development of the new Beijing, where the grown-up gangsters ride in limousines and drink expensive liquor, strongly contrasting with the austerity of the 1970s Beijing shown throughout most of the film. There were neither luxurious cars nor complicated flyovers back then, and people had little or no access to the outside world. The 1970s were an age of carefully managed information and knowledge that could be accessed only through state-controlled newspapers, radios and public loudspeakers. The few exotic cultural products were politically sympathetic songs and films imported from the Soviet Union — for instance, songs like 'Moscow Nights', 'Swan Lake' and the 'Internationale', and films such as *Lenin in 1918* (directed by Mikhail Romm, 1939).

Director Jiang Wen utilises a myriad revolutionary songs to represent the spirit of the city during that period, including 'Chairman Mao, Revolutionary Soldiers Wish you a Long Life' (*Mao Zhuxi, geming zhanshi zhu nin wan shou wu jiang*), 'Missing Chairman Mao — the Savior' (*Xiangnian enren Mao Zhuxi*), 'Ode to Beijing' (*Beijing songge*) and 'Sun Shining on the Jinggang Mountain' (*Jinggangshan shang taiyang hong*). The lavishly displayed revolutionary songs featured in the film, together with images of Chairman Mao's gigantic statue and portrait, and political plays such as *Red Detachment of Women* (*Hong se niang zi jun*, directed by Pan Wenzhan and Fujie, 1971), resurrect the intense political and passionate atmosphere of the Cultural Revolution. *In the Heat of the Sun* shows how entertainment is limited to listening to radio programs (political or military news, or revolutionary songs), or joining in political events and ceremonies. The leisure activities are so limited that people can only watch the same film repeatedly, with Jiang's characters accordingly reciting entire conversations from films, and a music-lover pretending to be a North Korean ambassador in order to be able to attend a concert only accessible to state officials. The media therefore functions almost solely as a political tool imparting revolutionary ideas and glorifying the army's victory. Growing up in the confined space of the compound and its neighbouring districts, and within such an intensified revolutionary milieu, Ma Xiaojun and his followers (being the descendants of warriors) admire the soldiers and dream of becoming war heroes who can one day stand high and boast of their courageous determination and deeds, harvesting applause and compliments from the masses.

Being brought up in the military compound, Ma and his friends intimately bond with each other, so that they fight for each other, chase beautiful girls to boast of their charisma, and hang out day and night together. The experiences that they share in time and space reflect Scott McQuire's observation that 'personal experience is framed with the broader collective frames of both mass media and urban form across a range of scales — the home, the city, the globe' (2008, p. 7). Without parental supervision or teachers' authority, and with older teens following Chairman Mao's call for the youth to embrace the vast rural area to 'ensure that a new generation was exposed to a version of the rustication experienced by early Chinese Communists in Yan'an days and before' (Clark 2005, p. 29), Ma proudly claims: 'This city is ours'. Equipped with this unfettered freedom, they throw away their schoolbags and skip classes, worshiping those gangsters who attract large bands of followers for their bloodied fights.

As a generation that misses the war and the subsequent political movements, the youth of Jiang's film are denied the opportunity to become war heroes. The city streets and alleyways of Beijing become their battleground, and those who can fight like heroic soldiers gain their genuine reverence. Metaphorically, the state's schools, institutions and media propaganda relentlessly broadcast ideas and slogans such as: the youth are the 'flowers in the grand "national garden" at the present, and will be masters of the country in the future' (Xu 2010, p. 98). Furthermore, these adolescents generate a sense that their mission is to master the future of the city and the country, influenced by their older generation's unparalleled contribution to the new country and by the awareness of the significance of their specially guarded residence (p. 98). As the masters of the city and even the nation, they wear military uniforms, imagining themselves as courageous soldiers fighting for their motherland, always ready to sacrifice themselves for the victory of the war. It is, however, within the limits of their city and its alleyways that their battleground exists.

Walking in the city

As noted, Michel de Certeau elevates walking, the most mundane daily movement, as an effective and tactictal way to either affirm or resist the strategies imposed by city planners or government bodies. He compares the act of 'walking' with the 'speech act', so that a pedestrians' walking 'affirms, suspects, tries out, transgresses, respects, etc., the trajectories it "speaks"' (1984, p. 99). De Certeau clearly elaborates on his idea of 'walking' as a recognisably semiotic activity, stating:

> Charlie Chaplin multiplies the possibilities of his cane: he does other things with the same thing and he goes beyond the limits that the determinants of the object set on its utilization. In the same way, the walker transforms each special signifier into something else. And if on the one hand he actualizes only a few of the possibilities fixed by the constructed order (he goes only here and not there), on the other he increases the number of possibilities (for example, by creating shortcuts and detours) and prohibitions (for example, he forbids himself to take paths generally considered accessible or even obligatory). He thus makes a selection … He thus creates a discreteness … He condemns certain places to inertia or disappearance and composes with others spatial 'turns of phrases' that are 'rear,' 'accidental' or 'illegitimate'. (1984, pp. 98-9)

In the context of *In the Heat of the Sun*, the socialist ideology of revolutionary years shrinks into the background as the young protagonist's subjective experience provides us with a fragmented yet representative detail of the city. Accompanied by friends, Ma Xiaojun bicycles around, mapping compounds, courtyard houses, alleys and streets into his personal memory of the city, as told to the audience in his voiceover at the beginning of the film. And he celebrates birthdays or fighting victories in the revolutionary-themed Moscow Restaurant, the most popular restaurant for sons of compounds. While at his most restless and adventurous age, Ma Xiaojun seldom 'walks' — he runs, jumps, rushes for fights, races on his bicycle or slips in and out of strangers' houses. He does walk sometimes, though not in the street, but on roofs, where he can absorb an aerial view of his territory. His unusual ways of walking the city help create his personal narration, of innocence, passion and friendship, which at times seems to be add odds with what the audience is experiencing. Apart from his tactile exploring of the city, Ma discovers a new and risky way to understand the city better — that is, to sneak into strangers' houses. He makes a skeleton key that can open any lock in the neighbourhood. At first, he opens his parents' locked drawers and then moves on to houses near his school. The key is a powerful tool, enabling him to peep into other's private lives while they are out working or at school, and so he turns into a 'powerful man' who knows strangers' secrets.

The scenes of Ma's illegal behaviour — beyond his compound but within the confines of the city's private residences — are thrilling, but the film does not condone breaking in as reasonable or acceptable; the protagonist is motivated by curiosity rather than by the desire to steal things. Through Ma's snooping, we get an opportunity to look at the ordinary households of Beijing. The stylish architecture of the government officers' dormitory building, with its delicately decorated facades and large windows that allow sunshine into private spaces, is a long way from the crowded and dingy *hutong* homes of Old Beijing. This exotic architecture possesses a sense of the mysterious, which echoes the fitful, fantastical sense Ma has as he falls in love with a girl whose photo he discovers when he sneaks into her house. Inside large housing blocks, long corridors are lined with identical doors that separate the public from the private; each corridor has a public bathroom and toilet attached to it. Breaking into strangers' houses time after time, the boy concludes that people in general do not possess much wealth, as rooms are poorly decorated or furnished, and electrical equipment (perceived as a necessity nowadays) is barely there.

> Yomi Braester comments on the implication of Ma's key that
>
> the skeleton key opens the doors to an alternative fantasy world for Xiaojun, to a place that is paradoxically truly his own. Yet the key brings him face to face with more mysteries he cannot sort out and more memories suspended between fiction and reality. (2003, p. 204)

To face and to come to know the alternative worlds — these are compulsory lessons for a boy becoming a man. The lock — with its key as the most common spatial trope — relates to the idea of resistance and exclusion, whereas Ma's breaking in and stealing, in particular, creates a sense of the fallibility of the lock. While Xiaojun has never stolen anything (apart from helping himself to fresh dumplings), he does consider doing so in one apartment that has a TV set, but as the television is too heavy, he feels it is not worth the effort. Therefore, as Zhang Ning points out, the lock/key binary can be interpreted metaphorically as 'secret — disclose, constrain — emancipate, reject — enter' (2010, p. 104). The lock in this context resembles the power of keeping one's private space, while the key offers the possibility of breaking through the inequality of power, enabling Ma to enter this forbidden space.

In the process of unlocking and exploring the urban space, as stated above, Ma comes across a girl's picture and immediately falls in love with her. After that, his aimless city roaming comes to an end. Although his key could unlock any physical locks across the city, he cannot unlock the girl. For a long time, the girl, Mi Lan (Jing Ning), remains a myth for him. After days and nights of waiting and prowling, he finally meets and becomes acquainted with her, but friendship is far from the relationship that he desires. At the end, Ma follows Mi Lan, riding across the city and entering her home, where he tries to rape her — a metaphor for the way he feels he has the power to unlock any other locks. But after a painful struggle, Mi Lan repells him and he is forced to escape from the building.

Riding his bike with bare feet, aimless, exhausted and gloomy, he re-enters the space of the city. With familiar compounds, narrow alleys and courtyards witnessing his frustration and disillusionment, the teenage Ma Xiaojun is moving toward a new self. His relationship with Mi Lan is permanently ruined and he becomes isolated from his friends. This use of his personal way of 'walking' through the city, 'walking' into the hidden private houses of strangers and endeavouring to 'walk' into Mi Lan's affection, reflects de Certeau's (1984) assertion that he is attempting a transformation, 'to be other and to move toward the other' (p. 100).

Mr Six

Mr Six begins with scenes of a man on a motorbike riding through narrow city streets in the late evening. He pulls up, then walks away from the motorbike, picking the pocket of a drunken man being helped from a restaurant by friends. The thief then removes a bundle of cash from the wallet and dumps the wallet in a bin. Unknowingly, he is being watched by an unseen Mr Six, who suddenly speaks, asking the thief why he threw the wallet away. The thief retorts, 'What's it to you?' Mr Six's response sets the scene for his own sense of pride in, and guardianship of, his part of the city: 'You dumped it here, so it's got everything to do with me'. He tells the thief to at least return the ID to the owner. The thief challenges with: 'What if I don't? What are you going to do?' The camera drops behind Mr Six, allowing a glimpse of his hand, holding a bamboo birdcage, an iconic badge of the elderly in China. Mr Six, now established as someone who is perhaps too old to be entering into a fight with a thief, replies: 'Don't want to behave? Try me. Let's see you make it outta here'. The thief considers this, and Mr Six is seen in silhouette with his birdcage by his side. The thief nods, understanding the seriousness of the matter. He turns and retrieves the wallet from the bin. As he walks away, Mr Six picks up the birdcage, muttering, 'Act right, keep walking'.

This simple scene (over which the film's opening credits appear) establishes Mr Six's territorial advantage. There is nothing glamorous about the city, an untidy collection of laneways and unkempt shopfronts. Yet the importance of the scene and its placement in the film assist in the audience's conception of the public space under the careful watch of the private citizen.

Mr Six turns and enters the shop behind him, before pulling down a noisy security door, stained with the name of the film in Chinese characters, and the English words 'A film by Guan Hu'. This opening scene in *Mr Six* creates an image of urban China far removed from the images of a technocratic, developed China and the futuristic architecture of Beijing and Shanghai so often promoted through the media. One could well be convinced that it is a film set in earlier days — the 1980s, perhaps, in a time before technology became a pervasive part of urban life. But it is some way into the film before technology makes a key appearance, showing that the film is in fact a post-2010 film. Mr Six makes his way around his neighbourhood on foot, assisting the elderly (for, despite the earlier scene where it was assumed he was quite elderly, he is only in his late fifties), and dishing out advice on manners to young people. It seems a much simpler world than most contemporary urban environments.

When a local disturbance occurs, with a policeman slapping one of Mr Six's friends (known as 'Lampshade') and then trying to confiscate his means of transport (a rudimentary three-wheeled delivery bike), Mr Six appears, as if out of nowhere. He places a firm hand on the bike, stopping it as the policeman, Zhang (Zhang Yi), is about to wheel it away. Officer Zhang looks up and recognises Mr Six, and pauses to hear what the older gentleman has to say. Mr Six is concerned that the bike is Lampshade's means to an income, a way that he can cover the city and earn a living. Zhang explains that Lampshade not only did not have a licence to operate the vehicle, but that he had also crashed it into a police car, breaking a tail-light. Mr Six listens and agrees that Lampshade is in the wrong and the bike is confiscated, wheeled off and loaded onto a truck.

The scene takes place under the close watch of a gathered crowd, a common scene in China where, again, private matters quickly become public. While it seems that Mr Six has resolved the issue, even paying the policeman $300 in compensation for the damage, Mr Six then turns the tables on Officer Zhang by suggesting that it is only fair that Lampshade is allowed to slap the policeman. At first Zhang thinks it is a joke, but the crowd soon grows restless, calling out for the slap to take place. Ultimately, it is Mr Six who lands two playful slaps across the face of the policeman as the crowd gasps at this public display of defiance. Reluctantly, Officer Zhang must acquiesce to the humiliation dished out by Mr Six.

In essence, Mr Six's conception of the community is based on an idealised, nostalgic idea of personal, human interaction: a public defined by its physical place. The generative technologies grasped by the younger protagonists in the film nullify Mr Six's sense of 'ownership' of, and connection to, a neighbourhood, defined by the ability to walk around. Instead, through their fast cars, the young people are able to claim the entire city as their 'turf'.

Conclusion

Both films have a strong consciousness of place: *In the Heat of the Sun* deploys Beijing landmarks such as Tiananmen Square, the large-scale military complex and the famous Moscow Restaurant, while in *Mr Six* the foot-worn streets and Beijing dialect become the most distinctive trademarks, alongside the well-preserved courtyard house and the lake near the Summer Palace. The two films focus on the memory of a city, creating a sense of nostalgia for the past way of life and values. The memory is articulated unambiguously by Ma Xiaojun's heroic imagination and passionate exploration of the urban space, and by Mr Six's reiteration and insistence of highly localised principles and rules for dealing with social injustice.

The creation of a sense of place in the two films detailed in this chapter is centred on the streets of Beijing and the intersecting concepts of public and private space. In *In the Heat of the Sun*, public space is shown as a site for demonstrations of support for the state; by the time of *Mr Six*, a more dystopian use of space is found as crime and corruption flourish, but with the city still romanticised in its use of its streets for daily trade and commerce. In both films, the flow of urban life can be seen to be counter to institutional regulations. This mirrors Brian Morris's explanation of how demonstration marches interrupt the regular use of public spaces, where '[t]he marchers participating are not confined by the pavement: they override traffic lights and "Cross Now" signs at intersections along the route, and they challenge the sovereign right of the motor car to dominate the space of the street' (2004, p. 680). Morris questions the idea of this as an act of resistance, yet as *Mr Six* shows, the streets of Beijing are easily disrupted for the public spectacles that amass around fights, accidents, arguments or arrests. De Certeau links the spatial practice of walking with memory, which Morris suggests makes walking 'a signifying practice that enables narrative entries and exits' (p. 688). Both *In the Heat of the Sun* and *Mr Six* rely on such constant entries and exits to illustrate the fluidity of life within the space of the city.

The use of space and the performance of walking in that space are shown in both films as ways of enabling a public event to take place. In both films, gangs meet in highly symbolic ways. In the earlier film, hundreds of rival gang members swarm to face off under the Marco Polo Bridge, before the fight is fortuitously averted. In *Mr Six*, the stand-off takes place several hundred metres apart, over a frozen lake behind Beijing's Summer Palace. The lake at first seems to be an unconquerable rift between them, but Mr Six valiantly staggers across the ice toward the gang on the opposite bank of the lake. The 'semiotic regimes' (Morris 2004, p. 689) of walking, in such key moments of anticipated force, are apparent in both films.

As with the questions raised by Soja's *Thirdspace*, Li Zeng notes the importance of acknowledging 'the symbolic meaning and ideological function of the gap between the concrete place and the conceived space' (2011, p. 115). The aural and visual properties of film can assist us in both recognising this gap and moving toward a greater aesthetic understanding of the role of the city film. The city imagination created in both films is to a certain degree neither political nor commercial. The filmmakers investigate alternative urban spaces and images, exposing the voices and values of the city's 'real' people, its true public, within contemporary social contexts that are so often strongly determined by commercialisation and estrangement.

Such techniques in film mirror Soja's Thirdspace, a site where one can translate 'knowledge into action in a conscious and consciously spatial effort to improve the world in some significant way' (1996, p. 22). It allows us, the audience members, to 'guide our search for emancipatory change and freedom from domination' (p. 70). The filmic Beijing provides verified and multifaceted images of the city which have been underrepresented by mainstream narration. But the city image and the special group of people represented by these two films also grant audiences (especially those with a lived spatial experience of Beijing) an opportunity to push away from the stereotypical images of the city to inhabit a Thirdspace as a more personal, intimate conception of Beijing: a lived public space.

References

Braester, Y 2003, *Witness against history: Literature, film, and public discourse in twentieth-century China*, Stanford University Press, Stanford, CA.

Braester, Y 2007, 'Tracing the city's scars: Demolition and the limits of the documentary impulse in the new urban cinema', in Z. Zhang (ed.), *The urban generation: Chinese cinema and society at the turn of the twenty-first century*, Duke University Press, Durham and London, pp. 161-180.

Chen, K 1993, *Farewell My Concubine* [*Bawang bie ji*], film, Beijing Film Studio and Tomson (HK) Film Co. Ltd, China.

Chen, X 1997, 'The mysterious other: Postpolitics in Chinese film', trans D Liu & A She, *Postmodernism and China*, vol. 24, no. 2, pp. 123-141, viewed 24 March 2016, <http://www.jstor.org/stable/303709>.

Cui, S 2001, 'Working from the margins: Urban cinema and independent directors in contemporary China', *Post Script*, vol. 20, no. 2-3, pp. 77-93.

de Certeau, M & Rendall, S 1984, *The practice of everyday life*, University of California Press, Berkeley.

Guan, H 2015, *Mr Six* [*Lao Paoer*], film, Huayi Brothers and Taihe Film Investments, China.

Howard, YFC 2008, *Remapping the past fictions of history in Deng's China, 1979-1997*, Brill, Leiden.

Lefebvre, H 1991, *The production of space*, Blackwell, Oxford, UK and Cambridge, MA.

Jia, Z 2004, *The World* [*Shijie*], film, Shanghai Film Co. Ltd and Hong Kong Xinghui Ltd, China.

Jiang, W 1994, *In the Heat of the Sun* [*Yangguang can lan de rizi*], film, China Film Co-Production Corporation and Dragon Film, China.

Li, Z 2011, 'Living for the city: Cinematic imaginary of the cityscape in China's transnational films', *Critical Arts: South-North Cultural and Media Studies*, vol. 25, no. 1, pp. 102-117.

McGrath, J 2008, *Postsocialist modernity: Chinese cinema, literature, and criticism in the market age*, Stanford University Press, Stanford, CA.

McQuire, S 2008, *The media city: Media, architecture and urban space*, Sage, Los Angeles, CA.

Mendes, S 2012, *Skyfall*, film, Eon Productions and B23, UK and USA.

Morris, B 2004, 'What we talk about when we talk about "walking in the city"', *Cultural Studies*, vol. 18, no. 5, pp. 675-697.

Soja, EW 1985, 'The spatiality of social life: Towards a transformative retheorisation', in D Gregory & J Urry (eds.), *Social relations and spatial structures*, Macmillan, UK, pp. 90-127.

Soja, EW 1996, *Thirdspace: Journey to Los Angeles and other real and imagined places*, Wiley-Blackwell, New York.

Tian, Z 1993, *Blue Kite* [*Lan fengzheng*], film, Beijing Film Studio, China.

Wang, S 2006, *Could be beautiful* [*Kan shang qu hen mei*], People's Literature Publishing House, Beijing.

Xu, M 2010, 'Wang Shuo yu wenge houqi de chengshi manyou: Yi Dongwu xiongmeng weili', in D Zhu & H Zang (eds.), *21 shi ji Zhongguo wen hua di tu. 2008 nian (Review of twenty-first-century Chinese culture)* 第1版, Tongji University Press, Shanghai, pp. 94-108.

Zhang, N 2010, 'Wang Shuo: Yige shidai de qiaosuozhe', in D Zhu & H Zang (eds.), *21 shi ji Zhongguo wen hua di tu. 2008 nian (Review of twenty-first-century Chinese culture)* 第1版, Tongji University Press, Shanghai, pp.104-110.

Zhang, Z (ed.) 2007, *The urban generation: Chinese cinema and society at the turn of the twenty-first century*, Duke University Press, Durham and London.

Zheng, Y (2016). *Writing Beijing: Urban spaces and cultural imaginations in contemporary Chinese literature and films*, Lexington Books, Lanham, MD.

Social media and news media: Building new publics or fragmenting audiences?

8

Kathryn Bowd

Introduction

Social media present both opportunities and threats for news media, affecting their relationships with their publics and the geographical places and spaces that they have traditionally served. Social media provide opportunities to create and expand audiences, increase geographical reach, respond more quickly than ever before to news events and issues, and interact with news consumers in more immediate and direct ways. Consequently, they may enable news media to develop new publics and shift understandings of their relationships with place. However, news outlets' capacity to respond to these opportunities may be limited by competition for audience from non-traditional news providers, dispersal of demand, and as-yet limited opportunities to profit from social media engagement. Further adding to the complexity of the picture is that these opportunities and challenges are occurring at a time when the news media are in a state of flux more broadly, with the destruction of established business models, the fracturing of audiences and the widely heralded demise of print newspapers threatening the ongoing profitability — and in many cases viability — of news organisations. The threat to newspapers is particularly profound: McCombs et al. describe them as having been in perilous decline for many decades (2011), but the decline has been hastened more recently by technological and societal developments that have both severely impacted their capacity to sustain themselves through advertising and dispersed audience demand for news and information.

At the same time as capacities for information distribution have expanded and audience expectations of instant, ubiquitous access to news have continued to grow, declining profitability has resulted in large-scale and ongoing redundancies (see, for example, New beats, n.d.; Paper cuts, n.d.). This declining resourcing puts newsrooms and journalists under severe and constant pressure — pressure that may be felt even more intensely in newsrooms outside major cities, as non-metropolitan newsrooms have traditionally operated with relatively few resources. A small number of journalists have to cover not only a wide range of news topics, but also, in countries such as Australia, a geographical territory that may span thousands of square kilometres. Further adding to the complexity of the news environment in regional areas are the historically strong relationships between audiences and traditional news products, which may limit both incentive and opportunity to comprehensively utilise online platforms.

Nonetheless, having and maintaining a social media presence has become central to practice in newsrooms small and large. While the frequency of engagement and updating may vary widely, news outlets in the Western world which are not represented on at least one social media platform are becoming increasingly rare. However, the impact of this on news media's publics has yet to be fully explored — not least because the territory is shifting rapidly as new platforms are introduced and patterns of usage and engagement change. Mitchelstein and Boczkowski suggest that fragmenting of audiences has begun to occur as audiences utilise both online and traditional media (2013). Social media may further this fragmentation by providing additional ways for news consumers to access information and interact both with it and with the providers of the information. Exploring ways in which newspapers — particularly smaller newspapers, because of their variety of publication frequencies and ownership patterns — engage with social media may help to provide some pointers to the ways in which news media and their publics are connecting in the networked environment, and to the ways in which these connections are being influenced by social media. It may also further understanding of the increasingly complex relationships between news outlets and their publics, and the ways in which these relationships are being navigated in response to societal and technological change.

A time of change

Journalism is undergoing a significant period of change, affecting 'almost every aspect of the production, reporting and reception of news' (Franklin 2014, p. 469). Academics and practitioners alike have identified a number of key themes in this change. For example, van der Wurff and Schoenbach suggest that the current media environment is characterised by intense competition, commercialisation, falling trust and growing opportunities for user participation (2014), while Picard suggests that 'mature and saturated markets, loss of audiences not highly interested in news, the diminishing effectiveness of the mass media businesses model, the lingering effects of the economic crisis, and the impact of digital competitors' have all taken their toll (2014, p. 488). Franklin, too, highlights digital media as 'creating economic difficulties for legacy media and a frenzied search for alternative business models' (2014, p. 469). Sheller suggests that

> new mobile interfaces are reshaping not only how we filter and access news, but also how we engage in communication and shape social space, and hence how news itself is packaged, presented, and connected to location, proximity, and place. (2015, p. 20)

All of these factors point to a media environment facing ongoing financial pressure, competition from non-traditional providers, shifting and fragmenting audience demand and upheaval of professional practice. While this raises questions about whether the fundamental nature of journalism is changing, there is a strong suggestion in the literature that the shifts being wrought by developments in technology and audience movement are part of a constant and ongoing revision and reinterpretation of practice, creating 'new imperatives' in journalists' work (Usher 2014, p. 5). McCombs et al. point out that many of the influences on journalism remain the same (2011), while Lasorsa, Lewis and Holton argue that 'audio, visual, and digital innovations have not by themselves redefined what it means to be a journalist … but they have contributed to changing the way journalists think about and engage in their work' (2012, p. 19). Shifts in practice are perhaps most evident where they are brought about by changing technology, as 'journalistic practices are integrally tied to the technologies available to and leveraged by practicing actors' (Barnard 2016, p. 191). Technology may be an ongoing influence on journalism (Pavlik 2000), but Fenton claims that the current wave of change is part of a complex convergence of economic, regulatory and cultural forces (2010). While the journalist's job now involves the use of 'multiple tools to produce multiple types of content for multiple delivery platforms' (Singer 2011, p. 217), practitioners must also contend with cuts in newsroom resourcing which have resulted in fewer journalists producing more content under greater time pressure (McChesney 2012; van Leuven, Deprez & Raeymaeckers 2014). This convergence of pressures creates unique challenges for news media in navigating relationships with their publics.

News and social media

The changing technological and social environment has necessitated the staking out of online territory by news organisations, but digital colonisation has not necessarily been a smooth or comfortable process. Initial moves online were relatively slow and limited, with early digital journalism relying on content from newspapers and decisions made by print newsrooms (Bastos 2015). More recently, such approaches have been increasingly replaced by corporate strategies emphasising and/or prioritising digital communication (see, for example, Fairfax Media, n.d.), as media companies restructure and branch out into new products and new audiences (Gade & Lowrey 2011). However, the pace of change has varied widely.

It can be argued that news organisations' early approaches to online publishing have been to at least some extent reflected in their moves into social media. In many cases, particularly among smaller news organisations, social media engagement was — and may continue to be — led by one or more enthusiastic individuals rather than being part of an outlet- or group-wide strategy. This may reflect a limited understanding of the impact and benefits of social media, but could also be seen as indicative of the financial and resourcing constraints affecting journalism:

> Amid shrinking staffs and fewer resources, journalists find their jobs expanding and their routines vastly altered … [J]ournalists are producing additional content, learning multimedia skills, creating content for multiple platforms, updating continuously for the Web and interacting more with the audience. (Gade & Lowrey 2011, pp. 31-2)

In 2013, Hedman and Djerf-Pierre identified three groups of journalist users of social media, stratified by factors including age, type of work, and professional attitudes and practices, suggesting that even within newsrooms there may be limited consistency in journalists' approach to, and use of, social media. The benefits of being able to provide news immediately to an audience that is not geographically bounded, and to interact directly with that audience, have to be weighed against the challenges of both producing additional content for extra platforms at a time when resources are already thinly stretched, and operating in an environment that may not be comfortable for some.

However, as social media have become more firmly embedded in everyday communication, their importance and relevance to news organisations have grown: 'As most newspapers have become multiplatform enterprises, their product lines have expanded from the print domain to include the Web and social media platforms' (Ju, Jeong & Chyi 2014, p. 3). Advantages of being visible on social media include the capacity to draw traffic to their websites (Ju, Jeong & Chyi 2014) and the opportunity for audiences to disseminate online content via social media (Hermida et al. 2012). While any economic benefits may be less immediately evident (Ju, Jeong & Chyi 2014), a social media presence is now largely seen as integral to news media operations.

Social media and news audiences

The impact of this shift on news publics remains unclear. Traditionally, news has relied on a one-to-many model of information distribution:

> For at least 500 years ... the basic relationship between publishers and their publics has been defined by a 'broadcast' model of communication. The broadcast model emphasizes a one (or few) to many communication flow, with little feedback between source and receiver (or journalist and audience) and a relatively anonymous, heterogeneous audience. (Pavlik 2000, p. 234)

Pavlik argues that traditional media communication is also asymmetric, with information flowing primarily from organisations to their publics. For news media, the 'audience has traditionally been viewed as the receiver of news and information created, packaged and distributed by professional media organizations' (Hermida et al. 2012, p. 816).

However, online media have disrupted this model. As far back as 2000, Pavlik noted the emergence of two-way news communication, at that time led by email. More recently, 'internet technologies ... have facilitated the involvement of audiences in the observation, selection, filtering, distribution and interpretation of events' (Hermida et al. 2012, p. 816). Hermida makes a case that social media are influencing news models because they 'facilitate the immediate dissemination of digital fragments of news and information from official and unofficial sources over a variety of systems and devices' (2010a, p. 298). This means that news is no longer solely the province of professionalised news media (Picard 2014). Sheller suggests that news is now being 'pushed' to audiences through social media, where it is 'mixed with commentary and recommendations from personal social networks, and where the audience/consumer can easily add comments, share items, and re-distribute it to their social networks' (2015, p. 19).

This disruption presents challenges for newsrooms and journalists in navigating understandings of who engages with the work they produce and how people engage with it. While in decades past it might have been possible to generalise to some extent about news publics in terms of geographic location or demographic detail — although Allan argues that most news workers know very little about their audience (2004) — these assumptions have been rendered largely obsolete by the removal of geographic barriers to information access and the growth of online interaction. This shift to what Hess and Waller (2014) have labelled 'geo-social' journalism, with audiences no longer bounded by specific physical location, suggests that news media understandings of the publics must be responsive to change, even to the point where the conventional term 'audience' loses currency. In the networked environment, audience, with its implications of one-way information transmission, may be a largely ineffective term to describe the publics with which news media engage and the numerous ways in which this engagement occurs.

The public sphere and the networked environment

These changes may also be influencing news media's public sphere role. Newspapers were integral to Habermasian conceptualisations of the public sphere (Habermas 1989), as the communication of news helped to enable 'the people to reflect critically upon itself and on the practices of the state' (Stevenson 1995, p. 49). Lee and Chyi note that news 'comprises raw material from which public opinions are formed' (2014, p. 706), and that the media can influence the issues people think about and how they think about them (p. 707). However, the growth of the networked environment — and particularly of social media — is impacting on understandings of the public sphere (or spheres), and through this the role played by news media. Skogerbo and Krumsvik argue that social media have become part of a networked and increasingly hybrid public sphere (2015), and that 'by their sheer ubiquity, these media contribute towards changing media ecologies and open new ways and forms of communication between citizens and their representatives' (p. 350).

Notable about these new forms of communication is the shift away from hierarchical approaches to news traditionally utilised by news media (Hermida et al. 2012). Instead, members of the audience are 'connected not just to the person who sends a message, but also to each other. What emerges is a networked means of communication that alters the publishing dynamics of a media system premised on the idea of a broadcast audience' (p. 816). Lewis, Holton and Coddington point out that

> [a]s the adoption of social media has risen, so too have opportunities for interactions based around the sharing of and commenting on content ranging from text, photos, music and videos to user-generated memes and mobile games. Spaces such as Facebook, Twitter and Instagram are built for audiences who want to seek and share specific bits of information with others. (2014, p. 233)

In shifting away from information hierarchies, social media blur boundaries between public and private (see, for example, Hess & Bowd 2015) and open up spaces for activities including opinion formation and news production (Skogerbo & Krumsvik 2015).

Social media and journalism practice

Van Leuven et al. identify the networked public sphere as allowing 'non-linear, decentralized and multi-directional information flows' (2014, p. 852), and this may be shifting fundamental understandings of news dissemination as social media become 'ever more ingrained in the news experience, both from the perspective of audiences and the journalism profession' (Hermida et al. 2012, p. 822). The public spheres facilitated through social media are becoming spaces for audiences to share, discuss and contribute information, and a growing body of work suggests this is increasingly central to people's experience of news. News is shared not only by traditional media gatekeepers but also among and between networks (pp. 817, 821), which play a key role in distributing information on niche topics to specialised communities (Bastos 2015). Veo describes the mass media market as fragmenting 'into thousands of niches' (2009, p. 24), and this presents both opportunities and challenges for news media in engaging with publics in networked spaces. While twentieth-century industrial models of journalism focused coverage on institutions such as government, ignoring or downplaying ordinary people and daily life (Picard 2014), the capacity of networked technologies for personalised news streams allows people to concentrate on content that interests them. For news organisations, social recommendation can extend reach, but may further undermine established business models (Hermida et al. 2012).

Nonetheless, one of the benefits for news media in operating in network spaces may be the transfer of existing trust relationships, as Hermida et al. suggest: '[u]sers are adding social networks to their sources of news, but not at the expense of mainstream media outlets, in which they have retained a degree of trust' (p. 822). Even though they may not be the most immediately responsive entities in the social media space (particularly not when compared with online start-ups such as Buzzfeed), their established trust relationships with their publics may privilege them as sources of information.

Twitter and Facebook

Aligning existing trust relationships with widely utilised social media platforms provides opportunities for news media to engage with their publics in a variety of ways. Facebook and Twitter are the dominant social media platforms in news communication, although others, such as Instagram, are also being utilised. Pew Research Center data from 2014 show Facebook as by far the most popular social media platform, used by 71 per cent of online adults (Duggan et al. 2015). While LinkedIn, Pinterest and Instagram were all slightly more popular platforms overall than Twitter, Twitter was more popular for news. In a 2015 Pew survey, 63 per cent of Facebook and Twitter users said they obtained news through these social networks (in Lichterman 2015; see also Barthel, Shearer, Gottfried & Mitchell 2015). Ju, Jeong and Chyi claim that even though Facebook has more users than Twitter, the latter is more widely used as a source of news (2014, p. 12). In particular, Twitter has been identified as a source of breaking news, with 59 per cent of Twitter users following it for breaking news, compared with 31 per cent of Facebook users (Lichterman 2015).

The ways in which news outlets pursue users through social media are many and varied (Lasorsa et al. 2012), with Twitter and other social messaging tools both shaping and being shaped by established journalistic norms and practices (Hermida 2010b, 2012). For news outlets, establishing a presence on more than one platform may be an effective way of engaging a wider range of users: 'Different SNSs come with different feature sets and different user bases. That is why most newspapers are pursuing users on both Facebook and Twitter' (Ju, Jeong & Chyi 2014, p. 5).

Smaller newspapers and social media

This indication of variety in the ways news outlets utilise social media raises questions about whether this is apparent across, or also within, media sectors. The content and format of posts may provide an indication of what news outlets aim to achieve through their social media engagement. For example, exploring the use of social media by smaller newspapers may provide a sense not only of whether there are broad trends in this engagement, but also of what kinds of messages are being communicated and how, and the extent to which these exchanges are breaking down or maintaining hierarchical news communication processes. It may thus provide pointers to the ongoing nature of relationships between news outlets and their publics.

In Australia, smaller newspapers are generally those located outside metropolitan areas, although this sector could also be considered to encompass suburban newspapers and niche publications. The non-metropolitan newspaper sector in Australia is diverse in type but relatively concentrated in ownership, ranging from locally owned, weekly publications with limited circulation to corporate-owned dailies covering population bases of several hundred thousand people. Whatever their size, these smaller publications are seen as being in many ways different to their metropolitan cousins. They are generally noted as being 'closer' to their communities, and as having a strong emphasis on local news (Bowd 2010; Kirkpatrick 2001; Pretty 1995). In addition, they fulfil a historic role as champions of community interest — a 'voice of the community' (Ekstrom, Johansson & Larsson 2011, p. 259; see also Bowd 2010; Pretty 1995) — although this role may be being impacted by the growth of corporate ownership in Australia. Nonetheless, community-focused journalism is 'about connectedness and embeddedness. It articulates and emphasizes the "local" in both geographic and virtual forms of belonging' (Lewis et al. 2014, p. 232).

Regional newspapers in Australia have been severely impacted by the changes affecting the broader news industry. While initially many were in a stronger financial position than their metropolitan counterparts, more recently they have been increasingly affected by falling revenues (Hess 2015), leading to restructuring and redundancies (Lynch 2015). Nonetheless, most have a social media presence. Lewis et al. (2014) argue that while local journalists may lag behind their 'elite' peers in technology adoption, they 'may be open to more process-level participation' (p. 231). And while, for example, the 'Digital First' strategy adopted by Fairfax Regional Media, Australia's largest regional newspaper publisher, has resulted in job cuts, its emphasis on digital communication has highlighted the perceived importance of this area to the company. In 2014, Fairfax claimed that 'mobile and social media represent the biggest growth in the way readers are accessing information' ('Fairfax Regional Media has set another record win' 2014).

Exploring smaller newspapers' social media use

To explore how regional newspapers in Australia engage with social media, and through this to consider questions of relationships between these newspapers and their publics, the Facebook and Twitter posts of sixteen Australian regional newspapers were monitored and analysed over a three-month period in 2015. Four newspapers in each of four states — South Australia, Queensland, New South Wales and Victoria — were included, with data gathered from each publication from 1 March to 31 May. Data were collected manually each week during the survey period, using screenshots of all of the posts by each newspaper on the two platforms. Only posts using official newspaper accounts were included (those by journalists under their own names were not). The newspapers represented a mix of locally and corporately owned papers, with publication frequencies ranging from weekly to daily. Included were:

- in New South Wales [NSW]: *Port Macquarie News, Daily Advertiser* (Wagga Wagga), *Northern Star* (Lismore), *Moree Champion*
- in Queensland: *North-West Star* (Mount Isa), *Whitsunday Coast Guardian* (Proserpine), *Beaudesert Times, Observer* (Gladstone)
- in Victoria; *Ararat Advertiser, Moyne Gazette* (Port Fairy), *Sunraysia Daily* (Mildura), *Castlemaine Mail*
- in South Australia [SA]; *Bunyip* (Gawler), *Border Watch* (Mount Gambier), *Naracoorte Herald, Recorder* (Port Pirie).

Analysis of the posts focused on the type of content that was posted and trends across each publication. While posts were counted to provide an indication of these trends, the emphasis of the analysis remained qualitative, concentrating on what information was included, how it was conveyed and the ways in which this might contribute to interaction and ongoing relationships between the news outlets and their publics.

Key elements of the coverage

All of the papers in the survey had Facebook pages, but three either did not have Twitter accounts or had accounts that showed no activity during the survey period. The frequency of posting on both platforms varied widely from publication to publication, and there was also wide variation between platforms, with a minority of newspapers tweeting more frequently than posting on Facebook. Numbers of Facebook posts over the three-month period ranged from ten by Victoria's *Moyne Gazette* to more than 900 by the New South Wales daily, *Northern Star*. Twitter similarly showed wide variation, from one tweet by the *Moyne Gazette* to more than 1000 by Victoria's *Sunraysia Daily*. The greater number of posts overall on Facebook across the publications may be attributable to journalists' level of comfort in using Facebook rather than Twitter, but may also reflect the non-urgent nature of much of the news covered by regional publications. Exploration of broad trends in post content revealed a high degree of variation, even between newspapers owned by the same company, suggesting that each publication may be adapting its social media use to what it perceives as its own needs and those of its social media followers. For example, while the Fairfax-owned *Moree Champion* made extensive use of a 'regional wrap-up' (called 'Up and At It') as a means of directing traffic to its website, some other publications owned by the same company used this technique rarely or not at all.

However, one consistent trend across the publications was the local nature of content. Local news focus has consistently been identified in the literature as a key element of regional newspaper publishing (Kirkpatrick 2001; Bowd 2010; Vine 2012), and this appears to be flowing through to social media. Some publications — particularly the smaller ones — posted only about local events, issues and people, while others included elements of state, national and international news, but at a low level of frequency. Where broader news was included, it tended to be on topics likely to be of direct interest to regional audiences, such as the death of former Australian prime minister Malcolm Fraser, the executions of Bali Nine pair Andrew Chan and Myuran Sukumaran, and — in Queensland and NSW — the State-of-Origin rugby. The local nature of content was more clearly evident in the Facebook posts than the tweets, but this reflects the nature of the platforms, with Twitter's 140-character limit rendering unclear the origins of more of the news items posted.

Several other broad trends were also evident. Unsurprisingly, the daily papers tended to focus more on breaking news and police news than their smaller counterparts, although most publications made use at some point of the immediacy of social media to post information on road accidents affecting traffic. Also worth noting was coverage of Anzac Day, an annual Australian armed services commemoration on 25 April, which fell within the data-collection period. All of the papers included social media coverage of Anzac Day commemorations, and this was arguably where some made the most effective use of the capacities of social media, by including not only pointers to online stories, but also photos and videos, and in some cases by providing running coverage of local Anzac Day events.

Beyond this, however, the newspapers showed extensive variation in post content and format. Unsurprisingly, common topics included police and emergency services news, council and government, sport, human interest and local events. But there was little similarity across publications in the extent to which these topics were a focus of social media content. For example, NSW's *Port Macquarie News* reported extensively on local sporting events through Twitter, but included only three council-related tweets, while the *Daily Advertiser* included little Twitter coverage of either sport or council, but concentrated on police and emergency services news; and SA's *Bunyip* tweeted similar amounts of council and sport news. Similarly, some used social media extensively to direct audiences to photo galleries on a newspaper's website or in its print edition —

for example, around 40 per cent of the Facebook posts by South Australia's *Recorder* newspaper directed the audience to image-based coverage (particularly archival photos) — while others used this technique little if at all. And some used social media as a form of direct promotion for their online or print editions — explicitly referring to content in the newspaper or to a competition being run by the outlet, but others did not. For example, South Australia's *Bunyip* and *Border Watch* newspapers regularly ran images of their front pages as part of Facebook posts, alerting audience members not only to the content of the print edition but also its appearance.

Despite the lack of consistency across the publications, the majority of posts suggested replication of established news communication practices, with newspapers providing information *to* an audience. While all social media platforms incorporate interactive capacity, such as the ability to 'like', re-post or comment, there was limited use of interactivity beyond this. Some papers, such as Queensland's *Whitsunday Coast Guardian* and Victoria's *Sunraysia Daily*, did not directly seek to engage their audiences at all during the data-collection period. Many of the Facebook posts by Victoria's weekly *Castlemaine Mail* appear to have been taken straight from the pages of the print publication, rather than having been adapted for the online environment. However, the publication did on several occasions make use of the capacity to post questions to its audience. In other cases where interaction was explicitly sought, this tended to occur at a relatively superficial level, and primarily through Facebook rather than Twitter. For example, the NSW daily *Northern Star*'s (n.d.) invitations to interaction included a question about predictions for the final score in the State-of-Origin rugby game (May 27). Another question was: 'Do you live in a street with an unusual name? We'd like to hear from you about addresses you love, or hate' (May 5). It also included 'throwaway' questions on many news reports, particularly 'What do you think?', on topics ranging from smoke-free outdoor dining areas (April 18) to the NSW state election (March 11). Nonetheless, while the questions were broad, the generally conversational tone of these questions suggests public responses would be welcomed.

One area where public interaction was specifically sought by some newspapers was in relation to photographs. This included calls for photos of local events taken by people who were there, and a regular 'photo of the day' poll in NSW's *Northern Star*, with readers invited to both submit photos and vote on those submitted. Two papers, the *Northern Star* and Queensland's *Observer*, regularly ran photographs (sometimes the same photographs) with a call to 'caption this photo'. These photos — usually featuring animals and usually also geographically non-specific — were evidently among the resources available to publications in the APN News & Media ownership network.[1]

---

1 Note that APN's regional newspapers have since been bought by Rupert Murdoch's News Corp (see Battersby 2016).

There were a small number of instances where journalists used the capacities of social media — predominantly Facebook — to seek people to interview on specific topics, but for the most part the social media posts appeared to serve a primary role of providing information to news consumers. While most were local and relatively conversational in tone, both the content and the phrasing suggested information provision as their main aim, with interaction — through the capacity to like, comment or retweet, or through more direct appeal for information and/or opinion — secondary. This suggests that regional newspapers have yet to fully embrace the networking possibilities offered by social media, instead falling back on established news communication conventions.

Conclusion

In an environment in which 'the contraction of legacy media continues apace, characterised by falling audiences, readerships and advertising revenues' (Franklin 2014, p. 470), news outlets' engagement with social media is not just a way of 'keeping up', but also a means of helping to ensure survival in a rapidly changing media landscape. The growing presence of smaller newspapers in this space indicates that they are — on an individual basis or as part of a corporate strategy — taking steps to avoid being left behind. Allan argues that journalists are at the centre of public life as a result of their mission of 'ensuring that members of the public are able to draw upon a diverse "market place of ideas"' (2004, p. 47). Social media, and the networks they generate, may help to expand this marketplace, reshaping public sphere understandings and the role of journalism within them: '[s]ocial networking sites represent an evolution of the public sphere, where the dynamics of publication and distribution of news are being reshaped by networked publics' (Hermida et al. 2012, p. 816).

Regional newspapers, with their established role at the centre of local communication networks and their longstanding relationships of credibility and trust, may be ideally placed to capitalise on these shifts in public sphere understandings. However, in order to do so they need to be able to maintain their relevance and centrality across both online and offline platforms. Adapting to new media platforms requires more than 'repurposing existing media products' (Wolf & Schnauber 2015, p. 771), and Mitchelstein and Boczkowski suggest that online news producers and consumers 'straddle between tradition and innovation in their daily practices' (2013), a perspective that could also be applied to social media. Franklin points out that 'the expansive popularity of social media, especially Twitter, offers a further development of consequence for the future of journalism' (2014, p. 472), but the extent to which the development is a positive one depends at least in part on how news media respond to it. It appears that at this stage Australia's regional newspapers are taking relatively tentative steps into the social media environment. While engagement with social media is widespread, and posts may cover a diverse range of topics, most generally replicate traditional one-to-many news communication practices. Where two-way communication with a news outlet's publics occurs, it tends to happen at a relatively superficial level.

In utilising social media primarily in a way that replicates established practice, regional newspapers run the risk of fragmenting existing audiences across a range of delivery platforms — print, website and social media — rather than expanding their reach to new publics and cementing their role in public life. Peters points out that 'old audience habits are certainly becoming de-ritualized and it is unclear what will replace them' (2015, p. 1). Ongoing replication of hierarchical communication practices may lead to news audiences choosing to engage with a preferred delivery platform rather than across the spectrum of communication options in the networked public sphere. As well as fragmenting existing audiences, this may limit opportunities for news outlets to build new publics. The uptake across the broader media environment of concepts such as 'participation, interaction, and openness' (Peters & Witschge 2015, p. 20) is less evident among the regional newspapers in this study, and may affect the extent to which such publications can build and maintain publics in the networked environment.

While regional newspapers have traditionally had relatively close relationships with their audiences because of their focus on local content and local interest, as the nature of the media landscape changes this relationship may not be secure. Peters suggests that in the past there was a 'certain stability and predictability to media consumption', but today such patterns seem 'increasingly anachronistic, at least with Western societies. The places, spaces, times, and further social aspects of news consumption are all changing … ' (2015, p. 5). This presents news media in regional areas with particular challenges. They may have been insulated to some extent by their longstanding connection with their — predominantly geographically bound — readerships, but as understandings of networks and public sphere engagement change, and understandings of place shift, they risk being left behind. While the study reported above has limitations in that it canvasses only the published social media outputs of the newspapers, rather than considering the motivations of journalists or the direct responses of audiences, it nonetheless is a first step in providing pointers to how Australia's regional newspapers are utilising social media and whether such utilisation places them in a position to expand their publics. It suggests that to a large extent established communication practices are being replicated through social media, supplemented by limited attention to new means of storytelling and superficial calls for interaction. Consequently, rather than being able to expand their publics as geographical and other communication barriers break down, and thereby consolidate their place as a central element of local communication networks, news outlets risk fragmenting existing audiences across the multiple platforms in which these audiences are increasingly engaged.

References

Allan, S 2004, *News culture*, 2nd edn, Open University Press, Maidenhead.

Barnard, SR 2016, 'Tweet or be sacked: Twitter and the new elements of journalistic practice', *Journalism*, vol. 17, no. 2, pp. 190-207.

Barnett, S & Townend, J 2015, 'Plurality, policy and the local', *Journalism Practice*, vol. 9, no. 3, pp. 332-349.

Barthel, M, Shearer, E, Gottfried, J & Mitchell, A 2015, 'The evolving role of news on Twitter and Facebook', viewed 1 March 2016, <www.journalism.org/2015/07/14/the-evolving-role-of-news-on-twitter-and-facebook>.

Bastos, MT 2015, 'Shares, pins and tweets', *Journalism Studies*, vol. 16, no. 3, pp. 305-325.

Battersby, L 2016, 'Rupert Murdoch's News Corp buys APN regional papers for $37 million', *The Sydney Morning Herald*, viewed 11 November 2016, <http://www.smh.com.au/business/media-and-marketing/rupert-murdochs-news-corp-buys-apn-regional-papers-for-37-million-20160621-gpnyt1.html>.

Becker, LB & Vlad, T 2009, 'News organisations and routines', in K Wahl-Jorgensen & T Hanitzsch (eds.), *The handbook of journalism studies*, Routledge, New York, pp. 59-72.

Bowd, K 2010, 'Local voice, local choice: Australian country newspapers and notions of community', PhD thesis, University of South Australia, Adelaide.

Chyi, HI & Chadha, M 2012, 'News on new devices', *Journalism Practice*, vol. 6, no. 4, pp. 431-449.

Duggan, M, Ellison, NB, Lampe, C, Lenhart, A & Madden, M 2015, 'Social media update 2014', *Pew Research Center*, viewed 29 March 2016, <http://www.pewinternet.org/2015/01/09/social-media-update-2014>.

Ekstrom, M, Johansson, B & Larsson, L 2010, 'Journalism and local politics', in S Allan (ed.), *The Routledge companion to news and journalism*, Routledge, Abingdon, pp. 256-266.

Fairfax Media n.d., 'Our portfolio', *Fairfax Media*, viewed 30 March 2016, <http://www.fairfaxmedia.com.au/portfolio-landing>.

'Fairfax Regional Media has set another record win', 2014, July 9, *Port Macquarie News*, p. 5.

Fenton, N 2010, 'News in the digital age', in S Allan (ed.), *The Routledge companion to news and journalism*, Routledge, Abingdon, pp. 557-567.

Franklin, B 2014, 'The future of journalism', *Journalism Practice*, vol. 8, no. 5, pp. 469-487.

'Friends with benefits? News companies and Facebook', 2015, *The Economist*, 16 May, vol. 415, no. 8938, p. 58.

Gade, PJ & Lowrey, W 2011, 'Reshaping the journalistic culture', in W Lowrey & PJ Gade (eds.), *Changing the news*, Routledge, New York, pp. 22-42.

Habermas, J 1989, *The structural transformation of the public sphere*, Polity, Cambridge.

Hedman, U & Djerf-Pierre, M 2013, 'The social journalist', *Digital Journalism*, vol. 1, no. 3, pp. 368-385.

Heikkila, H & Ahva, L 2015, 'The relevance of journalism', *Journalism Practice*, vol. 9, no. 1, 50-64.

Hermida, A 2010a, 'Twittering the news', *Journalism Practice*, vol. 4, no. 3, pp. 297-308.

Hermida, A 2010b, 'Tweet the news: Social media streams and the practice of journalism', in S Allan (ed.), *The Routledge companion to news and journalism*, Routledge, Abingdon, pp. 671-682.

Hermida, A 2012, 'Tweets and truth', *Journalism Practice*, vol. 6, no. 5-6, pp. 659-668.

Hermida, A, Fletcher, F, Korell, D & Logan, D 2012, 'Share, like, recommend', *Journalism Studies*, vol. 13, no. 5-6, pp. 815-824.

Hess, K 2015, 'Making connections', *Journalism Studies*, vol. 16, no. 4, pp. 482-496.

Hess, K & Bowd, K 2015, 'Friend or foe?', *Media International Australia*, no. 156, pp. 19-28.

Hess, K & Waller, L 2014, 'Geo-social journalism', *Journalism Practice*, vol. 8, no. 2, pp. 121-136.

Hindman, DB 2011, 'Changes in community power structures', in W Lowrey & PJ Gade (eds.), *Changing the news*, Routledge, New York, pp. 118-135.

Ju, A, Jeong, SH & Chyi, HI 2014, 'Will social media save newspapers?', *Journalism Practice*, vol. 8, no. 1, pp. 1-17.

Kirkpatrick, R 2001, 'Are community newspapers really different?', *AsiaPacific Media Educator*, no. 10, pp. 16-21.

Lasorsa, DL, Lewis, SC & Holton, AE 2012, 'Normalizing Twitter', *Journalism Studies*, vol. 13, no. 1, pp. 19-36.

Lee, AM & Chyi, HI 2014, 'Motivational consumption model: Exploring the psychological structure of news use', *Journalism & Mass Communication Quarterly*, vol. 91, no. 4, pp. 706-724.

Lewis, SC, Holton, AE & Coddington, M 2014, 'Reciprocal journalism', *Journalism Practice*, vol. 8, no. 2, pp. 229-241.

Lichterman, J 2015, 'New Pew data: More Americans are getting news on Facebook and Twitter', *Nieman Lab*, viewed 23 February 2016, <www.niemanlab.org/2015/07/new-pew-data-more-americans-are-getting-news-on-facebook-and-twitter>.

Lowrey, W & Gade, PJ 2011a, *Changing the news*, Routledge, New York.

Lowrey, W & Gade, PJ 2011b, 'Complexity, uncertainty, and journalistic change', in W Lowrey & PJ Gade (eds.), *Changing the news*, Routledge, New York, pp. 3-21.

Lynch, J 2015, 'Fairfax confirms job cuts in overhaul of regional publications', *The Age*, 17 April, p. 25.

McChesney, RW 2012, 'Farewell to journalism?', *Journalism Studies*, vol. 13, no. 5-6, pp. 682-694.

McCombs, M, Holbert, RL, Kiousis, S & Wanta, W 2011, *The news and public opinion*, Polity, Cambridge.

Mitchelstein, E & Boczkowski, P 2013, 'Tradition and transformation in online news production and consumption', in WH Dutton (ed.), *The Oxford handbook of internet studies*, Oxford Handbooks, Oxford, viewed 25 October 2016, <http://www.oxfordhandbooks.com/view/10.1093/oxfordhb/9780199589074.001.0001/oxfordhb-9780199589074>.

New beats n.d., 'Redundancy timeline', *New beats: A study of Australian journalism redundancies*, viewed 4 October 2016, <http://www.newbeatsblog.com/redundancytimeline>.

The Northern Star n.d., Facebook, viewed 25 October 2016, <https://www.facebook.com/thenorthernstar/?fref=ts>.

Paper cuts n.d., '1859+ jobs', *Paper cuts*, viewed 4 October 2016, <http://newspaperlayoffs. com>.

Paulussen, S & D'heer, E 2013, 'Using citizens for community journalism: Findings from a hyperlocal media project', *Journalism Practice*, vol. 7, no. 5, pp. 588-603.

Paulussen, S & Harder, RA 2014, 'Social media references in newspapers', *Journalism Practice*, vol. 8, no. 5, pp. 542-551.

Pavlik, J 2000, 'The impact of technology on journalism', *Journalism Studies*, vol. 1, no. 2, pp. 229-237.

Peters, C 2015, 'Introduction', *Journalism Studies*, vol. 16, no. 1, p. 1-11.

Peters, C & Witschge, T 2015, 'From grand narratives of democracy to small expectations of participation', *Journalism Practice*, vol. 9, no. 1, pp. 19-34.

Picard, RG 2014, 'Twilight or new dawn of journalism? Evidence from the changing news ecosystem', *Journalism Studies*, vol. 15, no. 5, pp. 500-510.

Pretty, K 1995, 'Rural newspaper journalists: Who are they?', in P Share (ed.), *Communication and culture in rural areas*, Centre for Rural Social Research, Wagga Wagga, pp. 199-217.

Rivas-Rodriguez, M 2011, 'Communities, cultural identity and the news', in W Lowrey & PJ Gade (eds.), *Changing the news*, Routledge, New York, pp.102-117.

Rosen, J 2006, 'The people formerly known as the audience', *PressThink*, viewed 30 March 2016, at <http://archive.pressthink.org/2006/06/27/ppl_frmr.html>.

Sheller, M 2015, 'News now', *Journalism Studies*, vol. 16, no. 1, pp. 12-26, DOI: http://dx.doi. org/10.1080/1461670X.2014.890324.

Singer, JB 2011, 'Journalism and digital technologies', in W Lowrey & PJ Gade (eds.), *Changing the news*, Routledge, New York, pp. 213-229.

Skogerbo, E & Krumsvik, AH 2015, 'Newspapers, Facebook and Twitter', *Journalism Practice*, vol. 9, no. 3, pp. 350-366.

Stevenson, N 1995, *Understanding media cultures*, Sage, London.

Usher, N 2014, *The new media world: Making news at The New York Times*, University of Michigan Press, Ann Arbor, MI.

van der Wurff, R & Schoenbach, K 2014, 'Civic and citizen demands of news media and journalists: What does the audience expect from good journalism?', *Journalism & Mass Communication Quarterly*, vol. 91, no. 3, pp. 433-451.

van Leuven, S, Deprez, A & Raeymaeckers, K 2014, 'Towards more balanced news access? A study on the impact of cost-cutting and Web 2.0 on the mediated public sphere', *Journalism*, vol. 15, no. 7, pp. 850-867.

Veo, V 2009, 'SBS: Engaging with news audiences in the new media age', *Media International Australia*, no. 133, pp. 24-25.

Vine, J 2012, 'News values and country non-daily news reporting: The online revolution's impact', *Rural Society*, vol. 21, no. 2, pp. 158-171.

Wolf, C & Schnauber, A 2015, 'News consumption in the mobile era', *Digital Journalism*, vol. 3, no. 5, pp. 759-776.

The use of Chinese social media by foreign embassies: How 'generative technologies' are offering opportunities for modern diplomacy

9

Ying Jiang

Social media platforms provide spaces for interaction and increased engagement, thus furthering the goals of public diplomacy. Due to the perceived ease with which social media can be accessed and the low cost in comparison with other methods, social media platforms are seen as attractive technology-based communication channels for many embassies and other organisations, particularly for those facing budget cuts and demands to increase engagement (Fisher 2013).

It is believed that social media provide the right channel to reach youth populations, which is one of the major goals of current public diplomacy efforts (Mershon 2012). For public diplomacy, it is equally important to listen to and understand young people's thoughts and aspirations, along with their information-seeking and other kinds of behaviours (Riordan 2004). In addition, social media provide the opportunity to reach the youth populations of other countries. In foreign embassies in China, for example, there are more than forty embassies that use the most popular Chinese social media platform — Weibo — to engage with the 'online publics' in China.

This chapter examines how 'generative technologies' are offering opportunities for modern diplomacy. Engagement and interactivity are what have been emphasised in using social media in public relation works. However, this chapter argues that interactivity is not necessarily linked to the success of the engagement with online publics via social media accounts. This chapter examines the interactivity of those embassies' Weibo accounts by looking at two aspects: the number of comments or retweets that each post receives, and the number of negative and positive comments that each post receives.

According to my previous research, it is evident that Weibo can be employed effectively to engage with online communities, which is one of the goals of public diplomacy, but it was difficult to measure its real effects simply by looking at the data collected at that stage. In fact, one of the important phenomena which my research illustrates is that the number of followers does not equal the influence Weibo has on its followers — that is, the level of 'conversational' or informal communication on Weibo accounts does not indicate the success of e-diplomacy. Indeed, the negative and hostile comments left on some of the embassies' Weibo accounts show that the outcomes of its public diplomacy tasks are unsuccessful.

This chapter focuses on measuring the interactivity of these foreign embassies' Weibo accounts. Through my research, I found that awareness does not imply positive influence. Defining public diplomacy [PD] as communication with foreign publics for the purpose of achieving a foreign policy objective, PD practitioners should be cognisant of the fact that *information* is different from *influence* (Wallin 2013). Other researchers have similarly found that an account's high number of followers does not necessarily equate to that account having a strong connection with an audience. An account might have 1 million followers, but even though a post from that account gets retweeted 1000 times per day, those followers may support or oppose the user's communication goals (Wallin 2013).

Literature review

Research on the government's application of new media has had a long existence. In 1986, Garramone, Harris and Pizante were the first researchers to discuss how computers could provide a two-way flow of information between elected officials and their constituents. McKeown and Plowman (1999) explained how 1996 US presidential candidates used the internet to reach voters during the general election; Trammell (2006) explained how blog-based attacks were utilised during the US election in 2004; Levenshus (2010) explained how Barack Obama's campaign utilised the internet for grassroots efforts in 2008. Other scholars have looked at how governmental organisations from the Middle East and the United Arab Emirates [UAE] used the internet (Curtin & Gaither 2004; Ayish 2005; Kirat 2007), as well as the role of culture, in country-sponsored tourism websites (Kang & Mastin 2008); how the diffusion of social media has affected public health communication (Avery et al. 2010); and what the impact of transparency laws is on Latin American government websites (Searson & Johnson 2010).

Research that examines the influence of organisations' impact or influence on people through the use of social media is not rare. For example, in 2013, the European Commission published a report entitled *Assessing the Benefits Of Social Networks on Organizations* (Martin & van Bavel 2013). This project aimed to analyse the current market situation for a limited number of social media stakeholders, to identify and analyse best practices for these selected stakeholders, and to define and prioritise relevant policy options. This report is one of the most comprehensive pieces of research on the topic so far. It conducted an exhaustive and critical review of the academic, business and policy literature on the organisational use of social networking tools and social media platforms, as well as regular engagement with academic experts in this area. It was observed that while social media technologies present several potential benefits to organisations, there are considerable challenges and bottlenecks affecting adoption that may warrant policy intervention.

Apart from this relatively large-scale project on social media's influence on organisations, scholars from a range of backgrounds have also examined the effectiveness of employing social media in different contexts. For example, Murthy (2015) investigated the relationship between social media and organisational collaboration, changes to organisations, and the effect of microblogging on organisations. Puijenbroek et al. (2014) focused on investigating the relationship between social media use and learning activities undertaken by employees. Kleinhans, van Ham and Evans-Cowley (2015) explored the potential of social media and mobile technologies to foster citizen engagement and participation in urban planning.

However, there is not much research into the influence of foreign embassies in China. One piece of research worth mentioning is a report written in Chinese and published by Chinalabs in 2013, which looked at the internet influence that Chinese foreign embassies have, analysing the level of each foreign embassy's online impact by looking at their websites and social media accounts. This report found that only 15 per cent of foreign embassies in China opened Weibo accounts, and most of these Weibo accounts lacked interactivity. According to this report (2013), Weibo is playing a 'media' role. In other words, this social media platform was used by foreign embassies to share information rather than to influence followers or initiate interactivity with followers. However, this research was conducted almost four years ago, and, given the rapid development of foreign embassies' use of Weibo, the research findings summarised in this report need an update.

Method

To address the above issues, I first gathered a list of embassies on Chinese social media platforms. For the purpose of this study, the definition of an embassy's Chinese social media account refers to the embassy's official account as verified by the service provider. It does not include any ambassador's personal account, nor does it include any consular or consular staff member's account.

To gather this list, I mainly used one simple method — trawling for known embassies through Weibo's celebrity plaza (Mingren Tang), where embassies are categorised by their countries. Following this, I then gathered a list of foreign embassy Weibo users. I collected numerical and descriptive data (such as the user's self-written Twitter biography, representative avatar, number of friends and number of followers) for each of our examined Weibo users. I then collected and archived further descriptive data (country, registered date) with both text and time/date tweeted. In order to analyse a similar series of tweets, I then edited this to a three-month period between September 2014 and December 2014.

Based on my Stage 1 research results, which will be published by Routledge in 2017 (Jiang, forthcoming), I selected the five foreign embassies' Weibo accounts with the highest number of followers. Canada has the most followers on Sina Weibo. Canada's followers have surpassed the US's followers, reaching a figure of more than 1.1 million. The US embassy has around 900 000 followers as of 6 December 2014. Cuba and the UK have the same number of followers and ranked third on the list, while the Korean embassy's Sina Weibo have slightly fewer followers than Cuba and UK. Echoing the method of Leavitt et al. (2009), I collected a three-month sample of those five accounts' Weibo comments, and then categorised the comments into three basic types: positive, negative and other (for example, irrelevant questions or advertisements).

Findings

Statistics on foreign embassies' Weibo influence (sample from 6 September to 6 December 2014)

The influence of each embassy through Weibo can be assessed by calculating the number of comments on their posts, and the number of retweets of their posts. After analysing the number of comments and retweets each embassy received on their Weibo account from September to December in 2014, I gathered the following results (Figure 9.1). As can be seen, the Korean embassy has the highest ratio of retweets and comments.

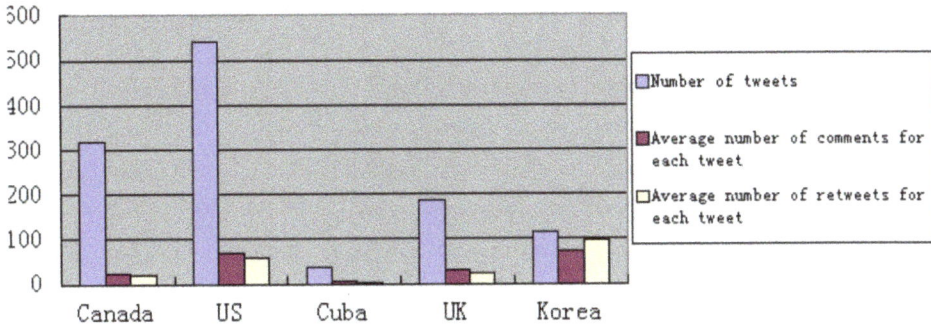

Figure 9.1: The number of comments and retweets per post by embassies.
Source: Y Jiang [Figure as provided].

After an extremely time-consuming manual collection of comments left on the Weibo accounts of the above-mentioned five embassies between 6 September and 6 December 2014, I found that although the US embassy has the highest level of interactivity (that is, the highest number of comments), more than half of the comments it received were negative ones (Table 9.1). Although Cuba has the least number of comments, most of the comments it received were positive. The Korean embassy is also leading the way in receiving positive comments. The percentage of negative comments received by the British and Canadian embassies is just under 50 per cent (Figure 9.2).

	Canada	US	Cuba	UK	Korea
Total number of comments	7632	37 800	195	5952	8658
Positive comments	2303	5670	120	1258	6925
Negative comments	3803	22 680	0	2542	760
Other (including questions not related to the topic or ads)	1526	9450	15	2152	946

Table 9.1: Analysis of comments left on the Weibo accounts of five embassies.
Source: Y Jiang.

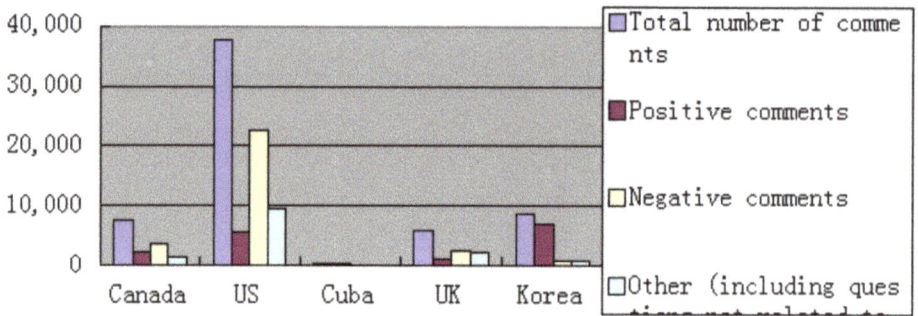

Figure 9.2: The number of positive and negative comments received per embassy.
Source: Y Jiang [Figure as provided].

Other findings

Among the collected valid comments, it was evident that nationalistic sentiments toward certain Western countries are frequently presented on the embassies' Weibo accounts. According to initial statistics, of 3000 negative comments received by the Canadian and the US embassies (which are the two embassies who received the highest number of negative comments), most of the themes of those comments were nationalistic. For example, this is a post made by the US embassy on 31 Oct 2014, which received 132 comments, most of which were negative (Figures 9.3 and 9.4):

> @US Embassy in China: Around 2 million voters in America started the prior-voting process for the mid-term election on 20 October. President Obama has also joined them. Among the 50 states in the US, 43 of them allow pre-voting. Both parties are working hard to win the voters during this period. Due to the high competitiveness of the election, both parties are going to all lengths to win voters from every corner. What else would you like to know about the mid-term election?[1]

Below is a sample of the comments that this post received[2]:

User name	Comment
Shua Qiang	Great! People in China won't be able to see one vote in their life!

---

1   Translation provided by the author.
2   Comments translated by the author.

Xianshi_Taobi	Reply @wobuqirenyoutian: What's the real meaning of China's election system? We don't agree.
Jiujiaowoaliaoshaba	Do you dare to give me the American visa?
Wobuqirenyoutian	China's election system is similar to most of the nations. 1200 candidates are not nominated by themselves, they are nominated by representatives from different areas, and will then be voted by people. What's wrong with this? Isn't it the same in Ukraine? Also the same in Japan, Korea? Isn't it all the same?
Wobuqirenyoutian	Those 'occupiers' in Hong Kong requested a 20% threshold for election, if a 20% support rate can represent the community, why can't a 50% supporting rate represent China's election system?
Djquan172	American people request REAL election.
Gangchushengjiuhensha	Fucking Americans! Why don't you sit down and talk to the people who occupied Wall Street?
Xianshitaobi	Reply @wobuqirenyoutian 'Representatives need to represent the majority of people, otherwise, people will be represented without knowing who are representing them'. Aren't you talking about China?
Wobuqirenyoutian	Reply @xiaoshitaobi Because there are 7 billion people in the world, the majority of us will be represented instead of representing others or ourselves. How can we have 7 billion mouths discussing one issue? Therefore, the most effective and realistic method is to elect representatives.
Qingcheshuilian	America will spend an estimated 4 billion US dollars on the election, where does this money come from? What's the motivation of people who are providing the funds? Why are they spending so much on the election?

回复@有秋意:选举团制度被创造出来时为了确保每个州都在总统选举中有代表。选举团制度迫使候选人到人口众多的地区以外展开竞选活动，照顾在直选体制下可能被忽略的地方。不赞成这种制度的人士则认为直接选举更简单明了。更多信息 🔗 网页链接

@美国驻华大使馆 V

10月20日，大约200万美国选民提前开始2014年中期选举的投票。奥巴马总统也加入了提前投票的队伍。在美国50个州中，有43个州允许提前投票。两党都正在努力争取提前投票的选民。由于很多职位的竞选比分十分接近，两党都全力以赴争取每一个角落的选民。你还想了解中期选举什么？

🔗 美国部分选民提前...

美国部分选民提前开始中期选举的...

2014.10.22大约200万美国选民提前开始2014年中期选举的投票。10月20

文章详情　👍71

2014-10-24 10:51 来自 新浪博客　　　　　　　　　　　　转发 596　评论 239　👍62

2014-10-31 15:12 来自 微博 weibo.com

收藏　　　　　　　　转发 75　　　　　　　　评论 123　　　　　　　👍25

😊 🖼 ☐ 同时转发到我的微博　　　　　　　　　　　　　　　　　　　　评论
　　　☐ 同时评论给原文作者 美国驻华大使馆

全部　热门　认证用户　关注的人　　　　　　　　　　　　　　　　　共123条

励增：真棒，在中国民众一生都见不到选票
2014-10-31 17:59　　　　　　　　　　　　　　　　　　　　回复　👍3

现黄_逃遥：回覆@我不杞人忧天: 中共的"普選"是什么内涵？是什么货色？我们不认同，你能怪罪我们吗？好好反省自己吧。删贴必再贴
2014-11-1 20:29　　　　　　　　　　　　　　　查看对话　回复　👍1

就叫我阿廖沙吧0：敢不敢给我签证
2014-11-1 16:50　　　　　　　　　　　　　　　　　　　　回复　👍2

Figure 9.3: Screenshot of the US embassy's post and received comments.
Source: Y Jiang.

我不杞人忧天：回复@现实_逃避:中共的普选方案是与当前世界多数国家的选举模式一样。1200多人不是代表自己提名，而是作为代表提出他们所处的人群、团体、阶层、政党里得票数超过半数的人选作为候选人，交由公民一人一票裁决胜负。这有什么不对吗？乌克兰不就是这样吗？日本、韩国不就是这样？------不都是这样吗

2014-11-4 09:52　　　　　　　　　　　　　　　　　　　　　回复　　👍

我不杞人忧天：占中者要求获20%支持就可以号称代表民意，就必须登堂入室执行权力，这让获50%支持的人情何以堪？这是外星球的国际标准吧。

2014-11-4 09:51　　　　　　　　　　　　　　　　　　　　　回复　　👍

djquan172：美国人民要真普选。

2014-11-4 09:13　　　　　　　　　　　　　　　　　　　　　回复　　👍

刚出生就很傻：操你妈了个比的美国佬，坐下来谈你妈，你怎么不和占领华尔街谈呢？操你妈了个比的美国佬，坐下来谈你妈，你怎么不和占领华尔个比的美国佬，坐下来谈你妈，你怎么不和占领华尔街谈呢？操你妈了个比的美国佬，坐下来谈你妈，你怎么不和占领华尔街谈呢？操你妈了个比的美国佬，坐下来谈你

2014-11-4 02:20　　　　　　　　　　　　　　　　　　　　　回复　　👍

信访脚步11：极度腐败福建省莆田市仙游县原建设局长借其媒友名挂森榕项目建私人豪宅，圈抢、炒卖农民宅基地耕地，伪造规划，以权谋私，其亲友原鲤城镇党委书记滥用职权，欺上瞒下，对多年信访村民实行放火烧宅等打击报复手段，以超生、默许私人卖地，安抚部分村民忍受掠夺。一张假规划，8年信访路，习近平管吗？

2014-11-3 12:55　　　　　　　　　　　　　　　　　　　　　回复　　👍

现实_逃避：回复@我不杞人忧天:"既然当代表就需要站在整体利益、多数人利益的立场上，那样才有人推举你当代表，否则就甘心被代表。"你真的不是在讽刺中共233

2014-11-3 10:57　　　　　　　　　　　　　　　查看对话　　回复　　👍

我不杞人忧天：回复@现实_逃避:😂因为我明白，在地球人口已经70亿的情况下，绝大多数民众都是被代表的身份，不然都去当代表，70亿张嘴怎么商讨问题？现实与有效的办法就是选举代表。不喜欢被代表，就去争当代表，既然当代表就需要站在整体利益、多数人利益的立场上，那样才有人推举你当代表，否则就甘心被代表。

2014-11-3 10:52　　　　　　　　　　　　　　　查看对话　　回复　　👍

清澈水涎：美国选举要预计花费40亿美元。这些钱来自哪里，出钱的人目的何在，花钱的人如何获得？为什么要花这么多钱，进行选举，对美国人民来说，是不是一种不正常的选举模式？楼下，这里谈美国，你脑袋锈逗啦！

2014-11-3 07:18　　　　　　　　　　　　　　　　　　　　　回复　　👍

Figure 9.4: Screenshot of comments left on the US embassy's posts.
Source: Y Jiang.

People might argue that the topic of this particular post was 'political', and that it might have attracted certain users who are in favor of China's voting system. However, even with 'non-political' topics, negative comments were apparent. For example, the following post made by the US embassy on the same day regarding 'Halloween' also received ironic and hostile comments (Figures 9.5 and 9.6).

> @US Embassy: Today is Halloween. It is a day deeply loved by American children although it's not an official festival, because they can wear any costume they like, and play 'treat or trick'. The other custom of Halloween is to decorate pumpkins. Children empty a pumpkin, sculpt a face on the outside, then put a candle inside of it. The pumpkin lantern, which is also called a 'Jack lantern', is then complete. Does China have similar festivals?[3]

Sample of comments received:[4]

User name	Comments
Barbie696	Why does your post sound so provocative? Of course different cultures have different festivals. We don't have Halloween in China, so what?
Moxisaixiansheng	Yes we do, people who play tricks will be beaten into a 'Jack-lantern' face.
Hongheixiaoqihao	This is a festival of Western devils, we don't need it.
Ruchunqiu	Yulanpeng festival. But it is not an entertaining day, kids will not allowed to go out after dusk.
Xiaonuan-Li	We have bo lantern!
Hsia SH	We have the Zhongyuan festival. We consider this a very important day although it's not an official festival. We use this day to commemorate our loved ones who have passed away. Do you have this type of festival in the US?
Yunjingchen	Do you have the Chongyang festival to respect your elders? Or Lantern's Day to eat sticky rice balls? Or Dragon Boat Day to eat dragon boats? Or the Qingming festival to sweep the tombs of those who passed away?

3   Translation provided by the author.
4   Comments translated by the author.

Biantailadexiaohuzhu	I feel like our spring festival is better than this festival.
Daduhuangweiwei	Feel like your post is so ironic. We have the warmth of strong family connection, do you American devils have it?
Yiyongjunjueqipingtianxia	Do you know you are retarded?
Huaren37276	So a lot of pumpkins will be wasted on this day?

今天是万圣夜，虽然不是官方节日，却深受美国儿童的喜爱，因为这一天他们可以穿上奇装异服，玩"不给糖就捣乱"的游戏。万圣夜的另一个风俗是装饰南瓜。把南瓜掏空，在外面刻出一张脸，然后在瓜中插上一支蜡烛，一个南瓜灯也叫"杰克灯"就大功告成了。请问中国有类似的节日吗？ 🔗 网页链接

2014-10-31 10:06 来自 微博 weibo.com

收藏   转发 75   评论 104   👍 56

☐ 同时转发到我的微博   评论

全部 热门 认证用户 关注的人   共104条

Barbie696：这话问的怎么这么挑衅呢。。不同的文化节日当然不一样，我们没有万圣节怎么了呀
2014-10-31 12:30   回复 👍1

默西塞先生 ★：有啊，谁捣乱直接打成杰克脸
2014-10-31 10:11   回复 👍1

红黑小7号：这是洋鬼子的节日，中国不需要
2014-10-31 10:13   回复 👍2

茹春秋 ★：盂兰盆会。但是我们一丁点没有娱乐的意思，我们就放河灯喂恶鬼烧纸钱，而且稍微懂点儿的都不让小孩儿天黑以后出门。

Figure 9.5: Screenshot of US embassy's post and the comments it received.

Source: Y Jiang.

小暖-Li ★ : 我们中国有波咯灯😲
2014-10-31 10:28   回复 👍1

HsiaSh : 中元节，虽然不是官方节日，但深受中国人民重视，因为这一天可以带上黄表，香纸，出去给祖宗焚烧祭拜。中元节的另一个风俗是普渡，择日以酒肉、糖饼、水果等祭品举办祭祀活动，以慰在人世间游玩的众家鬼魂。请问美国有类似的节日吗
2014-10-31 12:07   回复 👍4

云镜尘 : →_→你们有重阳节孝敬老人，元宵节吃汤圆，粽子节吃粽子。清明节扫墓么？
2014-10-31 10:10   回复 👍2

变态辣的小户主 : 感觉春节全家团聚比这个更好。。。玩什么时候不是玩。。。。
2014-10-31 10:30   回复 👍3

公民王海滨 V 🐕 : //@狗宫纪事: 党国只有洗脑节日！
2014-10-31 10:20   举报   回复 👍1

大肚黄雄雄 ★ : 这话的讽刺意味好浓啊!中国人过节有浓浓的亲情味，美鬼有吗？我们有中秋节如此诗情画意的节日，你们有吗？中国春节小孩得红包，你们有吗？
2014-10-31 10:24   回复 👍2

以上为热门评论，查看更多»

义勇军崛起平天下 : 博主你脑残知道吗？
2014-11-5 19:20   回复 👍

华人37276 : 那不是要浪费很多南瓜，
2014-11-5 14:47   回复 👍

刚出生就很傻 : 操你妈了个比的美国佬，坐下来谈你妈，你怎么不和占领华尔街谈呢？操你妈了个比的美国佬，坐下来谈你妈，你怎么不和占领华尔街比的美国佬，坐下来谈你妈，你怎么不和占领华尔街谈呢？操你妈了个比的美国佬，坐下来谈你妈，你怎么不和占领华尔街谈呢？操你妈了个比的美国佬，坐下来谈你
2014-11-4 02:21   回复 👍

现实_逃避 : 回复@大肚黄雄雄: 其实考虑到欧洲各国文化相近，最后一句不算什么讽刺吧...例如吧，圣诞节英美有圣诞老人，某些国家是圣尼克，设定也不相同。对应万圣节的简单回答也有中元节就

Figure 9.6: Screenshot of US embassy's post and the comments it received.
Source: Y Jiang.

The US embassy is not the only Western country that has received hostile comments on its posts. Nationalistic comments left on the Canadian embassy site are also apparent. On 23 October 2014, a post made by Canadian embassy says:

Yesterday, barbarian behavior and a violent terrorist attack occurred in the land of Canada, for the second time in a week. We send our prayers and memorials to the family and friends of sergeant Nathan. Sergeant Nathan died in the attack when serving in the guard of honour for the Canadian national war memorial museum yesterday afternoon.[5]

However, the comments left by users are not friendly at all. Here are the translations of the first ten comments:[6]

User name	Comment
Sad grassmud horse	Didn't you ask the eastern Turkish brothers in your care to say hello to the Arabs?
Huang pu zhong sheng	Soldiers were killed, policemen were injured; it happened in a governmental organisation's venue. The attackers are now dead, but there is no evidence. How can you be so sure it is a terrorist attack? If it happened in China, would Western media consider it as a terrorist attack or a desperate action?
Warriorantigreen	You deserve it! I thought you could speak their language.
Shandiren	People with 'zhuangbility' want to show their 'niubility' but only reflect their 'shability'.
Zifeifanxiejiaozhilouxiajiaotang	You deserve it.
Artyang77	What do you think of the terrorist attacks in Xinjiang?
Sheisheibushiwo	Come on, I hope you accept more Muslims. Take all Muslims from China.
Lan Xiao Tian	Hope Canada takes more Muslims and becomes a Muslim country one day.
Roger is a big chubby guy	This incident only happened yesterday, it still needs investigation before being determined a 'terrorist attack'. The Canadian government should respect the rights of people who are involved and allow international organisations to join the investigation.

5   Translation provided by the author.

6   Comments translated by the author.

Ziwuyingxiao	We encourage the Canadian government to communicate with the minorities and stop suppressing the minorities.

昨天，在加拿大的国土上出现了野蛮和暴力恐怖袭击，这已经是本周第二次出现这样的事件了。我们向下士纳森·奇里洛的家人和朋友寄予哀思及祈祷，纳森下士于昨天在加拿大国家战争纪念馆参与礼仪仪仗队活动时遇害。

2014-10-23 14:47 来自 微博 weibo.com

收藏　　　　转发 75　　　　评论 106　　　　👍28

☐ 同时转发到我的微博　　　　评论

全部　热门　认证用户　关注的人　　　　共106条

悲伤的草泥马：你们没让收留的东突兄弟向阿拉伯人弹问好？
2014-10-26 11:24　　　　回复　👍8

星雨钟声：被打死的是军人，受伤的是警察，袭击发生在议会大厦这个政府部门，行凶者已被击毙，死无对证！凭什么是说是恐怖袭击？如果这事发生在中国新疆，西方媒体会怎么说？这是恐怖袭击还是绝望的呐喊？
2014-10-24 10:49　　　　回复　👍9

Warriorantigreen：活该 你不是会飙维语吗？
2014-10-26 16:16　　　　回复　👍1

山鹿人：装逼被雷劈！说的就是你@加拿大大使馆官方微博
2014-10-26 16:30　　　　回复　👍1

自费反邪教之楼下桥塘：活该
2014-10-26 09:48　　　　回复　👍2

Figure 9.7: Screenshot of Canadian embassy's post and the comments it received, 10 October 2015.

Source: Y Jiang.

Figure 9.8: Screenshot of Canadian embassy's post and the comments it received, 10 October 2015.

Source: Y Jiang.

Discussion

These results and evidence demonstrate that 'conversational' communication enabled by 'generative technologies' does not necessarily equate to high engagement with online publics. Having a high number of followers and a high level of interaction with your audience does not link to positive action. Wallin's (2013) thoughts bear repeating here: PD practitioners should be aware that information is different from influence.

159

Based on my own research findings, it is also arguable that the number of followers do not necessarily equate a strong connection with an audience.

Conclusion

Future research can look at another channel of 'online publics' in China — Wechat — which is also used by some foreign embassies. Due to the different nature of Wechat, a couple of aspects might be worth comparing:

1. Are the 'spaces' created by those five embassies on Wechat consistent with their Weibo 'spaces'?

2. Does Wechat pose less challenges than Weibo for foreign embassies in China?

This chapter is intended to provoke thoughts about better ways to use these 'generative technologies' or other tools for public diplomacy practicioners. It is not intended as an argument against the use of local popular social media for public diplomacy purposes, but to encourage a critical look at its practice and to encourage those employing it to better analyse it.

References

Avery, E, Lariscy, R, Amador, E, Ickowitz, T, Primm, C & Taylor, A 2010, 'Diffusion of social media among public relations practitioners in health departments across various community population sizes', *Journal of Public Relations Research*, vol. 22, no. 3, pp. 336-358.

Ayish, MI 2005, 'Virtual public relations in the United Arab Emirates: A case study of 20 UAE organizations' use of the Interne', *Public Relations Review*, vol. 31, no. 3, pp. 381-388.

Chinalabs 2013, 'Report on the effectiveness of using the internet by foreign embassies in China', viewed 22 August 2015, <http://www.huanqiu.com>.

Curtin, PA & Gaither, TK 2004, 'International agenda-building in cyberspace: A study of Middle East government English-language website', *Public Relations Review*, vol. 30, no. 1, pp. 25-36.

Fisher, A 2013, 'The use of social media in public diplomacy: Scanning e-diplomacy by embassies in Washington DC', viewed 22 August, 2015, <http://takefiveblog.org/2013/02/19/the-use-of-social-media-in-public-diplomacy-scanning-e-diplomacy-by-embassies-in-washington-dc/>.

Garramone, G, Harris, A & Pizante, G 1986, 'Predictors of motivation to use computer-mediated political communication systems', *Journal of Broadcasting & Electronic Media*, vol. 30, no. 4, pp. 445-457.

Jiang Y (forthcoming), 'Weibo and e-diplomacy: Scanning embassies on Weibo', in N Chitty, L Ji, GD Rawnsley & C Hayden (eds.), *The Routledge handbook of softpower*, Routledge, London, n.p.

Kang, DS & Mastin, T 2008, 'How cultural difference affects international tourism public relations websites: A comparative analysis using Hofstede's cultural dimensions', *Public Relations Review*, vol. 34, no. 1, pp. 4-56.

Kirat, M 2007, 'Promoting online media relations: Public relations departments' use of Internet in the UAE', *Public Relations Review*, vol. 33, no. 2, pp. 166-174.

Kleinhans, R, van Ham, M & Evans-Cowley, J 2015, 'Using social media and mobile technologies to foster engagement and self-organization in participatory urban planning and neighbourhood governance', *Planning Practice & Research*, vol. 30 no. 3, pp. 237-247.

Leavitt, A, Burchard, E, Fisher, D & Gilbert, S 2009, 'The influentials: New approaches for analyzing influence on Twitter', *Web ecology project*, viewed 12 September 2012, <http://www.webecologyproject.org/2009/09/analyzing-influence-on-twitter/>.

Levenshus, A 2010, 'Online relationship management in a presidential campaign: A case study of the Obama campaign's management of its internet-integrated grassroots effort', *Journal of Public Relations Research*, vol. 22, no. 3, pp. 313-335.

McKeown, CA & Plowman, KD 1999, 'Reaching publics on the web during the 1996 presidential campaign', *Journal of Public Relations Research*, vol. 11, no. 4, pp. 321-347.

Martin, A & van Bavel, R 2013, 'Assessing the benefits of social networks for organisations: Report on the first phase of the SEA-SoNS Project', Report EUR 25928 EN, Publications Office of the European Union, Luxembourg, viewed 28 October 2016, <http://publications.jrc.ec.europa.eu/repository/bitstream/JRC78641/jrc78641.pdf>.

Mershon, P 2012, '5 Social media tips for finding and engaging your target audience', *Social media examiner*, viewed 22 August 2015, <http://www.socialmediaexaminer.com/5-social-media-tips-for-finding-and-engaging-your-target-audience-new-research/>.

Murthy, D 2015, 'Introduction to the special issue on social media, collaboration, and organizations,' *American Behavioral Scientist*, vol. 59, no. 1, pp. 3-9.

Puijenbroek, T, Poell, RF, Kroon, B, Timmerman, V 2014, 'The effect of social media use on work-related learning', *Journal of Computer Assisted Learning*, vol. 30 no. 2, pp. 159-172.

Riordan, S 2004, 'Dialogue based public diplomacy: A new foreign paradigm?', in D Kelly (ed.), *Discussion papers in diplomacy, no. 95*, Netherlands Institute of International Relations Clingendael, Netherlands, viewed 28 October 2016, <http://www.clingendael.nl/sites/default/files/20041100_cli_paper_dip_issue95.pdf>.

Searson, EM & Johnson, MA 2010, 'Transparency laws and interactive public relations: An analysis of Latin American government websites', *Public Relations Review*, vol. 36, no. 2, pp. 120-126.

Trammell, KD 2006, 'Blog offensive: An exploratory analysis of attacks published on campaign blog posts from a political public relations perspective', *Public Relations Review*, vol. 3, no. 4, pp. 402-406.

Wallin, M 2013, 'The challenges of the internet and social media in public diplomacy', *American security project*, viewed 12 January 2016, <https://americansecurityproject.org/ASP%20Reports/Ref%200112%20-%20Challenges%20of%20the%20Internet%20and%20Social%20Media%20in%20PD.pdf>.

Links

Weibo, <http://www.weibo.com/u/1743951792?topnav=1&wvr=6&topsug=1&is_all=1>.

An opinion leader and the making of a city on China's Sina Weibo

10

Wilfred Yang Wang

Introduction

> *Diaoyu* Islands are China's, but Guangzhou is ours!
>
> (*Diaoyu Dao shi Zhongguo de, er Guangzhou shi WoMen de!*)

The territorial dispute between China and Japan over the *Diaoyu* Islands (the *Senkaku* Islands in Japanese) in September 2012 triggered nationwide protests.[1] Since Guangzhou was one of the main protest sites, thousands of people from other parts of China travelled there to launch their campaign against Japan. However, the protest turned violent as protesters damaged private and business properties in Guangzhou. In responding to these disruptions, some local commentators launched a Weibo [microblog] campaign to boycott the anti-Japan protest to protect Guangzhou from chaos and disruptions. The phrase '*Diaoyu* Islands are China's, but Guangzhou is ours!' was the

---

1   Since the focus of this chapter is China, I will use the Chinese term '*Diaoyu* Islands' instead of the Japanese term '*Senkaku* Islands'.

campaign slogan.[2] Many Guangzhou's Weibo users were quick to follow by re-posting the message to their own networks.

This chapter examines the role of an opinion leader on Sina Weibo who conducted the online campaign that countered the nationwide anti-Japan protests in Guangzhou. Specifically, I focus on those online practices by the opinion leader and his followers which have reproduced the sense of locality of Guangzhou, the southern Chinese city near Hong Kong and Macau.

Current literature has established that the communication process in public communication is indirectly mediated through a few individuals — opinion leaders — who present their knowledge, expertise and authorities over the issue at hand in order to facilitate public engagement and participation (Katz 1957; Katz & Lazarsfeld 1955; Gökçe et al. 2014). However, Sassen (2011, p. 574) argues that contemporary political practices are increasingly related to 'the production of "presence"'. In other words, the formation of the publics and the reproduction of place are intricately connected, and this spatial-public dialectic redefines the role of opinion leader in the digital era. After determining one local media commentator as the opinion leader during the event, I ask two specific things. First, how did the opinion leader exploit Weibo's platform and Guangzhou's inhabitants' experience of place in order to construct himself as a spatial subject rather than merely as a 'political leader'? Second, how did he mobilise his Weibo followers to 're-make' Guangzhou during a period of hypernationalism in China?

In order to develop the line of inquiry that connects opinion leader, locality and digital media, I draw on the relational characteristic of place to examine Guangzhou's experience: the meaning of the city is undergoing constant rebuilding and changes. Because of factors such as Guangzhou's economic role in facilitating China's economic reforms since the late 1970s (Vogel 1989) and its geocultural affiliation with Hong Kong (Fung & Ma 2002) and the overseas Chinese communities (Faure 2007), the city has developed a distinctive local identity. These factors guide my analysis in the following ways. First, I provide a conceptual discussion about the notion of place and city below. Specifically, I draw on an interdisciplinary approach to develop a framework that focuses on the digital formation of local place in China. Following that, I frame the anti-Japan demonstrations in relation to Weibo use, and locate the social controversies caused by the demonstrations against China's asymmetric spatial arrangements. I then make a brief note on the research methods I have used. Finally, I discuss the role of the opinion leader in facilitating the sense of locality and place in Guangzhou.

---

2 This phrase was used by local mainstream media including the state-run *Guangzhou Daily*, which used this phrase in their official Weibo account on 18 September 2012 (http://www.weibo.com/1887790981/yCoKg96PI?from=page_1002061887790981_profile&wvr=6&mod=weibotime&type=comment#_rnd1474524387853) to call for rationality and calmness in the anticipated anti-Japan demonstrations in Guangzhou.

City, place — A brief overview

This chapter builds on two conceptual premises to develop an interdisciplinary approach. First, I draw on cultural geographers' concept of relational ontology to emphasise the pluralistic and transformative natures of a geographic place — such as that of Guangzhou. This is not new, as geographers generally conceive that a place has to be understood in relation both to its broader structural transformations (Relph 1976; Harvey 1969, 1989; Castells 1989, 2009), and to people's bodily practices and daily routines (de Certeau 1984; Kekou 2013). The intellectual origin I draw upon here is therefore similar to Kennedy et al.'s emphasis on the processual qualities of place as discussed in their chapter in this book (Chapter Twelve), seeing place as a site of discourse contestation and power interactions. In other words, even though a place is geographically fixed, its meanings shift over time. Second, I also accept that the communication process is mediated and filtered through a few individuals — opinion leaders (Katz & Lazaersfeld 1955). Opinion leaders present their knowledge, expertise and authorities over the issue at hand in order to enact public engagement and participation (Wright 2006; Dubois & Gaffney 2014).

These two approaches intertwine with each other in the sense that while they can complement each other's limitations, in doing so they also critically expand the conceptualisation of collective actions in a digital era. First, the study of geography is an inquiry into the multiple communicative processes that produce and disseminate geographic knowledge. Since public communication is always mediated by a small number of individuals, the dissemination of geographic knowledge has likewise always been processed by a handful of individuals/institutions — through, for example, textbooks, mass media and other cultural and social institutions. In the case of China, geographic knowledge and information are either mediated by social institutions such as school (Judge 2002), by online communities (Wang 2015), or by grassroots creative artists (Liu & Cai 2014). In the same vein, communication facilitated by opinion leaders is spatially defined. These individuals exert their authority and influence in relation to the social experience and cultural expression of the physical place. The knowledge and expertise of any given opinion leader are not universally applicable or recognised. In other words, opinion leaders are not merely political figures who represent a certain class ideology; they are essentially spatial subjects who narrate the lived experience for — and to — a spatially defined audience.

By synthesising the two approaches in relation to China, I am informed by William Hurst's (2008) study on Chinese laid-off workers' collective actions. In learning about the framing and discourse used by the protest leaders of laid-off workers' movements across China, Hurst (2008) identifies three different regional political economies (regional frames) which are used to mobilise and frame collective actions. As a result, the modes of action and the ways that protesters perceive potential gains or costs in seeking redress also differ across China. Hurst (p. 86) points out that 'specific lived experience of otherwise unconnected individuals shapes worldviews in important ways'. In other words, there are no universal 'working-class struggles' across China; instead, protest leaders in different regions 'localise' their framing rhetoric to enact different modes of collective movements, which carry different sets of demands and pursuits.

Hurst's study is telling, as it indicates that opinion leaders do not merely incite shared class-grievances; they 're-map' local people's collective memories and knowledge of the physical place to determine the mode, requirements and tactics of their actions. Henceforth, it seems as though any collective action is essentially an embodying process that encapsulates the experiential dimension of a place (Prieto 2011). Since the experience of place 'can be either real or imagined', the meanings of a physical place are being 'constantly reinterpreted and reclassified' (Sen & Silverman 2014, p. 3). In the same vein, de Certeau (1984, p. 93) states that a city is 'defined and created' by its citizens' mundane everyday practices. 'Walking', for example, is an elementary form of physical motion which we practise to experience the city (p. 94). Such bodily movements and physical motions map our knowledge of, and personal networks within, the spatial structure (de Certeau 1984) and bring us into different places (Casey 1993).

To think about de Certeau's illustration of the bodily mapping of a city in a digital context would require some clarification. While it is true that these embodiment practices are now increasingly 'digitised' (Kekou 2013), to simply conceive that digital media have provided the 'space' (Zheng 2007) and the 'resources' (Eltantawy & Wiest 2011) for us to perform these practices is problematic. It might instead be worth considering how digital media enact new bodily practices that enrich and complicate the embodiment of geography (Farman 2012). Digital media have primarily subsumed some of the duties of our bodies in mapping and making places — duties such as walking. The navigation and imagination of the physical location are increasingly expressed through the transmission and dissemination of data in the form of textual and audiovisual materials (Graham, Zook & Boulton 2012). However, these data are locally specific as our bodily practices, spatial movements and physical motions in the material world continue to define, characterise and attach meanings to these digital representations.

The digitisation of embodiment will facilitate new interpretations, dynamics and cultural understanding, thus inventing new bodily practices to be performed and carried out in a physical sense. These practices, as Farman (2012, p. 36) puts it, dissolve our sense of the virtual into the material world; they enact what he terms as 'the transformation of space into place', so that the virtual representations (re)produce our actual sense of the physical surroundings (p. 40). Farman (2012) links his arguments to Casey's notion of emplacement (1993), which emphasises the 'situational characteristics' of our sense of place. In other words, information is *non-transferrable* universally (Farman 2012, emphasis in the original, p. 42) but we (as social agents) 'contextualise' the information in accordance with different situations. The job of contextualising the knowledge and information rests on the shoulder of opinion leaders. As discussed, public communication is always mediated through the opinion leader who needs to renarrate and reproduce the sense of a place in order to foster the collective bodily practices of place remaking.

China's spatial politics and the anti-Japan demonstrations

The event of anti-Japan demonstrations was a result of a series of diplomatic disputes between China and Japan over the maritime sovereignty of the *Diaoyu* Islands, offshore of Taiwan, in 2012. The tipping point came as the Japanese government issued a formal statement claiming its acquisition of three of the islands in the region on 11 September (Fujimura 2012). The timing, however, coincided with the anniversary of the Mukden Incident — Japan's conquest of part of northeast China on 18 September 1931, which marked the beginning of its invasion of China during World War II. In 2012, Chinese people took their anger to the internet to call for street protests. In responding to the online campaign, more than 60 000 people staged protests at more than twenty-eight major Chinese cities (including Hong Kong) on 15 September (BBC Chinese 2012). However, many people did not protest in their local city but travelled to different major cities to voice their anger, one of those cities being Guangzhou.

Although the protests were initially peaceful, they later turned violent, as some protesters allegedly committed violent acts, including smashing Japanese-brand cars, shop fronts and even stealing properties from Japanese-owned shops. In Guangzhou, major business districts became paralysed and public transportation experienced major disruptions due to the protest and its related violent activities (Spegele & Nakamichi 2012). Protesters threw rocks to smash the windows of the luxury and heritage Garden Hotel because it hosts the Japanese consulate (Wu 2012).

While the issue in contention was that the protesters had seriously disrupted the lives and social order of Guangzhou, the city has a long history of struggle with the central state governed by the Chinese Communist Party [CCP] over the issues of cultural identity and geosubjectivity (Faure 2007; Wang 2015). China has one of the world's oldest and most enduring systems of territorial hierarchy, which can be dated back to the Han Dynasty (from 206 BC to 220 AD); this hierarchy was arranged vertically to ensure that imperial decrees and central policy guidelines were disseminated throughout the district, the county and the township (Oakes & Schein 2006; Wang 2005). Such a spatial arrangement aims to 'prevent power from slipping from centre to the periphery' (Whitney 1970 in Wang 2005, p. 10). The CCP then adopted this spatial administrative and ruling philosophy when it came to power in

1949. A Chinese local place is deemed to serve the agenda and interests of the national subject, rather than being able to assert its own subjectivity (Judge 2002).

In the case of Guangzhou, since the city is the 'transferring terminal' for millions of migrant workers moving to the Pearl River Delta region (Vogel 1989), the rapid economic and demographic changes underpin constant social tensions between locals and outsiders over employment, social security and even family stability (Cheung 2002). Further, Guangzhou's geolingual proximity with Hong Kong also ensures that it has developed a distinct local identity for itself. However, local identity can be problematic for the CCP, as it can fall outside of the agenda of nation building and nationalism. This was evident, for example, when the government attempted to abolish Cantonese broadcasting on television in 2010 (Wu 2010). The proposal triggered thousands of citizens of Guangzhou to protest on the street (2010). The CCP's cultural policy over time is a form of displacement (Relph 1976), which refers to the conquering of place as modernity displaces traditional folk traditions. In contrast, the formation of a place-centric identity and the project to renarrate those places are examples of efforts to counter what de Certeau (1984, p. 161) terms the expansion of the '"techno-structural" urban landscape'. In doing so, the geo-embodying process provides the moral justifications (purpose) and the contextual knowledge (information) needed to operationalise collective practices and movements (Farman 2012), which both are facilitated by, and enable the emergence of, opinion leaders.

A note on method

I collected two sets of Weibo posts as data from Guangzhou between 15 September and 18 September 2015 — during and after the weekend of the anti-Japan demonstrations. The first set of data helped to determine opinion leader(s), as I had little knowledge about who the individual(s) would be at the time of research. The second set of data helped me to gain insights into the opinion leader's practice and his interactions with followers in mapping Guangzhou's local values and identity.

I collected the first set of data through searching for two different but related key phrases:

1. 'Guangzhou is ours' (广州是我们的) — this was the campaign slogan
2. 'Anti-Japan' (抗日) — this was a broader reference to the incidents at the time.

I utilised Weibo's advanced search function, which offers the filtering options of 'time range' and 'location' to generate those Weibo entries from Guangzhou posted from 15 September to 18 September 2012. I retrieved 15 766 entries (original posts and comments) by searching the first key phrase and 4412 posts (original posts and comments). I followed established typologies which focus on the regularity of posting (Graham & Wright 2013) and the response rate in the forms of 're-post' and 'comments' (Cha et al. 2010; Bruns & Burgess 2012) at a particular time and space (an event) to determine the authority and potential influence of individuals. In relation to Weibo, Zhang and Pentina (2012, p. 316) further state that opinion leaders should display strong awareness of civic rights to provide moral judgments to controversial issues. This of course, relates to China's one-party political structure and the limited freedom of political expression (King, Pan & Roberts 2013).

By following these typologies, I determined that Chen Yang, a local media commentator, was the opinion leader during the anti-Japan demonstrations in Guangzhou. He has 267 414 followers[3] and posted regularly during the anti-Japan demonstration weekend — thirty-five entries in total, or more than eight entries per day. Excluding the most popular entry (posted at 02:45am on 16 September 2012), his entries on average were re-posted 2462 times and received 195 comments during the research period. These figures outperformed the average number of re-posts (7.5 re-posts) and comments (20.6 comments) of other opinion leaders in the data. Further, Chen's most well-received entry was re-posted 44 211 times, receiving 210 'likes' and 9615 replies (comments). In other words, this post alone accounts for more than 50 per cent of the total number of re-posts and comments in the dataset.

Having determined Chen as the opinion leader, I generated the second set of data by collecting all of his thirty-five entries during the research period. I then specifically focused on the fifteen entries he posted on 18 September 2012, the peak of the nationwide demonstrations. On average, each entry was re-posted more than 418 times and received more than 195 comments. I also collected all of the 9615 replies to the most well-received entry in order to examine the interactions between Chen and his followers. The remainder of this chapter discusses my major findings in relation to the formation of Chen as a spatial subject and his role in facilitating the bodily practices of remaking Guangzhou on Weibo.

Discussion

As the purpose of this chapter is to understand Chen's role in facilitating the formation of a local *public* through the reproduction of the *place* of Guangzhou during the controversies of the hypernationalistic sentiment in 2012, it is important to unpack the nature of an opinion leader in relation to Weibo's platform. Chen's status as an opinion leader was both platform-orientated and socially constructed. Since its launch in 2009, Weibo has been a 'celebrity forum' that preferences the views and opinions of established and well-known public figures (Wang 2015). Weibo has both verified and non-verified users. Verified accounts (V-accounts) affirm the social status and political power (both mainstream and grassroots) of certain individuals. Such accounts have gone through an identity verification process by submitting proof of identity

---

3   As of 23 April 2016, when I accessed his blog <http://weibo.com/fm1052chensir>.

(China's Identity Card, a passport, or documentation that proves the legitimacy of an organisation) to Weibo in order to be endorsed, and thus are generally perceived as more trustworthy (Huang & Sun 2014). The views expressed, and the information provided, by V-accounts normally attract more online traffic and attention than non-verified accounts. Consequently, V-accounts generally have more followers than non-verified accounts (Huang & Sun 2014). This fosters a culture on Weibo in which users are inclined to 'follow' established public figures (Zhang & Pentina 2012).

However, Weibo users are highly selective in the V-accounts they follow. Chen's Weibo posts during the research period actually outperformed the entries posted by such public accounts as the local police (@GZpolice), news outlets and other verified individual accounts. This is probably because Chen has been critical of the mainstream establishments in China, which is consistent with the view that an opinion leader generally works outside of the mainstream political institutions (Gökçe et al. 2014).

Chen's perceived detachment from the establishment relates to his ongoing efforts to construct himself as a spatial, local subject of Guangzhou rather than as a loyal media personality who follows the party line. In other words, Chen's status as an opinion leader is socially constructed and culturally embedded. This is illustrated through his Weibo account name, 'Guangzhou Chen Yang', which explicitly emphasises his association with the local city as part of his online persona. Chen's 'offline' reputation of being a critic of the local and state government's wrongdoings over time (RFA 2009) further reinforces his subversive persona. Chen hosts current affair programs at Guangzhou Television and writes columns for the *Southern Metropolis Daily* — one of the most well-known news outlets pursuing investigative journalism in China (Zhao 2008). He generally conducts his television programs in Cantonese instead of in the official Mandarin. This is in defiance of Article 21 of the State Administration of Radio, Film, and Television [SAPPRFT] code, which asserts that 'broadcasting hosts shall be the role model to actively promote the popularization of Mandarin, use standard and correct form of written Chinese, and defend the integrity of the motherland's spoken and written language' (Liu 2004). Chen's defiance not only reinforces his 'non-establishment' status but also allows him to facilitate the formation of a geopublic through the transmission and circulation of his Cantonese broadcasting.

As a result, Chen has received widespread public support in Guangzhou, with many Guangzhou citizens calling him 'Chen Sir'. The English word 'Sir' means 'teacher' and 'mentor', which, in contemporary Cantonese, is an expression of respect. Public support for Chen was evident when there was speculation that he had been axed from his regular television program because of making critical remarks against party officials (RFA 2009). In response to the development, thousands of posters with the phrase 'Chen Sir, I support you!' suddenly appeared across Guangzhou's streets and online forums (Southern Weekly 2009) in support of him.

By thinking of Chen as a spatial subject, whose authority and expertise are locally defined and embedded in Guangzhou's geography, we can understand his Weibo presence through the perspective of emplacement. As previously mentioned, the formation of a public is closely related to the creation of people's collective sense of geo-belonging. This involves the integration of bodily practices and digital media use. As I collected all of Chen's Weibo entries during the anti-Japan demonstrations weekend (15-18 September 2012), it became obvious to me that Chen mapped the spatial progressions and movements of the anti-Japan demonstrations on Weibo.

On 18 September at 19:03, for example, Chen posted: 'Just walked past some mass gatherings, and saw that people were communicating with each other through some walkie-talkie devices … [T]hey were all speaking in Mandarin!'[4] Later on, at 19:35, he re-posted a Weibo update from the Guangzhou police's Weibo account stating that 'a large crowd was gathering in the area near the zoo (a central city area), causing traffic delays'. Chen added his comments in the re-posting: 'Please beware and co-operate with the traffic police's jobs. Pray for our city!' Later on in the evening, at 20:33, he posted: 'Our [Guangzhou's] police have finished the cleanup of the demonstrations areas, which should put an end to the whole thing! Good job!' Towards the end of the evening, at 21:04, Chen questioned the demonstrations:

> So these protest brigades have been marching from Huanshidong Road [the main drive way in the western district] to Tianhe [an eastern district], circulating the entire Guangzhou. They created so much traffic chaos and inconveniences; can't they just stay at one place so we can express patriotism [*aiguo*] and live normally [*shenghuo*] at the same time?

These entries not only illustrate Chen's active presence on Weibo, but also show that in posting his entries he was effectively mapping Guangzhou in relation to the events. His entries became the new 'maps' of Guangzhou, which provided guidance and direction for locals to help them live through unexpected changes in their situation. These entries also underpinned Chen's strong awareness of the particular affordances Weibo has as a platform. While re-posting is a common feature that users (including Chen) used to disseminate news and information, it is worth noting that Chen has also made use of Weibo's portable feature (available as an app on smart phones) to maintain his regular posting. This is evident from the data as Weibo posts contain information on 'posting source' (*laiyuan*). Three out of the five entries mentioned above were posted via Chen's smart phone, and eighteen out of his thirty-five entries (over the research period) were posted via his smart phone.

We can thus contend that Chen's 'on-the-move' style of Weibo posting during the anti-Japan demonstrations constructs what McQuire (2008, pp. 146-7) calls 'the

---

4   Chen's posts were originally written in Chinese. All translations in this chapter are provided by the author of this chapter.

mobile public'. The public no longer stays at a specific location but has the flexibility to 'move' with the temporal and spatial developments of the events (the demonstrations) and the issues (the chaos and disruptions). This is not to say that the public becomes placeless; to the contrary, the making of the public now relies on the circulation and dissemination of the networks, which are enabled by the bodily practices of posting, recording and navigating on Weibo.

In addition to his own online mapping of the demonstration, Chen further utilised these techno-bodily practices to interact with his followers. As mentioned elsewhere, Chen's most well-received entry from the datasets was posted on 16 September 2012 at 02:45. The post reads as follows:

> Please do not describe those protesters on the street as 'patriots'; they are not emotionally charged and doing stupid things (destroying Japanese goods and shops in Guangzhou). They in fact knew very well what they were doing, and had everything planned in advance. Dear fellow Guangzhouers [*jiefang*], if any of you see them on the street, take a step back and photograph them (as evidence). Let's isolate them from the protesting scenes, so we know exactly who they are. *Diaoyu* Islands are China's, Guangzhou is ours. Please be safe, Guangzhou [*Guangzhou pingan*].

In this entry, Chen not only reconstructed the chaotic scenes, which resulted from the damage done by the protesters (whom he called the 'fake patriots'), but also called upon his followers to 'photograph' those who had caused troubles as a way to defend Guangzhou inhabitants' rights and ownership of their hometown.

In order to access his followers' response to these suggestions, I generated a sample of 990 posts from the 9615 comments through a systematic sampling method (every ninth post is sampled). The words *Pai* and *Zhao* (both mean 'photograph') were mentioned fifty-four times in the sample. Some Weibo users even made quite detailed suggestions about how to take photos of violent protesters. A Weibo user (16 September 2012) suggested:

> Use your smart phone to capture the image of those people; if you can, take a few more pictures with an SLR Camera as it can produce higher image quality, showing their faces, and then put on the internet for a human flesh search![5]

Another user posted at 12:48 on 16 September 2012, agreeing: 'Do not just *weiguan* [surround and look], but take and upload a photo of them, to make their face public, to let their friends and family know how ugly their actions are!' Not only have these responses reaffirmed Chen's opinion leadership status, but they have also clearly responded to his call for action. Such comments illustrate the convergence of Weibo's platform features and Guangzhou's society as Chen has effectively exploited Weibo's

---

5   Human flesh search (*renrou sousuo*) is a collective online practice to 'track down offline individuals by employing as many computer users as possible in the search' (Herold 2011, p. 129).

functions of visualisation and archiving to gather and foster collective response and participation.

The practice of photographing has two layers of implication. First, photographing enabled people to visualise Guangzhou's streets in order to provide needed geographic information and knowledge about the development of the nationalistic demonstrations. Second, the practice of photographing enacted the extended practices of 'archiving' and 'searching'. Boyd (2010) identifies four primary affordances of social media: persistence, replicability, scalability and searchability. These four types of affordances allow textual and audio-visual data to be preserved and transmitted across time and space. Photographing, as a bodily practice in a physical place, penetrates these four technical affordances of Weibo, as images can be stored (persistence), re-posted and shared (replicability) in order to enlarge the visibility of the campaign (scalability). Further, the practice of photographing allows extended techno-bodily practices of human-flesh search (searchability), as suggested by some of Chen's followers. The formation of a Guangzhou public at the time could be what Boyd (2010) calls the 'networked public', which was enabled by those bodily and digital practices initiated by Chen.

The integration between bodily and online practices shows that the virtual and the physical are not mutually exclusive but, to use Farman's (2012, p. 46) words, they are 'mutually constructed'. The mapping and visualisation of Guangzhou could not have happened without Weibo, but Weibo's platform features would have become meaningless and irrelevant without the lived experience of the city. Chen therefore did not 're-map' Guangzhou himself, but he mobilised his Weibo followers to use their physical bodies to remake Guangzhou collectively.

Conclusion: Renarrating China

Despite the anger and discontent evident on Guangzhou's Weibo, it is crucial to clarify that there was no suggestion that Guangzhou inhabitants thought anything other than that China's territorial ownership of the *Diaoyu* Islands was correct. In fact, Chen and most of his followers on Weibo clearly expressed the very strong view that the territorial sovereignty of the islands was critically important in developing a sense of pride for the Chinese identity. Hence, the formation of a geopublic in Guangzhou is not equivalent to a peripheral identity. Many of those comments in support of Chen's suggestion to 'photograph' those irrational protesters made the point that Japan and its people would not have suffered, because the shops and cars were the properties of Chinese and the Japanese firms employed Chinese people. In other words, the process of remapping Guangzhou was not a matter of simply rejecting the overarching national identity; instead, it emphasised Guangzhou's local interest in *parallel* with the overarching expression of nationalism.

The paradoxical treatments of the anti-Japan demonstration in 2012 as expressed by Guangzhou Weibo users (including Chen) seemingly illustrate Tilly's (2010) account of the 'ambivalent' state-city relation. While individuals living in the city seek protection and stability from the state, the state also relies on the resources of the city in order to prosper, develop and maintain its ruling legitimacy. The symbiotic relations between the two allows ongoing renegotiations to take place, as the two progress together in an evolving relational process. This ambivalent state-city relationship might have defined Chen's and his followers' practices on Weibo. Recreating Guangzhou became a process of renarration of the Chinese nation, thus presenting a vision and an interest that are alternative to those imposed by the nation-state.

This chapter has explored Chen's role as an opinion leader on Weibo in facilitating the formation of a geopublic in Guangzhou, amid the expansion of the nationalistic movement network in 2012. Chen's capacity to manipulate Weibo's technological affordances and the lived experience in Guangzhou enabled him, first, to construct himself as a spatial subject of the city and, second, to construct a geopublic that contested and questioned the legitimacy of a state-imposed notion of nationalism. The online practice of (re)posting, archiving, uploading and searching evolved into the bodily practices of photographing, observing and mapping the city. Such techno-bodily embodiment encapsulates Guangzhou's local values on the one hand and the national agenda of border sovereignty on the other. It has thus effectively renarrated an alternative vision of nationhood, one that differs from the state-imposed version.

References

BBC Chinese 2012, 'Internet users in the mainland China continue to call for anti-Japan demonstrations (Dalu Wangmin Jixu Haozhao Juxing Fanri da shiwei)', *BBC Chinese*, viewed 21 August 2014, <http://www.bbc.co.uk/zhongwen/simp/chinese_news/2012/08/120818_china_protest_japan.shtml>.

Boyd, D 2010, 'Social network sites as networked publics: Affordances, dynamics, and implications', in Z Papacharissi (ed.), *A networked self: Identity, community, and culture on social network sites*, Routledge, New York, pp. 39-58.

Bruns, A & Burgess, J 2012, 'Researching news discussion on Twitter', *Journalism Studies*, vol. 13, no. 5-6, pp. 801-814.

Casey, ES 1993, *Getting back into place: Toward a renewed understanding of the place-world*, 2nd edn, Indiana University Press, Bloomington.

Castells, M 1989, *The informational city information technology, economic restructuring and the urban-regional process*, Blackwell, Oxford and Cambridge.

Castells, M 2009, *The power of identity: The information age: Economy, society and culture, Volume II*, Wiley-Blackwell, Hoboken.

Cha, M, Haddadi, H, Benevenuto, F & Gummandi, KP 2010, 'Measuring user influence in Twitter: The million follower fallacy', in *Proceedings of the Fourth International AAAI Conference on Weblogs and Social Media*, Association for the Advancement of Artificial Intelligence, Washington DC, pp. 10-17.

Cheung, P 2002, 'Guangdong under reform: Social and politicla trends and challenges', in J Fitzgerald, *Rethinking China's provinces*, Routledge, London, pp. 125-152.

de Certeau, M 1984, *The practice of everyday life*, University of California Press, Berkeley.

Dubois, E & Gaffney, D 2014, 'The multiple facets of influence: Identifying political Influentials and opinion leaders on Twitter', *American Behavioral Scientist*, vol. 58, no. 10, pp. 1260-1277, DOI: http://dx.doi.org/10.1177/0002764214527088.

Eltantawy, N & Wiest, JB 2011, 'Social media in the Egyptian Revolution: Reconsidering resource mobilization theory', *International Journal of Communication*, vol. 5, pp. 1207-1224.

Farman, J 2012, *Mobile Interface Theory: Embodied space and locative media*, Taylor & Francis, New York.

Faure, D 2007, *Emperor and ancestor state and lineage in South China*, Stanford University Press, Stanford.

Fujimura 2012, *Press conference by the Chief Cabinet Secretary*, excerpt, 10 September, viewed 12 October 2013, <http://japan.kantei.go.jp/tyoukanpress/201209/10_p.html>.

Fung, A & Ma E 2002, 'Satellite modernity: Four modes of televisual imagination in the disjunctive socio-mediascape of Guangzhou', in SH Donald, M Keane & Y Hong, *Media in China: Consumption, context and crisis*, Routledge Curzon Press, New York, pp. 67-79.

Graham, M, Zook, M & Boulton, A 2012, 'Augmented reality in urban places: Contested content and the duplicity of code', *Transactions of the Institute of British Geographers*, vol. 38, no. 3, pp. 464-479.

Graham, T & Wright, S, 2013, 'Discursive equality and everyday talk online: The impact of "Superparticipants"', *Journal of Computer-Mediated Communication*, vol. 19, no. 3, pp. 625-642, DOI: http://dx.doi.org/10.1111/jcc4.12016.

Gökçe, OZ, Hatipoğlu, E, Göktürk, G, Luetgert, B & Saygin, Y 2014, 'Twitter and politics: Identifying Turkish opinion leaders in new social media', *Turkish Studies*, vol. 15, no. 4, pp. 671-688, DOI: http://dx.doi.org/10.1080/14683849.2014.985425.

Harvey, DD 1969, *Explanation in geography*, Hodder & Stoughton Educational, London.

Harvey, DD 1989, *The condition of postmodernity: An enquiry into the origins of cultural change*, Blackwell Publishers, Cambridge, MA.

Herold, DK 2011, 'Human flesh search engines' carnivalesque riots components of a "Chinese democracy"', in DK Herold & P Marolt, *Online society in China: Creating, celebrating, and instrumentalising the online carnival*, Routledge, Hoboken, pp. 127-145.

Hirokawa, T 2012, 'China calls on Japan to release arrested island activists', *Bloomberg News*, viewed 12 October 2013, <http://www.bloomberg.com/news/2012-08-15/japan-arrests-14-for-landing-on-island-claimed-by-china.html>.

Huang, R & Sun, X, 2014, 'Weibo network, information diffusion and implications for collective action in China', *Information, Communication & Society*, vol. 17, no. 1, pp. 86-104.

Hurst, W 2008, 'Mass frames and worker protest', in KJ O'Brien (ed.), *Popular protest in China*, Harvard University Press, Cambridge, MA, pp. 71-87.

Judge, J 2002, 'Citizens or mothers of citizens? Gender and the meaning of modern Chinese citizenship', in M Goldman & EJ Perry, *Changing meanings of citizenship in modern China*, Harvard University Press, Cambridge, MA, London, pp. 23-43.

Katz, E 1957, 'The two-step flow of communication: An up-to-date report on an hypothesis', *Political Opinion Quarterly*, vol. 21, no. 1, pp. 61-78.

Katz, E & Lazarsfeld, PF 1955, *Personal influence, the part played by people in the flow of mass communications*, Transaction Publishers, Pscataway.

Kekou, E 2013, 'Cities in digital format', *Technoetic Arts: A Journal of Speculative Research*, vol. 11, no. 3, pp. 263-271.

King, G, Pan, J & Roberts, ME 2013, 'How censorship in China allows government criticism but silences collective expression', *American Political Science Review*, vol. 107, no. 2, pp. 326-343.

Liu, C & Cai, X 2014, 'Performing Guangzhou and Guangzhou Ren: Analysing popular music in Guangzhou', *Social & Cultural Geography*, vol. 15, no. 7, pp. 769-785, DOI: http://dx.doi.org/10.1080/14649365.2014.924156.

Liu, H 2004, 'Code of professional ethics of radio and television hosts of China (Zhongguo guangbo dianshi boyinyue zhuchiren zhiye daode zhunze)', *State Administration of Press, Publication, Radio, Film and Television of the People's Republic of China*, viewed 29 September 2016, <http://www.chinasarft.gov.cn/articles/2005/02/07/20070920151122290946.html>.

McQuire, S 2008, *The media city: Media, architecture and urban space*, Sage Publications, London.

Oakes, T & Schein, L 2006, 'Translocal China, an introduction', in T Oakes & L Schein, *Translocal China: Linkages, identities and the reimagining of space*, Taylor and Francis, Hoboken, pp. 1-35.

Prieto, E 2011, 'Geocriticism, geopoetics, geophilosophy and beyond', in TT Robert, *Geocritical explorations: Space, place and mapping in literary and cultural studies*, Palgrave MacMillan, New York, pp. 13-27.

Relph, E 1976, *Place and placelessness*, Pion Limited, London.

RFA 2009, 'Guangzhou's famous TV host Chen Yang disappeared from his usual show leads to suspicions (Guangzhou Zhuming Jiemu Zhuchiren Chen Yang zai Jiemuzhong Xiaoshi re Caiyi)', viewed 22 February 2016, <http://www.rfa.org/mandarin/yataibaodao/chenyang-01082009093805.html>.

Sassen, S 2011, 'The global street: Making the political', *Globalizations*, vol. 8, no. 5, pp. 573-579.

Sen, A & Silverman, L 2014, 'Introduction to embodied placemaking: An important category of critical analysis', in A Sen & L Silverman (eds.), *Making place: Space and embodiment in the city space and embodiment in the city*, Indiana University Press, Bloomington, pp. 1-18.

'Sina Weibo: "China's Twitter", files for IPO', 2014, *Hindustan Times*, viewed 2 May 2014, <http://www.hindustantimes.com/technology/socialmedia-updates/sina-weibo-china-s-twitter-files-for-ipo-in-us/article1-1195375.aspx>.

Soja, EW 2010, 'Cities and states in geohistory', *Theory and Society*, vol. 39, pp. 361-376.

Southern News 2012, 'Traffic control lasted for nearly 10 hours in Guangzhou (Guangzhou Duochu Jiaotong Guanzhi jin 10 Xiaoshi)', viewed 22 September 2016, <http://gd.sina.com.cn/news/b/2012-09-19/07349304>.

Southern Weekly 2009, 'Chen Sir, Guangzhouers support you! (Chen Sir, wo cheng ni!)', viewed 22 September 2016, <http://www.nbweekly.com/news/people/200912/11201. aspx>.

Spegele, B & Nakamichi, T 2012, 'Anti-Japan protests mount in China', *Wall Street Journal*, viewed 12 October 2013, <http://online.wsj.com/news/articles/ SB10000872396390443720204578000092842756154?KEYWORDS=pan asonic+china+protest&mg=reno64-wsj&url=http%3A%2F%2Fonline.wsj. com%2Farticle%2FSB10000872396390443720204578000092842756154. html%3FKEYWORDS%3Dpanasonic%2Bchina%2Bpr>.

Tilly, C 2010, 'Cities, states, and trust networks: Chapter 1 of cities and states in world history', *Theory and Society*, vol. 39, no. 3-4, pp. 265-280, DOI: http://dx.doi.org/10.1007/s11186-010-9119-z.

Vogel, EF 1989, *One step ahead in China Guangdong under reform*, Harvard University Press, Cambridge, MA.

Wang, J 2005, 'Introduction: The politics and production of scales in China — How does geography matter to studies of local, popular culture?', in J Wang, *Locating China: Space, place, and popular culture*, Taylor and Francis, Hoboken, pp. 1-30.

Wang, WY 2015, 'Remaking Guangzhou: Geo-identity and place-making on Sina Weibo', *Media International Australia, Incorporating Culture & Policy*, vol. 156, pp. 29-38.

Wright, S 2006, 'Government-run online discussion Fora: Moderation, censorship and the shadow of control', *The British Journal of Politics and International Relations*, vol. 8, no. 4, pp. 550-568, DOI: http://dx.doi.org/10.1111/j.1467-856x.2006.00247.x.

Wu, WT 2010, 'Flash public activity at Guangzhou's People's Park: "I sing Cantonese for Guangzhou" (Guangzhou Renmin Gongyuan Xian "wowei yueyu dasheng chang" huodong)', *ifeng.com*, viewed 11 October 2016, <http://news.ifeng.com/mainland/ detail_2010_07/26/1830865_0.shtml>.

Wu, Z 2012, 'Beijing faces protests dilemma', *Asia Times online*, viewed 22 September 2016, <http://atimes.com/atimes/China/NI19Ad02>.

Zhang, L & Pentina, I 2012, 'Motivations and usage pattern of Weibo', *Cyberpsychology, Behaviour and Social Networking*, vol. 15, no. 6, pp. 312-317.

Zhao, Y 2008, *Communication in China: Political economy, power, and conflict*, Rowman & Littlefield Publishers, Lanham, MD.

Zheng, Y 2007, *Technological empowerment: The internet, state, and society in China*, Stanford University Press, Stanford.

Public audiencing: Using Twitter to study audience engagement with characters and actors

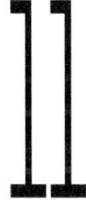

11

Kim Barbour

Introduction

In this volume, we speak to the making of publics. One of the ways that publics are made is through research, where the researcher defines the inclusion and exclusion of different individuals and groups when creating their sample. Audience research makes publics in two ways: the researcher defines the target population, and from within that population, individuals come together to identify as audience members. This necessarily complicates the process of determining how different audiences engage with different types of media products, as the views, behaviours and responses of those who are either excluded by the researcher, or who exclude themselves, are not represented in the research process. An ongoing issue in primary qualitative research, engaging with members of an audience — however nebulous or fractured that audience might be — without inconveniencing the participants of the research process has been facilitated in recent decades by access to online forums, discussion boards and social media streams, where collected views and behaviours can be studied 'in the wild'. Although these spaces are used by only a fraction of the viewers of any particular film, television show or concert, the ability for researchers to make a 'public' of these viewers gives us new ways to engage with audience research.

In this chapter, I present the preliminary results of an investigation into the way audience members of fictional television shows engage with actors and characters via Twitter. I propose that Twitter use by audience members makes visible an everyday practice that has yet to be fully acknowledged by research — that is, the way that we hold both the actor and the character in our heads while watching television, simultaneously acknowledging the 'realness' of both. To illustrate this proposal, I am using data collected during the first broadcast of the television drama *Love Child*, Season Two, on the Channel Nine network in Australia.

This project was designed to test a personal observation of Twitter user behaviour during the final season of *True Blood* (HBO). While following the live tweets of fans during the broadcast of the show in the United States, I realised that Twitter users were not only tagging the characters' official Twitter feeds[1], but often the actors' personal Twitter handles as well. The audience was engaging and acknowledging the actors and characters simultaneously. As audience members watching a television show, we hold in our heads the characters and their associated personality traits and personal histories, while at the same time we recognise the actors, with their personality traits, personal histories, and, I argue, all their previous roles and characters that we have encountered. Our capacity to suspend disbelief only goes so far, particularly within the confines of our well-lit homes, with all of their corresponding distractions to our attention. I will also argue that it is possible that in splitting our attention through the use of a second screen, we are more likely to hold multiple identities of character and actor in our heads while we watch and tweet.

Audiencing

Highfield, Harrington and Bruns (2013) define audiencing as 'the public performance of belonging to the distributed audience for a shared media event' (p. 336), while Cubitt (2005) describes it as 'the work that audiences do when they use media' (p. 80). We can therefore understand audiencing as more than the simple act of watching a show on television, or attending the screening of a film. Rather, audiencing is the public display of those activities, the claiming of one's place as a member of the audience. Fiske (1992) introduced this concept in relation to people deliberately gathering to watch a particular show (*Married... with Children*), stating that 'it was an attempt to get glimpses of culture in practice' (p. 356). This audience 'can only exist when hearing something' (p. 358), and prior to the widespread ubiquity of internet access, could only be studied through shared physical spaces. According to Highfield et al.'s

---

1 HBO set up feeds for each of the main characters — a kind of in-world fantasy Twitter.

and Cubitt's definitions above, the agency of audiencing has been transferred from the researcher to those performing as part of the audience. This 'performance' or 'work' of audiencing is happening increasingly publically — rather than watching a show together with friends, as studied by Fiske (1992), viewers share the experience with unknown, imagined communities online through the use of hashtags.

If we define a 'fan' of a media product as someone who displays 'an intense interest, affection, and attachment for the object of their fandom ... distinguished from non-fans through their respect, desire and commitments' (Lanier & Fowler 2013, p. 285), then many forms of audience engagement would necessarily be excluded from studies that focus on fandoms and fan practice. Public audiencing is useful as a framework for gaining insight into the way viewers engage with elements of a media text without soliciting or directing the discussion. Additionally, unlike the intensity of fan activity, the more mundane activities observed in briefly coalescing collectives of unknown individuals who may or may not have an ongoing relationship with the text in question can be studied by framing the behaviour as audiencing rather than as a 'fan practice'.

Tweeting television

Studying Twitter practices in relation to TV shows has taken a range of approaches and focuses. Buschow, Schneider and Ueberheide (2014) investigated social TV, and compared the different types of communicative activities by people tweeting while watching different types of shows. They state: 'While talent shows produce expressions of fandom and critiques of the candidates in the show, live events evoke a critical debate about the show itself and what's happening on screen. Political talk shows can stimulate a public discourse' (p. 129). All three of these show types fall into the category of reality TV, or non-fiction programming, so the connection between the character on screen and the 'actor' overlaps almost completely. Similarly, Giglietto and Selva (2014) studied the tweeting behaviour of the audience of Italian political shows, and their research showed that the types of tweets broadcast connects to the types of behaviour and discussion seen on the shows: where presenters, interviewees or participants presented personal opinion as fact, so did the social media responses. Quintas-Frouffe and González-Neira (2014) looked at the connection between the success of Spanish talent shows and Twitter usage by judges and contestants, while Wohn and Na (2011) have analysed Twitter use during synchronous television watching as a form of social interaction between people with similar interests who are not co-located. Again, the shows that are investigated in both these research projects are either reality/talent shows, or political broadcasts.

In Australia, Highfield et al. (2013) conducted a comprehensive study of audience tweets during the Australian broadcast of the Eurovision Song Contest in 2012 (in which Australia was not competing), alongside international Twitter use. Their study showed how Twitter had become 'an unofficial extension of the event, through which audiences can engage in direct, many-to-many communion, conversing, and connecting with other fans throughout Europe and around the world' (p. 318). Although the Highfield et al. study looked at live-tweeting a televisual event, their focus was on the fans' interactions with one another rather than directly with performers.

One project that did study the ways audience members used Twitter to engage with a fictional television show was Wood and Baughman's (2012) investigation of *Glee* fandoms. Here, the authors looked at the ways that members of the fandom are engaging with characters to continue the narrative beyond the broadcast episodes. This included setting up accounts in the character's name, and tweeting as the character. Sometimes this would be in relation to what was broadcast on the show itself but would extend beyond this, when the fan-controlled character handles would continue to tweet during the off-season, or between episodes. This is similar to the in-world Twitter accounts set up by HBO for *True Blood*, but differs in that the accounts are run outside the control of the writers and directors of the show.

Equally interesting for engagement with fictional television programs is the study of the fan practices of *The West Wing* (Hickman 2013). Similarly to Wood and Baughman's (2012) study of *Glee* fandoms, these studies explore how fans continue the diegetic world outside the boundaries of the program by performing the characters through Twitter. Hickman (2013) notes that the research 'focuses on Twitter accounts that represent characters from a show that is no longer in production' (p. 221), demonstrating that these Twitter users demonstrate a significant, ongoing attachment to the characters within the fictional world which is sustained not only between episodes, but also beyond the run of the show itself. The intensity of this attachment is well beyond the more casual or banal engagement analysed below.

Despite the variety of projects investigating the use of Twitter as a way to engage with television programs, research into the audience's use of *actors'* twitter handles is noticeably absent from the literature, as is discussion of the overlap between real-world and fictional-world references in individual tweets. This small study engages with that gap in the research. As outlined above, through Twitter we are able to see and study a practice that has likely always existed. This is not a case of social media changing the way we engage with television, but rather exposing or surfacing audience interaction with actors and characters as they watch a fictional world unfold. What is argued here is that through Twitter, this process of interaction is made visible, even normalised, through the incorporation of hashtags and handles that incorporate both the characters' and actors' names.

Indeed, some characters become so intrinsically linked to a particular actor that it is difficult to see them in another role, and this is described below as *character bleed*. This is related to, but distinct from, typecasting in the early Hollywood studio system described by Harris (1991), who looks at the way the images of Marilyn Monroe and Grace Kelly were carefully crafted through personal narrative and film role choice. It is also close to the translation of Patrick Stewart's fame across format boundaries as detailed by Jenkins (1992), where fans of Picard in *Star Trek* followed Stewart to theatre and to film. Similarly, Ralph and Barker (2015) identify audience members' reading of an actor's skill level on the basis of prior knowledge through their study of responses to *The Usual Suspects*. These studies provide a background to my reading of the Twitter interactions of fans of *Love Child*.

Audiencing *Love Child*

Nine Network's *Love Child* is an Australian historical drama, with the first season set in late 1969 and Season Two beginning on New Year's Eve and New Year's Day, 1970. This chapter focuses on Season Two, which screened on Australian broadcast television in a Tuesday 8.40 pm (Australian Eastern Standard Time) timeslot from 5 May to 23 June 2015. The show follows the lives of the staff and patients of the fictional Kings Cross Hospital and the subsidiary Stanton House, a home for unwed pregnant women. The story tells of the lives of those involved in the practice of forced adoption, common at the time in Australia, where young unmarried women had their newborn babies taken from them based on a presumption that they were unfit mothers and unable to care for the children by virtue of their age, marital status and supposed loose moral standards.

Through Season Two, the narrative focused on different members of the ensemble cast. Most often, the character of Dr Joan Miller, played by Jessica Marais, was central, as she negotiated life and relationships as a professional woman, along with the guilt of losing a patient. Each week, one of the young pregnant women in the cast would give birth, suffer a setback or otherwise become central to the narrative. During Season Two, there were a stillbirth, unexpected twins, an ongoing custody battle, a wedding, acknowledgement of the racist attitudes of the time towards Indigenous Australian peoples, death, assault, kidnappings and bribery, plus a look at the growing feminist movement of the time, when one of the characters discovers author and activist Germaine Greer.

For the purpose of this analysis, a particularly cogent point is that many of the actors on *Love Child* are recognisable to an Australian commercial television audience. Jessica Marais (Dr Joan Miller) played Rachael Rafter on *Packed to the Rafters* (2008-13), while Matt Le Nevez (Jim Marsh) was the romantic lead, Dr Patrick Reid, on *Offspring* (from 2010). Miranda Tapsell (Martha Tennant) starred in the 2012 film *The Sapphires* (2012), while Jonathan LaPaglia (Dr Patrick McNaughton) would be familiar to watchers of Australian dramas *The Slap* (2011) and *Underbelly: Badness* (2012). Other actors involved in the show have had roles in long-running Australian series such as *Home and Away*, making them recognisable faces prior to joining the cast of *Love Child*.

In order to capture Twitter data for analysis, I used the online application TweetDeck to capture all tweets with specific search terms (usually names), Twitter handles or hashtags, taking screenshots and saving the image files. I focused on those tweets that deliberately joined the live broadcast public conversation about the show by including #lovechild, but also followed specific actors' handles — @missmirandatap, @JessicaMarais, @ellaschmo, @JMcKenzie, @harriet_dyer, @hensoir, @mattlenevez — as well as the official Twitter account for the show, @9LoveChild. This ensured that I captured tweets aimed directly at the actors, as well as those that were referencing the characters and the show more generally.

In total, I gathered seventy-two tweets from forty-six distinct users, a comparatively small sample for this type of study. However, the purpose of this investigation was not to collect all tweets about the show, but rather to look at particular types of behaviour. Episodes One and Two showed the smallest number of relevant tweets (four), while during Episode Three I captured sixteen tweets — this episode had two deaths, with a stillborn child and the death of a lover from the first series both garnering attention from live-tweeting viewers. On average, I captured around ten tweets an episode for the remainder of the series. From a data collection perspective, the shifting nature of the narrative simplified the collection of tweets during a live broadcast — most members of the Twitter audience were focused on one character/actor within the cast each week, and tweeted largely about their story.

Actor handle, out-world content

The first behavioural element relates to audience members talking directly to, or about, the actors, as separate from their onscreen characters. This occurred most in the first episode of the season, when the character of Gail died shortly after giving birth. The character was played by Tessa James, familiar to the audience through roles on *Home and Away* and *Neighbours*, as well as through her well-publicised relationship to Gold Coast Titans player Nate Miles. James had been undergoing treatment for Hodgkin's lymphoma, a fact that has been widely reported on in tabloid newspapers and magazines (AAP 2015; Fairfax Media 2014; HelloMagazine 2014; Ravn 2015). Her appearance in Episode One of *Love Child* therefore garnered her some Twitter attention that referenced her cancer treatment:

> Tessa James was amazing tonight in #LoveChild, loved seeing her acting again #StrongWoman #FighterSurvivor.

> I think tessa james is on lovechild I'M SO HAPPY IF ITS HER SHE LOOKS SO HEALTHY.

James is not a Twitter user herself, but fans still tried to connect with her by tagging her husband instead:

> Amazing seeing Tessa James back on TV tonight for #lovechild . Looking great! @nate_myles.

Considering the plot of this episode, the separation of character and actor here is particularly telling: the fans clearly distinguished between the character of Gail, who died, and the actor James, who 'was amazing', 'looks so healthy' and was 'looking great'.

Another tweet connects back to the idea of in-world and out-world content combining together:

> Loving the fact that @lincolnyounes1 has made the jump from @homeandaway to @9LoveChild #LoveChild.

Here, the tweet is referencing the actor's movement between shows, without referencing the character that he played in either space. This connects the actor to the two shows (through the use of the official handles for both) but does not reference the characters that the actor played in either.

Actor handle, in-world content

The second behavioural element I observed in tweets about *Love Child* reflected what I had seen within the *True Blood* fandom: that is, the tagging of actors' handles while tweeting responses to in-world situations on the show. This was a particularly common response, which itself has a few identifiable categories.

Although still speaking directly to the actor, three tweets referenced the story world and the actor's portrayal of a character. In one instance, the death of a favourite character from the first season was lamented, with the fan talking directly to, and tagging, the actor:

> @Ryan_Corr um excuse u, what are you doing dying on #LoveChild I refuse to accept this death. What the hell. Not ok. #longlivejohnny.

In a second example, the characters' decisions are questioned, while the actress is complimented, leading to an interesting blend of in- and out-world discussion in a single tweet:

> @ellaschmoo Shirley and the dr just doesn't feel right, but god damn girl, you rock the character Ella!! Xoxox.

And finally, this fan of the show is tagging the actors while actually speaking about their characters, collapsing the boundaries between fiction and reality further:

> Ohh can't wait for #JessicaMarais & @mattlenevez to get together on @9LoveChild #channel9 #LoveChild.

185

By utilising the affordances of Twitter, particularly through the use of the actors' Twitter handles, these fans are in essence speaking directly to the actors involved in the show. In the case of the first two, this is achieved by addressing their tweets firmly at the actors' accounts (by including the handle as the first element in the tweet); and in the second, the tweet tags the two actors involved — one through the use of their handle, and the other by the use of a hashtag of the actor's name as a replacement for the lack of a Twitter account.

A second subset of this type of behaviour sees the tagging of the actor as secondary to the content of the tweet, which is entirely focused on the story world. These tweets are commentary on the characters' behaviour in-world, while directly acknowledging the actors; in a sense, this could be read as a kind of critique, both of the actors' performances, but also of the writing of the show. One example again references the death of Season One favourite Johnny, played by Ryan Corr:

> I suppose ghost Johnny is better than no Johnny at all #lovechild @9LoveChild @Ryan_Corr.

Because of the placement of the actor's handle at the end of the tweet, this can be read as almost incidental, rather than an attempt to engage the actor in discussion. A connection is made to the actor, but it's not integrated into the flow of the text, nor does it substitute for a character's name. This was a recurring approach:

> Awww poor Patty, why doesn't she go to the club where Annie works or go to Annie's place? @9LoveChild @harriet_dyer #LoveChild.

In Episode Six, Miranda Tapsell's character Martha, a young Indigenous woman who worked in an administrative role at Stanton House, became the focus of a romantic storyline. Fans tagged the actor, with the tweeters supporting and praising the character while tagging actress Miranda Tapsell.

> When does Martha get a happy ending? When??? @missmirandatap #lovechild.

> Oh Martha you are so kind and giving and such a strong lady you don't deserve tobe treated like that @missmirandatap @9LoveChild #lovechild.

In contrast to the above tweets, where the actor is tagged after the comment, the following tweeter addresses their comment directly to both Miranda Tapsell and the official *Love Child* account, possibly in an attempt to engage in conversation about the show:

> @missmirandatap @9LoveChild Martha has the best one liners! And slaps. #carryingonlikeaporkchop #LoveChild.

By converting the character line into an extended hashtag, the tweeter not only saves valuable character space, but also transforms elements of the show into a Twitter-friendly format while locating his more general comment within the episode.

Character bleed

The final series of tweets discussed in this chapter relate to what I am calling *character bleed*. This occurs when an actor becomes well known in a particular role, and this role then bleeds into other performances. This is a risk for any actor in weekly television, but it's particularly so for actors in smaller markets such as Australia. The tagging practices of Twitter, along with the live nature of fan engagement with television shows through the use of Twitter as a second screen, make this process of character bleed visible.

> I can only see the guy who played Andrew Farriss, as Andrew Farriss #LoveChild.

This tweeter implies the process of character bleed directly. The tweet refers to the actor Andrew Ryan (handle @andyryansyd), who played musician Andrew Farriss in the television miniseries *INXS: Never Tear us Apart*. In *Love Child*, Ryan played Simon Bowdich, but for this tweeter, the *INXS* character has much greater resonance.

For other tweeters, it was Lincoln Younes's (@lincolnyounes1) participation on *Love Child* that was noticeable:

> Definitely weird seeing Casey Braxton on @9LoveChild @lincolnyounes1 #lovechild.

Casey Braxton was Lincoln's character on *Home and Away*. He left the show in 2014, so for regular audience members, he would still have been fresh in the mind as Casey. Indeed, this tweeter is inferring that the character Younes is playing on *Love Child* is being interpreted as his character on *Home and Away*; the second is being read as the first. The direct referencing of previous characters appeared frequently in these discussions, as can be seen in this more cryptic tweet about a *McLeod's Daughters* character:

> Harry was a shit in McLeod's Daughters and he's a shit in this too. #lovechild.

In this case, a significant amount of intertextual knowledge of Australian television was required to decode the message. Harry Ryan was actor Marshall Napier's character on *McLeod's Daughters*, and this tweeter is connecting that performance with Napier's performance as Greg Matheson, the most central villain of Season Two of *Love Child*. Another tweeter made a similar point the following week:

> Why does Marshall Napier always get the scheming two faced characters? #mcleodsdaughters #LoveChild.

In essence, the second tweeter is challenging what could be seen as typecasting of Napier, where his well-known character performances are similar enough to be readily identifiable as 'baddies'. It would be interesting to note whether this could affect Napier or other actors in similar positions, where the audience assumes new characters will fulfil the villain role, based solely on previous appearances in other programs.

Offspring vs *Packed to the Rafters*

Despite the fact that many of the cast of *Love Child* have worked on Australian staples *Home and Away*, *Neighbours* or *McLeod's Daughters*, the biggest character bleed related to two recently concluded shows: *Offspring* and *Packed to the Rafters*. Both these shows were warmly received by the commercial television audience, winning a number of Logie [Australian television industry] nominations and awards through their time on television. The casting of *Rafters* alum Jessica Marrais and *Offspring* leading man Matt Le Nevez as a potential couple in Season Two of *Love Child* was a fruitful area for character bleed. Rather than suspending disbelief and accepting the actors in their new roles, *Love Child* tweeters instead absorbed the existing narrative points into the new story. This was particularly true of fans of *Offspring*, likely because of the fact that fans were devastated by the death of Dr Patrick Reid (played by Le Nevez), who was the father of lead character Nina's baby and who died in a car crash in the lead-up to his wedding and the birth of his child. The fact that the character was written out of the show because the actor wanted to leave may have also made it harder for fans to let go of this beloved character.

Many tweeters resisted the movement of the actor from *Offspring* to *Love Child* by referring to Le Nevez's character as Patrick, his character's name on *Offspring*. They also connected Le Nevez's character's becoming a father on *Love Child* with the fact that this was not possible on *Offspring* due to his untimely death:

> at least patrick got to hold his child :'(#lovechild.

> And Patrick gets his baby at last. #lovechild.

One fan not only referred to Le Nevez's character as Patrick, but also referenced other parts of Le Nevez's background by asking where Nina was. This could be interpreted as a resistance to the possibility of a new romantic partner for a distinct character played by the same actor.

> Patrick on #LoveChild is confusing me. Where is Nina?

This could be confusing if you did not understand the intertextual reference to *Offspring*, as there is a character called Dr Patrick McNaughton (played by Jonathan LaPaglia) on *Love Child*, further complicating things.

In one of the few conversations between fans in these data, a tweet from an *Offspring* fan account commented on a plot point where Le Nevez's character had suffered a brutal beating in *Love Child*:

> Just caught up on #LoveChild seeing @mattlenevez being bashed up has ruined my Wednesday.

and another fan responded with:

> @[fanaccount] @mattlenevez Quite frankly, he deserves it for going and dying on Nina like he did! #damnyoupatrick.

Essentially, the second tweeter is saying that Le Nevez's bashing on *Love Child* is in some way retribution for his character's death on *Offspring*, leaving Nina to raise their child without him. Here, not only is the character's behaviour or expected role in the show linked back to prior roles played by that actor (as with Marshall Napier above), but plot elements are also connected together. However, this plot point also led to the most direct acknowledgement of character bleed in action, with a tweeter connecting together the two characters with the actor through the use of their personal names:

> Totally can't handle seeing Patrick/Jim/Matthew all banged up like that, brings back painful memories #LoveChild #Offspring #stillhurts.

This tweet demonstrates that the tweeter is simultaneously seeing and reading the past character of Patrick from *Offspring*, the present character of Jim in *Love Child*, and the actor Matthew Le Nevez, and that the older character informs and drives her reaction to the characters and plots in the present show.

Another example of this idea can be seen in a fan's acknowledgement that the character *has* changed, but her affections have not:

> Even though Patrick is not Patrick in #LoveChild I still love him like I loved Patrick.

This could be understood as a form of affective transfer here. The bleed of one character into another means that audience identification and acceptance are simplified — the transference of the affection towards a character that built up over many years streamlines the acceptance of the new character into a different fictional environment. However, for those who cast well-known faces who have played beloved characters in other shows, there are risks — fans may feel that their emotional involvement with the former character deserves recognition in the way the plot of the following show writes the story of the newer character. For example, here fans are voicing fears, echoed a number of times, that *Love Child* will kill off the character of Jim as *Offspring* killed off the character of Patrick.

> OK @9LoveChild you are not allowed to kill off @mattlenevez got it? Good #LoveChild.

> They're going to kill off Patrick (I mean Jim) again, aren't they? NOOOOOOO #sopredictble #offspring #LoveChild.

As the narratives became more closely aligned — Le Nevez's character plans to get married in *Love Child* as he had in *Offspring* — a fan commented on the differences between the plots: Joan agrees to marry Jim (*Love Child*), in contrast to Nina refusing Patrick (*Offspring*):

> At least Joan said yes…while Nina unexpectedly said no;) #Offspring #LoveChild.

Other fans turned the connection between the two shows into a joke:

> I'm confused. Who's that woman marrying Patrick? #lovechild.
>
> [in reply] Remember in Rosanne when Becky was replaced and played by a different actress? Well this is the new Nina …

Again, the first tweet makes the connection between *Love Child* and *Offspring*, while the second deepens the bleed between the two shows, by alluding to the character of Joan as a replacement for Le Nevez's character's prior romantic partner.

The final connection between Australian television dramas was made in relation to this wedding, introducing a prior role of Jessica Marrias (Rachel Rafter, in *Packed to the Rafters*), connecting it to the prior role of Le Nevez:

> So Rachel Rafter and Patrick Reid are getting married. #LoveChild #Livinginthepast.

Here, not only is the tweeter alluding to prior characters played by the actors, but also connecting disparate stories together in the third space of the *Love Child* plot. This displays the simultaneous recognition of multiple plots, characters and actors, and the capacity to connect them together in an interesting way.

Tweeting as audiencing in public

As the findings of this small study indicate, Twitter gives researchers a way to explore the ways that audiences of fictional television shows understand and read actors and characters across a range of performances. In particular, the analysis identifies three key behavioural elements: direct address to the actors, either inside or outside the diegetic space; tagging actors while referencing character behaviour; and character bleed. In a sense, Twitter has allowed researchers to get a feel for what I have no doubt has always occurred in private during television shows. Indeed, Fiske (1987) described the capacity of both audience members and professional critics to understand the 'realness' of both character and actor in his important book *Television Culture*. Fiske states that 'the fans and the literary or dramatic critics both retain, even if in a suppressed form, the awareness of the difference between a character and a person: the illusion of realism is only as complete as we allow or wish it to be' (p. 152). Fiske argued that television actors are distinct from other media stars of the time because they are frequently on the screen, through weekly or daily programming — they 'have a familiarity that offers their fans a much more intimate, equal role' (p. 150).

As discussed at the outset of this chapter, the tweets included in this study are conceptualised as a form of audiencing, of publicly claiming membership of the audience of a shared media event. Audience members tweet their thoughts, playing along with the show in the comfort of their homes, drawing on their pre-existing knowledge of actors and characters to joke around with the narrative. In doing so, they give audience researchers insight into the complex interpretative processes we use while watching TV. The tweeters do this publicly; their tweets are designed, through the inclusion of the #lovechild tag or the @9LoveChild handle, to join the public discussion of the show, even if only in the manner of a stream of consciousness.

In the collection of this dataset, the study of the everyday engagement with fictional television is facilitated by the affordances of Twitter as a second screen. The conversations, throwaway comments and in-jokes all contribute to an understanding of how viewers of *Love Child* are able to engage with multiple narratives simultaneously, smoothly transitioning between seeing the character on screen, the actor as a person, and the roles that actor has previously played. The playfulness visible in many of the tweets included above demonstrates the inherent creativity and interpretative nature of the act of watching television, even if one is not invested sufficiently in the program in question to be considered a 'fan'. This capacity to study the everyday, the banal, and the ephemeral engagement with fictional television through the use of Twitter or other second-screen applications offers scholars of audience studies many opportunities to further examine the continuing role of small-screen fictional narratives.

References

AAP 2015, 'Celebrities get behind Tessa James', *The Advertiser*, viewed 24 March 2016, <http://www.adelaidenow.com.au/news/breaking-news/celebrities-get-behind-tessa-james/story-fni6ul2m-1227066987948>.

Buschow, C, Schneider, B & Ueberheide, S 2014, 'Tweeting television: Exploring communication activities on Twitter while watching TV', *Communications: The European Journal of Communication Research*, vol. 39, no. 2, pp. 129-149.

Cubitt, S 2005, 'Consumer discipline and the work of audiencing', in S Cohen & RL Rutsky (eds.), *Consumption in an age of information*, Berg Publishers, Oxford, pp. 79-96.

Fairfax Media 2014, 'Tessa James returns to Australia following cancer diagnosis', *The Sydney Morning Herald*, viewed 24 March 2016, <http://www.smh.com.au/lifestyle/celebrity/tessa-james-returns-to-australia-following-cancer-diagnosis-20140922-10k7gj.html>.

Fiske, J 1987, *Television culture*, Methuen, London.

Fiske, J 1992, 'Audiencing: A cultural studies approach to watching television', *Poetics*, vol. 21, no. 4, pp. 345-359.

Giglietto, F & Selva, D 2014, 'Second screen and participation: A content analysis on a full season dataset of Tweets', *Journal of Communication*, vol. 64, no. 2, pp. 260-277.

Harris, T 1991, 'The building of popular images: Grace Kelly and Marilyn Monroe', in C Gledhill (ed.), *Stardom: Industry of desire*, Routledge, New York, pp. 40-44.

HelloMagazine 2014, 'Former Home and Away star Tessa James battling cancer', *Hello!*, viewed 24 March 2016, <http://www.hellomagazine.com/celebrities/2014092121051/home-and-away-actress-tessa-james-cancer-battle/>.

Hickman, J 2013, 'Continuing *The West Wing* in 140 characters or less: Improvised simulation on Twitter', *Journal of Fandom Studies*, vol. 1, no. 2, pp. 219-238.

Highfield, T, Harrington, S & Bruns, A 2013, 'Twitter as a technology for audiencing and fandom', *Information, Communication & Society*, vol. 16, no. 3, pp. 315-339.

Home and Away 1988-, television series, Seven Network, Sydney, Australia.

Jenkins, H 1992, *Textual poachers: Television fans & participatory culture*, Routledge, New York.

Lanier, CDJ & Fowler, ARI 2013, 'Digital fandom: Mediation, remediation, and demediation of fan practices', in RW Belk, & R Llamas (eds.), *The Routledge companion to digital consumption*, Routledge, London & New York, pp. 284-294.

Love Child 2013-, television series, Nine Network Television, Sydney, Australia.

McLeod's Daughters 2001-09, television series, Nine Network Australia, South Australia.

Offspring 2010-14, television series, Network Ten Australia, Melbourne, Australia.

Quintas-Froufe, N & González-Neira, A 2014, 'Active audiences: Social audience participation in television', *Comunicar*, vol. 22, no. 43, pp. 83-90.

Ralph, S & Barker, M 2015, 'What a performance! Exploring audiences' responses to film acting', *Participations: Journal of Audience & Reception Studies*, vol. 12, no. 1, pp. 739-761.

Ravn, M 2015, 'Former Home and Away star Tessa James celebrates final chemotherapy treatment', *Gold Coast Bulletin*, viewed 24 March 2016, <http://www.goldcoastbulletin.com.au/news/gold-coast/former-home-and-away-star-tessa-james-celebrates-final-chemotherapy-treatment/news-story/43eb6b3259a12400c00c46d17614b079>.

True Blood 2008-14, television series, HBO, California, USA.

Wohn, DY & Na, E-K 2011, 'Tweeting about TV: Sharing television viewing experiences via social media message streams', *First Monday*, vol. 16, no. 1, viewed 7 February 2015, <http://firstmonday.org/ojs/index.php/fm/article/view/3368>.

Wood, MM & Baughman, L 2012, 'Glee fandom and Twitter: Something new, or more of the same old thing?', *Communication Studies*, vol. 63, no. 3, pp. 328-344.

Overcoming the tyranny of distance? High speed broadband and the significance of place

12

Jenny Kennedy, Rowan Wilken, Bjorn Nansen, Michael Arnold and Mitchell Harrop

Introduction

In 2009, the Australian federal government decided to fund the construction of the National Broadband Network, or NBN. At a total projected cost of A$44 billion, it was the largest engineering and public infrastructure project in Australia's history, with the intention of laying 200 000 km of fibre optic cable to the doors of 93 per cent of Australian premises. For the remaining 7 per cent of people, who lived in rural and remote areas, wireless and satellite would replace fibre. However, in 2013, this fibre-to-the-premises [FttP] model was subsequently replaced by a much slower, hybrid model that used a mix of optic-fibre, co-axial cable and copper infrastructures alongside wireless and satellite in regional and remote areas (see Arnold et al. 2014 for installation history).

One of the stated key goals of the various plans for high speed broadband networks in Australia is to overcome the challenges of distance and the concomitant difficulties for transport implicit in distance. For example, in the initial scheme, the then Minister for Broadband, Communications and the Digital Economy, Stephen Conroy, signalled broadband-enabled benefits relating to social inclusion, economic productivity and geographic connectivity. He stated that 'every person and business in Australia, no-matter [*sic*] where they are located, will have access to affordable, fast broadband at their fingertips', and that high speed broadband [HSB] 'will help drive Australia's productivity, improve education and health service delivery and connect our big cities and regional centres' (2009). Australian geography has had a major impact on the history of telecommunications in the nation (see, for example, Given 2010). The National Broadband Network [NBN] has been promoted as a way of overcoming the 'tyranny of distance' experienced by people in remote and rural regions (Swan & Conroy 2011).

In this chapter, we seek to examine the dynamics of this process, exploring what high speed broadband infrastructure means for overcoming (or ameliorating the effects of) the 'tyranny of distance' for those living in regional and remote areas, and what HSB means for the social and material significance of these places. We are interested in examining how this distance is remediated and remade by NBN infrastructure, asking: What are people's *actual* experiences once they have subscribed to the NBN (especially in first-release sites) and have high speed broadband? Is the infrastructure of the NBN delivering on those early promises (especially given the switch of models)? And what implications does HSB use carry in terms of shaping the experience, meaning and significances of place (Stillman et al. 2010)? In thinking about place, digital infrastructure and social connection, we are also interested in the implications HSB has in terms of interaction with various publics (from the intimate publics of family and friends, to those involving local communities, to an array of wider networked publics), and the means of fostering and supporting these publics.

Methods

In responding to these questions, this chapter reports on data from a longitudinal research grant funded by the Australian Research Council [ARC], which brought together researchers from the areas of human and computer interaction, social studies of technology, and media and communication, to examine how HSB is configured in the production of place through the services provided by the NBN in Victoria, Australia. The project employed mixed methods to explore how the introduction of high speed broadband changes or affects the way people interact with media devices and technologies in the household (Nansen et al. 2015), and how HSB is configured in the production of place through the services provided by the NBN.

Over the life of the project there have been three waves of data collection, with each wave consisting of three methodological steps, in order to explore in depth the varied patterns of HSB appropriation within our sample households. Each wave commenced with a technology tour, where participants walked us through their home, describing the media devices and rhythms and routines of the household. The tour is an immersive strategy that provides us with contextual information about the existing media and communicative environment within the home. In addition to the tour, the second step we took was to interview the members of the household about their experience of high speed broadband and device use, thus extending insights drawn from the technology tour. The third methodological step was derived from the cultural probes method employed in the field of human-computer interaction. We extended this approach using digital media in order to collect situated snapshots of domestic technology use based around a number of playful media-oriented tasks. Each home was given an iPad mini. Participants used the iPad functions to take images and videos for tasks such as making a brief 'nature documentary', a 'news report', a 'diary room entry', or a 'chat show interview'. The second and third waves of data collection repeated these processes, building a diachronic profile of HSB appropriation and impact.

The data constructed in this project therefore consist of technology tour videos, media-rich entries, interview transcripts and observational notes, supplemented and interpreted in relation to data sourced from mass media, policy and commercial documentation, in order to represent the full complexity of high speed broadband appropriation and impact.

The ARC project study sample consisted of twenty-two technologically and geographically diverse households in Victoria, Australia, drawing out properties of connectedness and distinction. These were all early-NBN-release sites: Brunswick (inner urban); South Morang (suburban); Ballarat and surrounds (regional); and East Gippsland (rural). Technological differences in HSB access applied in relation to geographic locations: with fibre-to-the-premises available to homes in urban areas; fixed wireless available in regional areas not served by fibre-to-the-premises; and satellite in remote areas without access to wireless. Whilst each of these technology types had particular spatial implications, and different implications for place relations, which we will go on to describe, different connection infrastructures are not spatially exclusive: some households in our sample made regular use of more than one type of connection.

Fibre-to-the-Premises [FttP] refers to fibre optic cable deployed 'to the front door' of households. FttP has typically been implemented in selected inner-urban, urban and new developments in high-population regions. As a direct, material connection to each home, it is the most costly form of connection per household, but it also affords the best speeds. The inner-urban and urban homes in our study on the Australian government's NBN were connected via FttP. New housing developments in urban Ballarat also have FttP.

Fibre-to-the-Node [FttN] refers to fibre optic cable deployed to discrete neighbourhoods or blocks of premises. The fibre only goes as far as the principal connection. The 'last mile' of the connection to households is completed with existing copper cabling, which frequently has a lower speed and capacity than the equivalent cabling completed with fibre optics, but which is also available at a lower rollout cost. FttN is, at the time of writing, the preferred technology by the current Australian government for regions that would have been serviced with FttP under the former government. No houses in our sample were at the time of writing on FttN, though, given the present uncertainty about the FttN footprint to be delivered by the current NBN model, it is probable that future connections will be FttN.

Fixed wireless refers to broadband connection via radio signals conducted at ground level. The signal occurs between a ground station, similar to a mobile phone tower and an antenna or small dish on the receiving property. A transmission requires a line of sight from the tower to the property. Fixed wireless is typically installed in areas where it is not feasible to install FttP or FttN — that is, properties in rural areas, such as those outside Ballarat. The planning of the NBN rollout means that homes already connected to the NBN via fixed wireless in outer areas of Ballarat experience internet speeds far in excess of their urban counterparts yet to be connected to FttP or FttN. Despite Ballarat's regional hub status, it is still regional Victoria and there are assumptions of service limitations compared to Melbourne. Good fixed wireless coverage, however, is dependent on a clear line of sight from the radio signal tower to the property. For two of our participants in East Gippsland who live just 200 metres away from the closest tower, their house is in shadow, meaning that the house sits underneath the signal path and so, rather than fixed wireless, they have to connect to HSB via satellite.

Satellite broadband is used for only a small percentage of Australian homes, typically in the most rural and remote areas. Currently, households on satellite connections are on an interim service, with one new NBN Co. satellite launched in October 2015 — which, however, at time of writing, is yet to be connected to households. Homes with this connection type typically have satellite dishes installed on the roofs. While a direct line of sight is not required, satellites do need to be positioned accurately to receive the signal without interference.

Furthermore, each of these locations have particular socioeconomic characteristics, and, in order to contextualise the households we studied, the distinctions between these areas are summarised in Table 12.1. In this chapter, however, we are only concerned with exploring the last two of these four settings — the regional and the rural.

Figures 12.1 to 12.11 provide some examples of the settings in which our participants reside, and these images demonstrate varying proximities to other homes, servicing roads and infrastructures, and technological resources such as satellite or antennae.

Setting	Brunswick	South Morang	Greater Ballarat	East Gippsland
Distribution of sample households	6	6	5	5
Location type	Inner-urban	Urban	Regional	Rural
HSB type	FttP	FttP	Fixed wireless	Satellite
Size of area	5.2 km²	5.9 km²	740 km²	20 931 km²
Distance from state capital	6 km	23 km	115 km	280 km
Population	22 764	20 873	93 501	42 196
% employed	88.8%	89.8%	88.2%	84.1%
Median age	33	31	37	47
Average persons per household	2.3	3.1	2.4	2.3
Average weekly income per household	$1433	$1567	$988	$798
Number of homes occupied by owner	4632	5074	24 043	12 315
Number of homes rented	4417	1186	10 504	3922

Table 12.1: Technological, geographic and demographic distinctions between household locations, adapted from Australian Bureau of Statistics Census Data 2011.
Source: Australian Bureau of Statistics [ABS], 2016.

In many streets in Melbourne and other large towns in Victoria, houses are built in close proximity to one another. In the street shown in Figure 12.1, the houses have an FttP connection to the NBN. Decent roads connect the street to local amenities, the city centre, public transport and major highways.

Houses on the outskirts of regional towns, such as that in Figure 12.2, tend to be on larger blocks of land and may be several kilometres from their nearest neighbour.

These homes connect to the NBN through wireless connections. Homes may also make use of mobile internet services.

Regional roads have lower traffic volumes than do major roads connecting towns. Roads connecting hamlets of houses may be tarmacked like the one in Figure 12.3, while roads serving fewer properties are typically made of gravel. Regional townships are connected to other towns by tarmacked roads. Townships such as that pictured in Figure 12.4 have few amenities for residents, who must travel to larger towns to physically access goods and services. Railway lines run through regional townships (see Figure 12.5), but residents must travel to regional town centres to make use of railway services.

The rural homes we visited were in townships of no more than twelve other houses. Many of the roads into rural townships are gravel, and are pitted and difficult to navigate (see Figure 12.6). Each home is connected to the NBN by satellite, if it is connected at all. Figure 12.7 shows a rural home with a satellite dish on the roof. Although there are wireless towers at a workable distance, the typography of the local area means that these houses cannot connect directly (see Figures 12.8 and 12.9). Telecommunication structures make use of the affordances of the local typography, sometimes resulting in lines of sight being blocked between signal towers and houses, thus making preferable internet connection options impossible. Rural households have limited mobile internet access.

Rural townships are located in varying distances from larger towns, which provide many of the amenities and services residents require (see Figure 12.10). Some also provide transport links to other major towns and cities. The train station pictured in Figure 12.11 links the town and surrounding areas into Melbourne. In this case, the train journey into central Melbourne takes two and a half hours.

In this chapter, we are particularly interested in examining how HSB intersects with the other spatial elements that make regional and rural place meaningful for our participants. We take the standpoint that the uptake and appropriation of a technological infrastructure, such as HSB, is a process rather than a one-off event. We seek to examine the dynamics of this process — what HSB means for the 'tyranny of distance'.

Figure 12.1: A suburban street in Melbourne.
Source: J Kennedy, 2015.

Figure 12.2: A regional home in Victoria.
Source: J Kennedy, 2015.

Figure 12.3: An example of regional roads.
Source: J Kennedy, 2015.

Figure 12.4: A typical regional township of fewer than 200 people.
Source: J Kennedy, 2015.

Figure 12.5: Railway lines serve regional areas, connecting town centres to other town centres and larger cities.

Source: J Kennedy, 2015.

Figure 12.6: Example of rural roads.

Source: J Kennedy, 2015.

Figure 12.7: A rural home in Victoria.
Source: J Kennedy, 2015.

Figure 12.8: Visible telecommunication structures in the rural landscape.
Source: J Kennedy, 2015.

Figure 12.9: Visible telecommunication structures in the rural landscape.
Source: J Kennedy, 2015.

Figure 12.10: A rural town, with banks, a post office, pubs, supermarkets and local businesses.
Source: J Kennedy, 2015.

Figure 12.11: A rural train station.
Source: J Kennedy, 2015.

Connectivity and relational place

In developing this account of HSB, we draw on conceptions of place developed within human geography which emphasise relationality. A relational approach draws out the processual qualities of place — that it is something that is produced and, as such, 'ceaselessly changes over time' (Ek 2006, p. 51). According to a relational way of thinking, place can be understood, as Jeff Malpas (1999) suggests, as a bounded but open and contested site: a complex product of competing discourses, ever-shifting social relations, and internal (as well as external) events and influences. In this way, Malpas (p. 39) argues, any given 'place' is both a product of, and 'dependent upon[,] the interconnectedness of the elements within it' and on 'its interconnection with other places'. Or, as Steve Harrison and Paul Dourish (1996, p. 3) put it, our understandings and experiences of place derive 'from a tension between connectedness and distinction'. Nowhere is the tension between connectedness and distinction more apparent than in the socially, technically, economically and geographically varied Australian landscape.

According to Doreen Massey (1994, p. 154), one of the pioneers of this relational way of thinking, place is thus best understood as 'articulated moments in networks of social relations and understandings' which are both immediate in their impacts and also carry implications that extend beyond 'what we happen to define for that moment as the place itself'. This perspective emphasises the importance of thinking place both through, and in relation to, what Massey (2005, p. 181) terms a 'politics of connectivity' (here understood as connectivity between places, and between places and publics). While Massey refers to connectivity in a number of different senses (2005, pp. 181ff), it can be taken to include networked information and communications technologies, and the infrastructures that support them (see Rodgers 2004). It is in this context that we employ relational place as a productive concept for framing the ensuing examination of the increasingly crucial role that HSB infrastructure plays in mediating and shaping place-based experiences, interactions and interrelations (Massey 1992, p. 80), and in mediating and shaping the publics that form with, through and around these HSB-mediated experiences of place.

A key contribution of this chapter is to respond to criticisms that HSB provision and research on it tend to exclude those outside of metropolitan areas (Gregg 2010). Our approach in the broader research informing this chapter has been to conceive of the urban, regional and rural as 'topological spaces that are performed by particular networks and flows' (Cloke 2011, p. 568), including telecommunications networks and the various 'flows' (flows of communication, data and people) that are generated by, through and around this media infrastructure (Parks & Starosielski 2015).

The chapter aims to extend the work of Stillman et al. (2010) from the single context of the anonymised town of approximately 500, dubbed 'Wheatcliffs', to different regional and rural contexts (the urban sites in our research are not examined in detail in this chapter). Stillman et al. (2010) established five themes related to participant appropriation and negotiation of technology which are relevant here. These are summarised as follows:

- *distance and proximity* — finding place in relation to other places near and far
- *work and leisure* — making place, with convivial work and leisure energy expenditure
- *connection and disconnection* — between public and private realms, and between people, evidenced in different modes of connection/disconnection
- *technology access and exclusion* — parameters of sociotechnical choice, and acting strategically with choices
- *comfort and anxiety* — seeking control over sociotechnical to minimise negatives.

To pursue this argument, and to mobilise the above-mentioned themes, we focus on places that are regional and rural, what services facilitate or hinder residence in these places (distance and proximity), how these places are made through and in relation to everyday activities (work and leisure), and the issue of connection to others (connection and disconnection). Important to HSB in its contribution to the constitution of place is HSB infrastructure (technology access and exclusion), and the affective experience of all of the above for our informants (comfort and anxiety). What we are interested in, and seek to draw out here, is how place is constituted differently in each setting, especially as a result of the high speed broadband infrastructures provided in each place, and of the participants' experiences of these technologies in connecting to distributed places and publics.

The significance of connectedness

We take up the above concerns and explore them in relation to three properties of connectedness which have emerged from our study. These are

1.   connections to work

2.   connections to services

3.   connections to other people.

Each of these relations of connectivity is significant to our understandings and experiences of place, just as places are significant in constituting our connective relations.

Connections to work

Participants in the inner-urban and urban households predominantly worked outside the home, except for three households in which members ran a home business. Young professionals in inner-urban homes, like participants Riley and Ashley, commuted to work on public transport or made use of Melbourne's extensive bike lane network to cycle. Their journey times were under thirty minutes and there were multiple means of transport available to them. Those in the outer urban suburbs, such as Diane and Scott, typically drove to work. Work was twenty minutes away for Scott, and a 'good run into the city' for Diane took around forty minutes. Other households described similar car journeys to work, university or school in local areas. Few households made use of the railway line. Talaketu was the only person to mention making use of it. He commuted an hour each way from South Morang into the city each day. Those working in Melbourne's city centre mostly performed professional roles, while those working in the outer suburbs were employed in sectors ranging from retail, health services and education.

While many participants had opportunities to work from home, they only did so on a casual or ad hoc basis. Three exceptions were Malcolm, Dennis and Carl, each of whom ran a home business. Malcolm ran an urban regeneration organisation, Dennis worked as an interpreter, and Carl had recently established a new venture, running an affiliate marketing company selling advertising. All three had designated home office spaces, though Carl's was more makeshift than the others, as he used his stepdaughter's room while she was away studying. He saw this as sufficient until he had decided whether to continue with the venture, at which point he would make more appropriate working arrangements. Both Malcolm's and Carl's home businesses were assisted by HSB, enabling greater efficiencies through the running of multiple applications and faster upload speeds on which their business activities depended. Dennis's business, however, had been made more difficult as a result of access to HSB via the NBN. A steady form of income for him had always been Centrelink, a government service that provides assistance and benefits to their clients. Much of their correspondence is serviced by the legacy media of fax, but following his connection to the NBN, Dennis could no longer run his fax machine:

> I used to have one which worked on a combined line but that set-up isn't available on the NBN. I don't hear from Centrelink very often but they prefer to fax things. Centrelink are aware of NBN and are going to change their processes, but in the meantime they prefer to post things. It is too risky to scan. This is a bit of a drag, as Centrelink were a good provider of work. Not having access to a fax machine means less work through Centrelink. It was never a huge amount of work but could have been. (Interview with Dennis 2013)

For these inner-urban and urban households, place in relation to work was largely configured by connection to transport infrastructure rather than to internet infrastructure.

Working from home was much more common in the homes of our regional participants living on the outskirts of Ballarat, each of whom had a fixed wireless connection. Scott described himself as a 'cyber-commuter', sitting in his lounge room logging in via a VPN each day to servers in Europe. Through a 'local' company (some 100 kilometres away), he was contracted to a large mobile and tech company located in Europe to design and develop software. Working with multiple colleagues on different time zones, he conducted most meetings by telephone. Deborah also worked from home on a regular basis, providing administration support to a local farming business (typically fifteen hours per week). Her partner, Donald, ran a home pest-control business, which Deborah also helped with. Donald maintained the company website, and both of them responded to email enquiries about their services. The nature of Donald's work meant that he was away from the home for most of the day. Deborah also had an additional job working with livestock, so both of them were out of the home during all daylight hours. They typically spent time in the evening responding and making updates to the business website, or dealing with administrative duties.

Two further participants, Jackie and Craig, a couple in the same Ballarat area, also ran a home business. Having the office at home (Craig occupied the home office, while Jackie actually worked at the kitchen bench) complicated the division of work and family time. However, since having HSB, they reported fewer issues, as they could complete work tasks more quickly and give attention to other members of the family, placing less stress on family relationships, as their daughter Megan describes:

> I can sit down and watch a footy game with the family when I get home from work because with the NBN they have gotten their own work done quicker. It makes work/home life less stressful. (Interview with Megan 2013)

For these regional households, place in relation to work was configured by connections enabled via internet infrastructure rather than via transport infrastructure.

Living in urban Ballarat, in contrast to the outskirts of Ballarat, Michael and Angela had connections to work which were similar to those of the urban households in Melbourne. They rented a house in a newly developed suburb of Ballarat and had an FttP connection. In some ways, the suburbs of Ballarat are very much like the outer suburbs of Melbourne in terms of proximity to the workplace. Michael, a graphic designer who runs his own web design studio, used to work from home but moved to an office space in Ballarat's town centre, a couple of kilometres away, though working from home remained an option. Angela worked part-time for the local church, which she drove to twice a week.

For those participants living more remotely (our rural participants), working from home was a desired, but sometimes less than convivial, option, given the poor performance of satellite connections to HSB. For example, Donald lived with his wife Kara and their three children in a small town to the east of one of the National Parks that cover East Gippsland, after moving in 2013 from an outer suburb of Melbourne. They had been looking to move to the country, and when Donald's workplace moved locations (to the other side of Melbourne) he took it as an opportunity to change jobs. He began a new job working for a local food production company. Kara kept her job as a logistics manager for a Melbourne-based company and telecommuted, working in a designated office space in the family home. Because the home satellite connection was intermittent, Kara's company provided a 4G mobile wireless connection, which was strictly for work-related activities.

Another participant, Joan, also had her own office space in the home, and attempted to work from home when the satellite connection allowed. She taught at the TAFE [Technical and Further Education] College in Bairnsdale, some 100 kilometres away. However, to minimise commuting, she worked from home as often as the connection allowed. A further participant, Eliza, a manager in a government department, expressed her desire to work from home more often, but was unable to do so on the satellite connection she had at home. Though she had remote access to the department's file system, her work was often time-pressured, meaning that any latency or lag from satellite connection was detrimental:

> If the Prime Minister's office is chasing a document you've got to be able to go into the drive and quickly find stuff. Or, when parliament is sitting, you've got to do PPQ [possible parliamentary questions], which normally arrive at 8.30, and I have to write them by 10.30-11. I've got to have instant access to people and to the files. (Interview with Eliza 2013)

Further interviews in later waves of data collection reinforced the necessity of being connected at all times: 'People expect instant answers so it doesn't matter whether I'm working here or working in the office. The expectation is that you'll respond instantly' (Interview with Eliza 2015).

The necessity to have a fast connection meant that Eliza commuted into Melbourne's city centre four days a week and worked from home just one day a week. To reduce travelling time, she commuted in on Monday, stayed at her mother's in an inner suburb overnight, then returned home on Tuesday. Each Wednesday she worked from home, and each Thursday she commuted in and stayed at her mother's again. To make the commuting time-accountable and productive, she used the hours on the train in the mornings to go through her emails, and had normally caught up with emails by the time she got to work. Thus Eliza saw the time spent commuting as beneficial: the journeys home provided her with 'head space' from her demanding job, so she was refreshed by the time she arrived home. Her daughter, Dawn, similarly commuted into Melbourne to go to university. Living at a distance to university was less desirable for Dawn, who was 'forced' to live in East Gippsland due to lack of funds for living and studying closer to the city: 'I can't work enough hours to afford living in the city and go to uni. My brother didn't care for uni, he got a job and moved to the city' (Interview with Dawn 2013).

Of our rural participants, only one, Jaume, was running a home business. He operated a distributed cluster of computers, located across Europe, to conduct data crawling, which he leveraged into business opportunities. His office was located in a room in a neighbour's home; with a young family, it was often difficult for him to concentrate on work in his own home and so he found working outside of the home, albeit in another home, more productive.

Across these examples, connections to work were impacted directly but differently as a result of the specific configurations between geography and HSB technology provision and access. For regional participants of our study, connections to work were constituted principally in relation to, and were enabled by, HSB internet infrastructure. In contrast, for rural and more remote participants, these same connections were constituted in relation to both transport and internet infrastructure — both were important for rural/remote participants, because neither form of connection was adequate in and of itself.

Connections to services

Unsurprisingly, places in urban locations demonstrated greater proximity to consumption options and domestic services. For instance, when we visited the share-house of Christine, Shawn and Alexis, the housemates had just returned home from work and were having a drink and planning what takeaway to order for dinner. While we were in their home, Christine's grocery shopping arrived, which she had ordered online earlier that day. She preferred shopping this way as she found it easier to budget. Other urban households in our study made use of similar online purchase options, also facilitated by transport connectivity:

> I'm often at home during the day. Nysha's at work and I'm just going, 'oh, more of the internet arrived'. She will not rest until the entire internet is in the house. Every single physical object. I tend not to buy objects online. I tend to buy services. (Interview with Malcolm 2015)

Those in regional and rural areas also made considerable use of online purchasing options, which was enabled through the postal service. For example, Karl and Jean moved from Adelaide to Gippsland roughly ten years ago. The move was in part to set up 'the good life': living off the land, making food, and creating an income through crafted items. They regularly visited eBay and wine websites, and undertook internet banking. Via transport, their home was half an hour's drive to the nearest bank, and, in general, 'everything is at least half an hour away'. The result of this was that they viewed services such as online shopping and banking as a good thing.

While proximity of place to services is required to reduce travel time, and is generally regarded as convivial, for others the remoteness of place was desirable, in that it reduced having to interact or connect with a public of unknown others. For instance, for Deborah and Donald, HSB allowed items to be purchased online from home, avoiding a presence in town, affording an isolation they desired:

> I like isolation. I like the country, like not having to deal with people. I can't stand suburbia, the compact nature, there are too many people, it's too busy. Donald is the same. We like to be in the middle of nowhere, pottering around doing our own thing. (Interview with Deborah 2013)

While Deborah and Donald sought geographical and social isolation, Craig and Jackie's family valued the degrees of social interactions their home and HSB connection afforded. Having lived for a number of years in more remote parts of Victoria, when an opportunity to move closer to Melbourne, and support in terms of schools, infrastructure and family came up, they took it: 'We socialise in our own way. Not a particularly social person per se. We can all hold a conversation but we like our privacy'

(Interview with Craig 2013). Having HSB meant they could do away with many types of social situations which required impersonal communication, such as attending to business or personal matters through the local bank branch. Set on bushland not far outside the regional town centre, their home was a solace from such encounters.

Thus one of the most striking things to emerge out of the interviews with the regional households was the way in which HSB enabled their desire for isolation, and for connection on their own terms. In short, it offered flexibility. These households were already satisfactorily connected, and HSB enabled them to focus on the social connections and publics that were meaningful to them, rather than enabling opportunities for further encounters which they did not, in fact, desire. Even Dawn, who lamented that she was forced to live in a remote location, preferred to live without the 'noise' of neighbours: 'We don't have neighbours, which is great. I stayed with friends in the suburbs and you can hear neighbours talking, which is horrible!' (Interview with Dawn 2013). Isolation and connectivity would each appear to be ambivalent terms when considering the properties of place.

Connections to others

Another of the defining connections of place was the connection to family and loved ones — what we might call intimate publics. Each household defined its home and its place in terms of its proximity to family.

Certainly, some urban, regional and rural participants chose their home location based upon its proximity to family via transport. Diane and Scott purchased their house in South Morang because it was close to where they both grew up, and to where their families continued to live. Charles, a retired engineer who lived with his son Scott on a rural property approximately half an hour's drive outside of Ballarat, had selected the property with his late wife because it was centrally located to his children, who all lived a good distance away in other regional centres. For another couple, Donald and Kara, moving to East Gippsland meant living closer to family, their children's grandparents and related work opportunities.

Meanwhile, for others, communication technologies made up for a lack of proximity to transport. Udantika, who had family overseas, used Skype to talk twice a week to her mother. Angela's two boys, whose grandparents only lived a couple of hours away, used Michael's iPad to Skype their grandparents. And, for Joan, connection to HSB was a condition of her moving with Ivan from Canberra. She liked to keep in touch with family (she had two daughters living interstate, each with young children), and with friends interstate and abroad. However, she was unable to use Skype because of upload speeds; she could see and hear others, but they couldn't see her. Because the satellite connection was problematic for Skyping, they created a work-around: Joan found a mobile handset that worked with an external antenna, and Ivan erected a mobile aerial to the back corner of the house, which Joan connected to when making phone calls.

Of the participating households, Jaume and Erin, with their young family of three, had one of the more striking connections to local community. They lived in a community in East Gippsland of five or so households who shared external resources, such as produce and livestock, and collectively ordered fresh organic produce and maintained a local co-op. At one stage, the households also shared internet access, but with the introduction of data limit charges it became more problematic to distribute evenly, and so they reverted to individual household access.

The significance of place: Technology in action

The notion of relational place, outlined at the outset of this chapter, is productive for understanding the myriad factors guiding our participants' choices of location in which to reside. For some, decisions and ongoing experiences were characterised by familial connections; for others it was connection to work that was important in the relationality of place, while for others it was isolation, or the opportunity to disconnect from city life. Across all these households, key factors in these decision-making and experience-making processes were communications infrastructure and access to HSB, in relation to transport infrastructure and its implications for connectivity. What sociologist Manuel Castells (2011) famously called the 'space of places' was intertwined with the 'space of flows' in this decision making and experience. As this chapter shows, it is the relationality of HSB with other elements of place — transport, work, services and connection to different publics — that made it significant or meaningful.

HSB promises, however, to install important changes to the experience, meaning and significance of place (Stillman et al. 2010). For example, demonstrating the centrality of technology to the vitality and growth of regional and remote communities, Eliza talked about a local event she attended, called 'Connecting women across Gippsland', which brought together 600 women from regional and remote areas of East Victoria. One of the most striking aspects of the event for Eliza was the use of technology in facilitating the women's industriousness:

> It was about all of these businesses that women had created across Gippsland, unbelievable. There was one who has created a website for women travellers so women traveling alone [can] share homes across the world, but for a maximum of three days. She runs this from Bairnsdale or somewhere. There is a whole lot of food-based people selling their stuff online and there is one in Warringal [that's] grown to about 400 clients a week now. It's grown locally in South Gippsland, and there is a lot in the Far East. There were retreat centres, well-being-ness and I was just staggered.

They're all coming together and then, all of a sudden, you realise they were similar stories, but [technology] enabled them all to come together ... It was technology. Technology in action. (Interview with Eliza 2015)

Eliza observed the potential, but also the experiences of poor connectivity. Remote participants, especially, face extended delays and disappointments in getting the access they require. Progress in connection to NBN services is slow, with little communication from service providers as to when things will progress and even less faith in the current government's ability to implement the scheme satisfactorily:

Eliza: *My provider sent an email out ... [Y]ou could respond back saying if you're willing to be a test station as they calibrate the satellite or whatever. I said, 'Oh, yeah. Why not? I'm in this. I may as well do that'. Anyway, they contacted me a month or two ago and put another dish on my house ... and a box in the house. I don't believe we'll have access to it, but rather it'll be a test station.*

Interviewer: *So you won't actually be able to make use of it?*

Eliza: *I don't think so. We are first up the rank when that comes out.*

Interviewer: *Did they give you a timeframe?*

Eliza: *No. Don't be silly. That would require foresight and planning ... on the part of our government. Yeah, the federal governmental at that.* (Interview with Eliza 2015)

So, whilst we are now over five years into the rollout of the NBN in Australia, shifts in governments and policies, which have fractured along ideological lines, alongside inevitable delays encountered by a large technology infrastructure project, have meant that the opportunities of a national HSB network for reshaping place-based connectivity have also become fractured, though here along the lines of geography and technology for those in different regional and remote locations.

Conclusion

In this chapter, we have reported on three initial themes that emerged from our research examining how connectivity is configured in the production of place through the related services provided by HSB and by transport across twenty-two technologically, geographically and socioeconomically diverse households in Victoria, Australia. A key finding from this research is that, out of urban, suburban, regional and rural participants, it is the regional residents who have the greatest opportunity to realise the affordances of HSB for amplifying the relational qualities and significances of place. This is in part due to the relative inadequacy of transport connectivity, combined with more stable and higher-performing HSB access, along with the ways that such HSB access affords flexible arrangements in navigating different places and publics. Remote participants are faced with even more inadequate transport connectivity, but they often had to struggle to overcome a number of technical, environmental and other obstacles to access HSB services. For many remote participants, unlike those in the regional catchment of our study, these struggles over reliable and high-performing access meant that participating in remote work or social connections was not always a viable option.

Even so, despite variable quality of access to HSB services across sites, the findings to date do suggest that increased bandwidth is accompanied by increased participation in the digital economy, in online activities, and in the use of entertainment and communication services and technologies; and the responses of our informants indicate that increased digital literacy emerges through experience and use of HSB..

A key concern of this chapter has been to examine what HSB means for the significance of place and social interaction. The interrelated concepts of 'relational place' and 'politics of connectivity' have been central to this analysis, assisting us in seeking to understand the increasingly crucial role that HSB plays in mediating and shaping place-based experiences, interactions and interrelations, *and* the publics that form through and around these HSB-mediated experiences of place.

One of the more striking findings from this study relates to participants' views on the latter — how HSB assists (or not) in providing access to, and in the maintenance of, various publics. This came through most clearly with the rural participants, many of whom moved into these areas in order to enjoy the place-related benefits that these locations offer. For some of these rural participants, physical isolation was offset by access to both intimate publics (family and friends) and wider publics due to HSB provision. In a number of cases, the promise of HSB did not live up to the reality, thus requiring a number of ingenious if frustrating work-arounds in order to sustain social connections with loved ones elsewhere. Then there were regional cases where HSB provision permitted participants the opportunity to enjoy place-based isolation alongside engagement with local and wider publics on their own terms because of HSB connectivity. Thus, while the clearest benefit in terms of HSB for labour, learning or services from home appears to be for regional participants, the variable quality of HSB access beyond regional centres suggests that, in many respects, it still remains to be seen how the processual qualities of place in relation to the infrastructural affordances of HSB will alter what it is to be regional, rural and remote.

Acknowledgements

This work was supported by the Australian Research Council. The authors would like to thank the research participants for their enthusiasm, time and support. Participant permission has been granted for the use of images in this publication.

References

Arnold, M, Apperley, T, Nansen, B, Wilken, R & Gibbs, M 2014, 'Patchwork network: Spectrum politics, the digital home and installation of the Australian National Broadband Network', in J Choudrie & C Middleton (eds.), *Management of broadband technology innovation*, Routledge, New York, pp. 25-42.

Australian Bureau of Statistics [ABS] 2016, 'Census of population and housing: Data by region', *Australian Bureau of Statistics*, viewed 21 July 2016, <http://stat.abs.gov.au/itt/r.jsp?databyregion#/>.

Castells, M 2011, *The rise of the network society: The information age: Economy, society, and culture*, vol. 1, John Wiley & Sons, Chichester.

Cloke, P 2011, 'Urban-rural', in JA Agnew & DN Livingstone (eds.), *The SAGE handbook of geographical knowledge*, Sage, London, pp. 563-570.

Conroy, S (Minister for Broadband, Communications and the Digital Economy) 2009, *New National Broadband Network*, joint media release, Parliament House, Canberra, viewed 27 February 2012, <http://www.minister.dbcde.gov.au/media/media_releases/2009/022>.

Ek, R 2006, 'Media studies, geographical imaginations and relational space', in J Falkheimer & A Jansson (eds.), *Geographies of communication: The spatial turn in media studies*, Nordicom, Göteborg, Sweden, pp. 45-66.

Given, J 2010, '"The most connected place on the planet"', *Communication, Politics & Culture*, vol. 43, no. 1, pp. 120-142.

Gregg, M 2010, 'Available in selected metros only: Rural melancholy and the promise of online connectivity', *Cultural Studies Review*, vol. 16, no. 1, pp. 155-169, viewed 14 August 2014, <http://epress.lib.uts.edu.au/journals/index.php/csrj/article/view/1450/1546>.

Harrison, S & Dourish, P 1996, 'Re-place-ing space: The roles of place and space in collaborative systems', *Proceedings of the 1996 ACM Conference on Computer Supported Cooperative Work*, Boston, MA, 16-20 November, viewed 14 August 2014, <http://www.dourish.com/publications/1996/cscw96-place.pdf>.

Malpas, J 1999, *Place and experience: A philosophical topography*, Cambridge University Press, Cambridge.

Massey, D 1992, 'Politics and space/time', *New Left Review*, vol. 196, November/December, pp. 65-84.

Massey, D 1994, *Space, place, and gender*, Polity, Cambridge.

Massey, D 2005, *For space*, Sage, London.

Nansen, B, Wilken, R, Kennedy, J, Arnold, M & Gibbs, M 2015, 'Digital ethnographic techniques in domestic spaces: Notes on methods and ethics', *Visual Methodologies*, vol. 3, no. 2, pp. 87-97.

Parks, L & Starosielski, N (eds.) 2015, *Signal traffic: critical studies of media infrastructures*, The University of Illinois Press, Chicago.

Rodgers, J 2004, 'Doreen Massey', *Information, Communication and Society*, vol. 7, no. 2, pp. 273-291.

Stillman, L, Arnold, M, Gibbs, M & Shepherd, C 2010, 'ICT, rural dilution and the new rurality: A case study of "WheatCliffs"', *Ci: The Journal of Community Informatics*, vol. 6, no. 2, viewed 4 October 2016, <http://ci-journal.net/index.php/ciej/article/view/620/592>.

Swan, W & Conroy, S 2011, *Joint media release with Senator Stephen Conroy Minister for Communications and the Digital Economy — Second mainland site connected to the NBN*, Australian Government: The Treasury, 29 July, viewed 30 July 2011, <http://ministers.treasury.gov.au/DisplayDocs.aspx?doc=pressreleases/2011/091.htm&pageID=003&min=wms&Year=&DocType=0>.

This book is available as a free fully-searchable ebook from
www.adelaide.edu.au/press

www.ingramcontent.com/pod-product-compliance
Lightning Source LLC
Chambersburg PA
CBHW051312020426
42333CB00027B/3312